WEAVING NARRATIVE

PENN STATE ROMANCE STUDIES

EDITORS
Robert Blue (Spanish)
Kathryn M. Grossman (French)
Thomas A. Hale (French/Comparative Literature)
Djelal Kadir (Comparative Literature)
Norris J. Lacy (French)
John M. Lipski (Spanish)
Sherry L. Roush (Italian)
Allan Stoekl (French/Comparative Literature)

ADVISORY BOARD
Theodore J. Cachey Jr. (University of Notre Dame)
Priscilla Ferguson (Columbia University)
Hazel Gold (Emory University)
Cathy L. Jrade (Vanderbilt University)
William Kennedy (Cornell University)
Gwen Kirkpatrick (Georgetown University)
Rosemary Lloyd (Indiana University)
Gerald Prince (University of Pennsylvania)
Joseph T. Snow (Michigan State University)
Ronald W. Tobin (University of California at Santa Barbara)
Noël Valis (Yale University)

WEAVING NARRATIVE: CLOTHING IN TWELFTH-CENTURY FRENCH ROMANCE

MONICA L. WRIGHT

THE PENNSYLVANIA STATE UNIVERSITY PRESS
UNIVERSITY PARK, PENNSYLVANIA

LIBRARY OF CONGRESS
CATALOGING-IN-PUBLICATION DATA

Wright, Monica L., 1968–
Weaving narrative: Clothing in twelfth-century French romance / Monica L. Wright.
    p.   cm. — (Penn State Romance studies)
Includes bibliographical references and index.
Summary: "Analyzes the relationship between twelfth-century French material culture, especially with regard to attire and personal adornment, and the compositional and narrative techniques used in the emerging genre of courtly verse romance"
—Provided by publisher.
ISBN 978-0-271-03565-9 (cloth : alk. paper)
ISBN 978-0-271-03566-6 (pbk. : alk. paper)
1. French poetry—To 1500—History and criticism.
2. Material culture in literature.
3. Clothing and dress in literature.
4. Literature and society—France—History—To 1500.
5. Romances—History and criticism.
I. Title.

PQ178.W75 2010
841.109—dc22
2009029464

Copyright © 2009
The Pennsylvania State University
All rights reserved
Printed in the United States of America
Published by The Pennsylvania State University Press,
University Park, PA 16802-1003

The Pennsylvania State University Press
is a member of the
Association of American University Presses.

It is the policy of The Pennsylvania State University Press to use acid-free paper. Publications on uncoated stock satisfy the minimum requirements of American National Standard for Information Sciences—Permanence of Paper for Printed Library Material, ANSI Z39.48–1992.

This book can be viewed at:
http://publications.libraries.psu.edu/eresources/978-0-271-03565-9

IN MEMORY OF MY MOTHER,
Mary Sue Wright

IN HONOR OF MY FATHER,
Bill Wright

WITH GRATITUDE AND LOVE TO MY HUSBAND,
Robin Hermann

AND WITH ALL MY HOPES AND DREAMS FOR
Peri Grace Wright

CONTENTS

Acknowledgments ix

Introduction 1

1
Romance and the Fabric of Feudal Society:
Conjointure and Change   7

2
Material Matters: Clothing in Changing Contexts   23

3
Dressing Up the Character: The Elucidation of
Characters Through Clothing   43

4
Clothing Acts and the Movement from Code to
Signifying System   79

5
Clothing as a Structuring, Thematic, and
Narrative Device: The Art of Weaving Romance   123

Conclusion   167

Bibliography   173

Index   185

ACKNOWLEDGMENTS

THIS BOOK WOULD NOT have happened without the guidance, teaching, mentoring, advice, and support of Norris J. Lacy. It was he who introduced me to medieval and Arthurian literature and scholarship, he who taught me to read Old French. And it was he who, one day in a graduate seminar, asked a question that launched this work, whose topic has been a source of endless interest for me since. His is the model—scholar, teacher, mentor—that I have tried to emulate, imperfectly, but earnestly, all these years. If I have seen my way clear to the end of this long project, it is because I have stood on his shoulders to do so. Thank you so much, Norris.

This book is also immeasurably indebted to Robin Hermann, a great historian and even greater husband, who has read everything I have written many times over, and who, inexplicably, continues to find my work interesting. Without his sharp insights, continuous support, and love when most needed, this book would be little more than scattered files on my Mac.

Many other colleagues and friends have lent their encouragement during the course of the writing of this book. I thank Colette Winn, Elyane Dezon-Jones, and Harriet Stone for reading this work when it was at its roughest, and for making the suggestions that helped it first to form into something more than an academic exercise. My endless gratitude goes out to Robin Netherton and Gale Owen-Crocker, who have become great friends over the years and to whom I turn for all the answers about historical clothing. I thank Keith Busby for publishing my first article, thereby introducing my work to the scholarly world, and for sitting with me in the B. N. showing me how to read Guiot's manuscript. I thank Douglas Kelly for the many wonderful, kind, and generous discussions about my work and how his work on medieval rhetoric informed it; I thank him, too, for reminding me that what is not there is just as important as what is. I thank Kristin Burr for being the friend who understands everything, absolutely everything, without explanation.

Rupert Pickens and Logan Whalen have been on more panels with me and heard me speak more often than anyone else in the field, and their comments on my work at the very earliest stages have encouraged me to publish and continue to pursue new projects, but I especially thank them for the way they make being a medievalist so very fun.

I extend my thanks to Nancy Goldberg and June McCash for bringing me "home" to French in the first (and second) place. I also wish to thank many colleagues and friends both far flung and close to home who have encouraged me at various points along the way, or at least just made the way a little brighter. They include Catherine Jones, Elizabeth Poe, William Kibler, Valerie Wilhite, Joe Sullivan, Susan Hopkirk, Fabrice Leroy, Zan Kocher, Barry Ancelet, Emily Guignon, Elizabeth Allen, Sarah-Jane Murray, and all my colleagues at the University of Louisiana at Lafayette.

This project was partially supported by a Faculty Research and Creative Activity Grant at Middle Tennessee State University, for which I am grateful. I would also like to thank the helpful library staff and Interlibrary Loan staff at the Olin Library at Washington University in St. Louis, the James E. Walker Library at Middle Tennessee State University, the Jean and Alexander Heard Library at Vanderbilt University, and the Edith Garland Dupré Library at the University of Louisiana at Lafayette, as well as the generous librarians at the Richardson Memorial Library at the St. Louis Art Museum, the St. Louis Room of the Pius XII Memorial Library, and the Institut du Monde Arabe in Paris.

Some of the material in this book has previously appeared in articles and is included here with the kind permissions of the publishers. The section on making textiles in Chapter 4 relies heavily upon my essay "'De Fil d'or et de soie': Making Textiles in Twelfth-Century French Romance," in *Medieval Clothing and Textiles* 2, ed. Robin Netherton and Gale R. Owen-Crocker (Woodbridge, U.K.: Boydell, 2006), 61–72. The last section of Chapter 5 is a slightly reworked version of "*Chemise* and *Ceinture*: Marie de France's *Guigemar* and the Use of Textiles," in *Courtly Arts and the Art of Courtliness: Selected Papers from the Eleventh Triennial Congress of the International Courtly Literature Society*, ed. Keith Busby and Christopher Kleinhenz (Cambridge: D. S. Brewer, 2006), 771–77. Sections of my article "Dress for Success: Béroul's *Tristan* and the Restoration of Status Through Clothes," *Arthuriana* 18.2 (2008): 3–16, appear in Chapters 3 and 4. Portions of the essay "Their Clothing Becomes Them: The Narrative Function of Clothing in Chrétien de Troyes," *Arthurian Literature* 20 (2003): 31–42, are to be found throughout my analyses. I thank the publishers for granting me permission to reprint here.

I wish to thank the Romance Studies Series at the Penn State Press for its support of this project, especially Patrick Alexander, the general editor. I extend my gratitude to the anonymous readers of the manuscript whose time and effort I greatly appreciate and whose comments have, I hope, made this a much improved work, although I take credit for all its shortcomings. I appreciate also the thorough and thoughtful copyediting of Romaine Perin.

Finally, I thank my family for the kind of support that only family gives.

INTRODUCTION

ENIDE'S TATTERED DRESS AND Erec's fabulous coronation robe; Yvain's nudity in the forest that prevents maidens who know him well clothed from identifying him; Perceval proudly sporting his rustic Welsh costume, eschewing proper courtly attire to the derision of the court; Tristan disguised as a leper, begging from his peers; the utter abjection and degradation of the three hundred *tisseuses* toiling in rags while making fine, golden silk; Lanval's fairy-lady parading about in the Arthurian court scantily dressed for all to observe: just why is clothing so important in twelfth-century French romance? These images dazzle us with their splendor, confuse us with conflicting messages about courtliness, or unsettle us with frightening portraits of an unsavory material reality threatening to manifest. Moreover, these representations are not mere embellishments to the text; they and many other vestimentary depictions help actually to form the textual weave of the romances in which they appear. This book is about how these descriptions are constructed and what they mean, but it is also about how clothing becomes an active part of romance composition: the ways in which writers use it to develop and elaborate character; to advance, or, conversely, stall, the plot; and to structure the narrative generally.

This study seeks to understand the ways in which the writers of twelfth-century French romance used clothing as a signifier with multiple meanings in a variety of ways and for many narrative purposes. An exploration of the relationship between material culture and literary expression will help to elucidate how societal changes influenced and were influenced by the literary use of clothing. Essentially, this relationship is one of expansion: the possible meanings for clothing items were increasing and broadening in the society as new wealth was being created by and for the traders of luxury clothing items. In other words, the preexisting symbolic, unequivocal social meaning of clothing (for example, that if one dressed like a noble, one must be a noble) was being called into question by the merchant class and its members' ability to profit from providing the nobles with extravagant and exotic clothing. However, the literature pushed the boundaries of this ambiguity even further, creating meanings for clothing that seem improbable for the reality. For instance, in Chrétien de Troyes's *Erec et Enide*, the noble but poor heroine wears her tattered dress into Arthur's magnificent court, only to be met with unanimous admiration for her inherent nobility, which shines brightly despite her impoverished exterior. One has only to consider this first image of Enide to understand how useful vestimentary ambivalence could be to a writer proposing a less rigid conception of nobility to the very nobility that stood to lose something with the change. Moreover, through the use of clothing, the writers inscribed into their texts not only this kind of class ambivalence, but also gender ambivalence (as in the case of Camille, the warrior-queen in the twelfth-century version of *Enéas*), identity ambivalence (through the extensive use of disguise), and sexual ambivalence (for instance, when a character's attire communicates a complex and sexualized image). What is fascinating about this process is that, although romance was *the* courtly literature par excellence, it also presented the nobility with images of itself that must have been shocking, if not outright threatening, since romance writers questioned the social order of the nobility in so many ways. The writers seem to have been conscious of this threat: they tended to reinscribe order into their romances, taking their audience on an exciting voyage in which idealized members of the nobility faced and overcame challenges to their social order. This order, however, was changed in the process, just as the real social order of twelfth-century nobles was changing around them. Clothing is at the very heart both of the actual changes taking place and of the idealized, literary representation of those changes.

The present work attempts to generalize across works regarding the use of clothing in the context of a complex and dynamic signifying system in order to view the phenomenon of clothing globally in the corpus of romance of the period. Beyond the more comprehensive nature of this study, the aim is also to contribute to our understanding of the genre of romance and its conventions by relating the history of costume and material culture to the process of writing. I am concerned, moreover, not simply with the historical implications of literary clothing depiction from a remote period; my greatest interest lies, rather, in a shift in the representational system at large and how this shift becomes important to all of the narrative elements of twelfth-century romance.

The methodology employed involves the close reading of a number of texts in the corpus of twelfth-century verse romance and the cross analysis of the clothing references within these texts. I have interpreted each clothing instance in three different contexts: their specific narrative context, the sociohistorical context, and the context of the process of signification. From the set of analyses, I have extrapolated the broad tendencies of the writers of romance as they use the vestimentary code, and have charted another tendency of transforming the code into a signifying system capable of creating new meanings. I intend to elucidate of the process of signification valued by the writers and audience of the period as well as its mechanics in order to understand better the principles of representation of the twelfth century.

I am examining clothing as a signifier in the context of a developing signifying system, which allows me to see how the textual structure of romance is related to textile—in other words, how the process of romance composition is a technique of weaving. By this, I do not mean that the relationship between text and textile is simply metaphoric: it actually describes the relationship between the thematic and the formal and between the actions of characters and the process of composition. Eugene Vinaver first noticed this structure when he called romance a tapestry because of the way it creates meaning from patterns; that is, formally similar episodes, tropes, or motifs must be viewed in combination in order to be understood fully, and this is the major organizing principle of romance (*Form* 12). Romaine Wolf-Bonvin has more recently reminded us of the etymological reasons: "Le texte est avant tout tissage, texture" (*Textus* 11).

In Chapter 1, I focus upon the extratextual factors that to some extent determine the parameters of the use of clothing in the literature of the period. Included in this discussion are the contexts in which literary expression occurred: the context of the literary project as it was conceived by the writers of the period; the context of the representational mentality and its shift from a symbol-dominated system to one more closely related to the sign; the historical context, in which major changes were occurring that are eventually inscribed in the literature; and the context involving the process by which clothing has meaning within societies.

In Chapter 2, I describe the reality of clothing in the period, to the extent that we can make such determinations. The historiography of clothing for the twelfth century is problematic for two reasons: first, there are no extant garments, certainly not of the kind described in courtly romance, and second, the art historical record is scanty, with few manuscript illuminations dating from the twelfth century depicting lay clothing of the period. There are many dating from the thirteenth and fourteenth centuries, but these tend to depict contemporaneous clothing styles rather than twelfth-century modes. Moreover, for what visual evidence that does remain, mostly in the form of statuary, there is no way to match terms to forms. I extend my discussion of clothing items into the materials used to produce those garments, their origins and the economics involved in obtaining them, finishing the chapter with an overview of how clothing has meaning within human societies.

In Chapter 3, I discuss the function of description in romance and how clothing helps to elaborate characters' identities, paying particular attention to the dynamism of the emerging clothing system and the way it inscribes flexibility into the descriptions. For example, in Chrétien's *Chevalier de la charrette*, or *Lancelot*, right as Guenevere meets Lancelot for their tryst, she appears to her lover in a window. She is described as wearing a *chemise* covered with only a mantle. This image, as I analyze more thoroughly in my article "What Was Arthur Wearing? Discrepancies in Dress Descriptions in Twelfth-Century French Romance," is interesting because it combines two incongruous articles of clothing: the very public, ceremonial garment of the mantle—in fact, the only garment to be exclusively noble during the period—and the most private of garments, the *chemise*, a garment usually equated with nudity, thus shameful in public. This could be seen as the twelfth-century equivalent of wearing a mink stole with nothing but lingerie underneath. The juxtaposition of these two garments creates a clothing image of the queen that underlines and enhances a crucial duality in her character in this romance: she is both queen and Lancelot's lover. She is of the highest nobility (the queen of the noblest king) and an adulteress. This image is both public and private, both noble and base, and completely sexualized. This clothing description is extremely dynamic because it incorporates into itself the duality that defines Guenevere's character. My discussion leads me to an examination of code manipulation by which the writers altered the process of signification by code duplication but with different conventions, changes in community that result in multiple meanings for clothing instances, and subversion of the code until it effaces.

I continue my analysis of code manipulation in Chapter 4 but focus upon clothing acts rather than description and upon code manipulation with regard to context. I examine acts such as gifts, which are largely normative acts that provide evidence that although a clothing signifying system is emerging, the vestimentary code persists in its usage and in acts of dressing and undressing, for which meaning is mediated through changes in context and that must be interpreted in light of context. For example, clothing acts may have different meanings when viewed from different perspectives. My assertion that, in fact, the signifying system does not replace the code but subsumes it is reinforced by my discovery that romance writers model the very process of fashioning new meanings from old material and in which they themselves are engaged when they show characters making cloth or clothing.

Chapter 5 is an investigation of how the clothing signifying system interacts with different levels of the text: structural, thematic, and narrative. Clothing provides structure as instances open and close narrative threads and as they create links among episodes through both formal and thematic analogy. The clothing system also helps elaborate and illustrate the major themes of a given romance, providing thematic cohesion to the work as a whole, which is a form of structuring device. In Chrétien's *Chevalier au lion*, or *Yvain*, the hero fails to fulfill a promise he has made to his lady that he will return from his exploits after one year's absence. She sends one of her ladies to reclaim the ring that she had given him as a token of her love, and when the lady comes into court, she removes her mantle. She does this to honor the court, but it also prefigures and precipitates two other acts: Yvain's removal of the ring but also of all his clothes as he slips into madness and becomes a social outcast. This major undressing act makes his madness and outcast status material in the text, but is later reversed as Yvain regains his sanity, and of course, his clothes, and as he slowly regains his social status through the repeated fulfillment of obligations. This clothing cycle is emblematic of the major theme of the work: failure to fulfill an obligation, then compensation for the mistake through gradual fulfillment of the obligation. And just as this theme structures the romance, so do clothing instances, since Yvain's undressing/dressing cycle is reflected in a number of thematically similar episodes. This kind of structuration—analogical—is characteristic of the romance genre, and clothing plays an extremely important role in this weaving of romance. Finally, Chapter 5 concludes with the close reading of two works of courtly literature, *Guillaume d'Angleterre*, signed by a "Crestïens" whose identity scholars still debate, and Marie de France's *Guigemar*, for which it is possible to read the narrative through the clothing, and my conclusion emphasizes and confirms the contribution that clothing makes to a narrative as a whole.

In virtually every way, in twelfth-century France, clothing reached a new level of significance. Because it was so important, it is not surprising that it would enter so dramatically into the literature. My assertion is that clothing holds a privileged place in romance for two reasons: first, the structural similarity between the weave of cloth and the romance narrative, and second, the importance of clothing in the society at large. The nobility was having to prove itself more and more in ways other than its prowess in war, the twelfth century being a period of relative peace, so nobles had to seek out alternative means to assert their power. The major way they sought to do so was through the ostentatious display of wealth, and there is no better way to display one's personal wealth than by wearing it. Yet, ironically, the acquisition of luxury clothing items required the nobility to fuel the mercantile economy, which in turn enriched the merchant class, thereby threatening the situation of nobles still further. Feeling this pressure, nobles would also seek out new forms of self-representation, this impulse undoubtedly contributing directly to the rise of courtly romance.

Romance, in which the behavior of the knight at court was just as valued and scrutinized as his behavior on the battlefield, perhaps more closely reflected the image that male nobles, who had increasingly fewer opportunities to prove their prowess, wished to project of themselves: as finely and expensively dressed, well-behaved gentlemen. Moreover, the shift in setting from the battlefield to the court allowed for more depictions of ladies and their magnificent attire. Clothing and textiles, along with all of their possible mutations, quickly became part of the romance writers' repertoire of narrative tools, permitting them to weave the social concerns and material reality into a new literary genre.

1

ROMANCE AND THE FABRIC OF FEUDAL SOCIETY:
Conjointure AND CHANGE

IN FRANCE DURING THE second half of the twelfth century, from about 1160 until 1200, a period in which culture and the arts flourished and the economy was expanding, the writers of Old French verse romance showed an unprecedented interest in clothing. Whereas the *chansons de geste* that were popular before the rise of romance gave little notice to a character's clothing, the works of authors such as Chrétien de Troyes, Marie de France, and Béroul interspersed narrative with often lengthy descriptions of costume.[1] These descriptions do not simply provide character development or realism through accumulation of detail; they also structure the plot, providing thematic coherence through repetition, reflection, or analogy.[2] Moreover, significant instances of clothing are not confined to description; actions involving clothing, such as dressing and undressing, giving gifts, and making clothes, have particular narrative functions as well. For the purposes of this study, I will define clothing as broadly as possible, to encompass all types of vestimentary and adornment items worn. Along with the traditional articles of clothing of the period, including *bliauts*, mantles, *chainses*, and *chemises*, I discuss other

---

1. In *La Chanson de Roland* there is a significant amount of description of armor. The emphasis that the poet places on this one vestimentary item reflects the primacy that the society of the tenth, eleventh, and early twelfth centuries placed upon the military role of the sons of the nobility and royalty. With the shift from a wartime society to a largely peaceful one, the military role of the nobility becomes less crucial for the society, and the romances, although they continue to celebrate the knight, reflect this change both in representing knights as individuals and in according a great deal more attention to other aspects of courtly life. Correspondingly, the writers of romance expand the vestimentary repertoire to include clothing, softer and more supple than its wartime equivalent, armor.

2. All these terms refer to processes by which comparisons are invited among episodes and thematic units for the purpose of creating multiple relations among textual parts; they differ, however, in technique. Repetition is the process by which an image, motif, or action is directly and explicitly repeated; reflection and analogy are less direct; they rely on similarity without replication. Reflection occurs when an image, motif, or action is structurally similar to another, analogy when they are thematically similar.

worn items and place them under the general heading of clothing because they are all signifiers that belonged to the vestimentary code of the day. Such items include all the various pieces of armor, particularly hauberks and helmets; jewelry, with special attention to rings; and articles made of cloth, such as swaddling material and even, in one case, bedsheets, when they envelop a character and function as clothing. I have also included gifts of cloth under the heading because the raw materials for clothing are potential clothes and because their value for the vestimentary code is unmistakable.

The primary audience of the French courtly romances of the second half of the twelfth century were nobles whose contacts, whether firsthand or otherwise, with faraway, materially wealthy cultures intensified their interest in luxury items and, particularly, in luxurious clothing. It is not surprising that courtly authors, wishing to please their patrons and audiences, would include a new emphasis on clothing in the works they presented to them. In keeping with the notions that governed the art of composition, writers of romance exploited every expressive or instrumental quality of clothing they could in order to foster contemporary appeal in the stories they most often inherited from older sources. Clothing in the romance of the period became part of the weave of the text, appearing and disappearing at intervals, like a thread in a tapestry, structuring as it embellishes.

The authors of romance not only accommodated the tastes of their audience but also acclimated them to a world of change. As feudal society shifted from a period of ongoing war to one of relative peace, the mobilization of resources for war became focused on the acquisition of wealth. At the same time, the noble warrior class witnessed a shift in the justification for their elevated social status: no longer did their military prowess guarantee their place in society.[3] In this new era, they had to base their status on wealth, power, their capacity for largess, and their ability to effect an impressive appearance (Duby, *Guerriers* 262). Their increased need to express their status created greater demand for luxury goods, often unavailable locally. This demand stimulated trade, which, in turn, created possibilities for the enrichment of the merchant class.[4] The new wealth of the merchants began,

---

3. It is worth noting that throughout the twelfth century the nobility experienced a gradual displacement from positions of power in the government as Capetian rule was slowly consolidating and transforming into an administrative monarchy. In this new climate, the king was increasing appointing commoners to positions in the royal administration that had previously been held by members of the nobility. See Baldwin, "Capetian Court," and Luchaire, *Louis VII*.

4. Duby discusses this process at some length in *Guerriers et paysans* (269–77), claiming that the towns, in particular, favored the merchants and that among these merchants, "quelques-uns même, tout comme les principaux officiers des grands seigneurs, purent forcer l'entrée de la chevalerie" (271).

in some cases, to rival that of the nobility.[5] The resulting material ambiguity introduced by the enrichment of the merchants through foreign trade for the luxury items the nobles needed to express their status threatened these same nobles by destabilizing their world.

The shift in material stability in the world of the twelfth-century French noble was concurrent with a shift in the imaginative and conceptual universe that is discernible in the literary expression of the day. Writers of romance created for their noble audience the illusion of a safe though fictive world in which they could imagine themselves performing great deeds and in which the merchant offered no possible threat to the stability of the system.[6] Thus, the writers invited their audience to project itself into the roles of these heroes as they triumph in a idealized world. This world is woven together with the luxurious clothing that the nobles require to preserve and express status.[7] Having created what appeared to be a reaffirmation of the nobles' social position and their values, these writers nonetheless inscribed the very ambiguities that so threatened their audience in the material world. At the same time that the writers provided an illusion of stasis, they were shifting the world on its axis, shifting from absolute meaning to contingent meaning as they exploited the representational powers of the sign.

I am using the term *sign* in light of the distinction that Saussure and, later, Kristeva make between the symbol and the sign.[8] The distinction derives from a difference in relationship between the signifier and its meaning. Saussure defines this relationship as being arbitrary for the sign and motivated for the symbol. He emphasizes that *"le signe linguistique est arbitraire"* (100) inasmuch

---

5. Duby makes clear the link between the aristocratic need for luxury goods and their agents of exchange: "Mener cette fête permanente qui se tient au coeur du comportement aristocratique, c'est donc recourir nécessairement à des spécialistes de l'approvisionnement en denrées inconnues, merveilleuses et lointaines—à des marchands (*Guerriers* 262).

6. The merchants were often denigrated in the courtly romance of the period, as in *Guillaume d'Angleterre* when the narrator comments extensively and throughout the romance upon the base nature of the merchants who foster the king's two sons. However, merchants found a more sympathetic representation in the fabliau, where writers "describe the merchant's profits, but they also point out his qualities: ability, energy, courage, and a fondness for dangerous ventures. . . . [They] deserved much consideration, since their services were important for the church, for the knightly caste, and for all of society" (Gurevich 263).

7. Duby notes the society's reliance upon clothing in order to distinguish among classes and to determine social rank and role: "A l'époque, les catégories sociales sont clairement désignées par le vêtement, la forme des souliers, la coupe des cheveux—car il convenait que l'on reconnaisse au premier coup d'oeil à l'habit le moine, le pénitent, le prince, le rustre, la femme honnête et celle qui ne l'est pas" (*Trois Ordres* 74–75).

8. Saussure makes this distinction in his *Cours de linguistique générale* (101), and Kristeva throughout her essay "Du symbole au signe." I discuss this distinction in more detail later in this chapter.

as "[le signifiant] est *immotivé*, c'est-à-dire arbitraire par rapport au signifié, avec lequel il n'a aucune attache naturelle" (101; emphasis in original). The symbol, on the other hand, is a less flexible signifier because its meaning is motivated, that is, *not* arbitrary and, moreover, dependent upon some sort of resemblance or other intrinsic connection to that meaning. The sign's arbitrary connection between the signifier and the signified naturally allows for greater flexibility with regard to the assignment of meaning. In other words, the sign, because of the arbitrary connection between its form and meaning, can simply mean *more*, by having differing meanings and by undergoing a different process of signification from that of the symbol. Therefore, the sign's representational potential is greater than that of the symbol.

Confronted with their changing world, the members of the nobility would not surprisingly wish to cling to a disappearing, glorious past, and the writers who wrote for them understood this attitude. Like their patrons and audience, the writers of romance, most of whom belonged to the educated elite, although not necessarily to the nobility, also looked to the past, albeit a different past.[9] In the scholastic tradition of the day, the antique and classical authors provided both instruction and source material for literary creation. The artistic merit of a literary work was measured by how well it could mediate between past masterworks and the concerns of the present. Writers rewrote and modified existing works, using their antiquity as a source of authority while using their own skill to incorporate contemporary elements into the work. This mode of literary production was ideally suited to its audience because, like its audience, it derived its authority from the past while striving to make itself appealing to contemporary ideals. Moreover, twelfth-century French courtly literature and its noble audience both placed a great emphasis on clothing.[10]

---

9. Roberta Krueger points out that these writers were most often clerics who found themselves ideologically at odds with the subject matter presented to them by their patrons, and she further asserts that "Chrétien embellishes and partly obscures the stark realities of men's power over women and dresses them up so that they may appear benign and even beneficial; this is the process I refer to as 'mystification.' But he does not attempt to hoodwink his readers into blind acceptance of the ideals of chivalry and courtly love. He lays bare the process by which women are appropriated in such a way that the reader may criticize romance mystification" (*Women Readers* 34).

10. Dyan Elliott claims that during this period, "dress became something of a Western obsession" (286). Very little direct evidence of this enhanced awareness has survived from the twelfth century: we have no manuals of dress, if indeed such existed in that period, nor do we have many sources that document attitudes about dress. However, we do know from sermons of the church fathers that clothing styles had undergone several important changes during the twelfth century, including lacing the sides of garments to accentuate the wearer's figure and the lengthening of sleeves and trains (for more detail, see my discussion of costume history in Chapter 2). Moreover,

Conjointure

Douglas Kelly points out that twelfth-century writers would "imitate, but also recreate the received *materia* to fit new emphases, new intentions, and new audiences" (*Conspiracy* 111–12). The very form of romance was new in the twelfth century and therefore invited, created, and even required new meanings. Additionally, societal concerns in the period differed from those of previous periods, both in that society had shifted from a wartime period to one of relative peace and in that it was witnessing dramatic changes in the social structures that formed it. The *chanson de geste* had been remarkably effective as a literary expression of the national pride necessary in wartime, but it proved to be less valued in the courtly circles to which the knights had retired after their military service was no longer needed. Romance, on the other hand, emphasized the new values of the society: chivalry, *courtoisie*, courtly love, and the material luxury that distinguished the court.[11] However, the audience of romance did not reject the knightly exploits that made up the action of the *chanson de geste*; rather, they desired to see their military glory cast into a new courtly context, just as they themselves had been. The project of writing romance, then, became a project of rewriting: writers chose material from antecedent sources to rewrite into different contexts, and the court and its concerns are at both the origin and the center of romance.

Chrétien de Troyes, in line 14 of his prologue to *Erec et Enide*, claims that, unlike his predecessors who mangle and corrupt their sources, he is about to draw from an adventure tale *une molt bele conjointure*. He is evoking here the medieval notion of *conjointure*, in which the author of romance would use various source material and his or her skills as a writer to weave together a cohesive and beautiful text from divergent material, forming a new, original version. Eugène Vinaver defines the term, after a short review of its etymology, as "ce qui réunit, rassemble ou organise des éléments divers et même dissemblables, . . . ce qui les transforme en un tout organisé" (*Recherche* 107). Marie de France, in her prologue to the *Lais*,

---

we have substantial evidence that cloth figured as the most extensively traded commodity throughout the twelfth century, with a premium placed on the fine woolens from Flanders and the silks imported from the Levant. This fact, although it does not directly indicate a heightened awareness of clothing among the nobility, certainly suggests that there was a great deal of attention paid to and much expenditure made for the acquisition of the materials to produce luxury clothing.

11. Eugène Vinaver contends that romance differs from the *chanson de geste* in that "love interest and the pursuit of adventures unrelated to any common aim . . . displaced the theme of the defense of Christendom and the preoccupation of feudal warfare" (*Rise* 1).

provides more information than does Chrétien concerning the provenance of the method. She explains that the ancients, among whose heirs she counts herself, intentionally left aspects of their works obscure so that "pur ceus qui a venir esteient / E ki aprendre le deveient, / K'i peüssent gloser la lettre / E de lur sen le surplus mettre" (for those who would come along later and learn them could gloss the text and add more significance from their insight) (vss. 13–16).[12] Chrétien and his contemporaries would have seen their literary projects as the skillful use of classical techniques and devices (which conformed to their scholastic tradition) to translate or transform *materia* from various sources into compelling and beautiful new works that their audiences would find pleasing and in which everything has meaning and purpose. Their works, then, would need to reflect an amplified social reality to which their noble patrons could relate and would require inclusion of those textual features that were of the greatest interest to the society of the period. Kelly has pointed out that "authors like Chrétien when retelling and rewriting received *matières*, along with those who imitated his stories, themes, motifs, and lines of verse, did so in a cultural context that favored rhetorical training" (*Conspiracy* xi). Chrétien himself refers to his debt to Macrobius in *Erec et Enide*, explaining, "Macrobes m'ansaigne a descrive" (Macrobius teaches me to describe) (vs. 6741). The choice of places in the text, or *topoi*, to amplify and embellish depended first and foremost on the tastes and ideals of the audience, particularly in a system of artistic patronage. One such area of interest, as we shall see, was clothing, and a signifying system based on clothing would have appealed to the noble audience of Chrétien and his contemporaries, since the social ideas about clothing were beginning to change with certain other changes in society.[13]

The authors of the period were in a very real sense *weaving* a narrative. They transformed older material by infusing it with the ideals and nostalgia of the present, all through the use of age-old methods of composition. Their production bridged the gap between past and present. The means by

---

12. Krueger, writing about gender differences and how they are portrayed in the literature, says of Marie: "Partly because Marie's fictions imagine unusual answers to ordinary, yet intractable problems, they highlight the constraints and tensions faced by men and women in 'real' life, where no ideal solutions can be found. By assembling twelve diverse stories [in her *Lais*] that fail to converge around a simple moral truth, Marie invites her audience to add their own 'surplus de . . . sens'" ("Questions" 139).

13. Michel Pastoureau and Dominique Simonnet assert about the twelfth century that "à cette époque, on est pris d'une vraie soif de classification, on veut hiérarchiser les individus, leur donner des signes d'identité, des codes de reconnaissance" (*Petit livre* 19).

which the transformation occurred was through topical invention, which Kelly defines in the following way: "The author identifies (invention) those places (*topoi*) which he or she can elaborate upon (amplification) in order to represent persons, things, and actions as he or she intends for them to appear" (*Conspiracy* 38). Invention is a threefold operation, which includes drawing on source material (*ab auctore*), using material from the writer's mind (*de suo*), and skillfully employing the art (*ex arte*) (66). "Topical invention encompasses authorial interpretation of *matière*, disposition of parts, amplification, and choice of ornamental devices and vocabulary" ("Rhetoric" 247), and includes such features as versification, embellishment, and description (*Romances* 192). The term *description* (*descriptio*) in the context of medieval rhetoric has a broad range of meanings. "*Descriptio* overlaps in meaning with rewriting as copying, paraphrasing, imitating, and emulating; that is, with any original description by which an antecedent matter, motif, or theme is rewritten in order to enhance, improve upon, or correct the prior version or versions" (*Conspiracy* 42).

The medieval art of rewriting provided the writers of the late twelfth century with a poetic enterprise perfectly suited to appeal to their audience. Through their use of *conjointure*, writers were able to give their noble audience the best of both worlds. They could commit to parchment the idealized fantastic world of knights and great deeds, fulfilling the nobles' need to remember or invent their glorious ancestral past, conjoined with the new world of fantastic material goods needed by the nobles to reassert their status in the void left in the wake of wartime. The distinction between the *chanson de geste* and the romance will again serve as an illustration of this point: whereas the *chanson de geste* relates the knightly exploits of the warrior class in the context of one country's war against another, the romance relates not only individual knightly exploits but also knightly behavior at court. The romance adds the component of the court as the ultimate context for all action and incorporates female characters as well.[14] Thus, the romance sets knightly exploits firmly within a courtly context in which both deeds and the accouterments of proper courtly behavior allow

---

14. Although romance is often perceived as empowering women by casting them in larger roles within the works, Simon Gaunt and Krueger have both argued that, in the framework of a feminist reading, the shift from epic to romance in fact marginalized them more, primarily reducing them to objects of exchange between men. Both have also remarked that the patronage of Marie de Champagne for Chrétien's *Lancelot*, a feature of the romance that seems to confer to the female power over the male cleric, is, in the end, a pact between two male clerics that allows for completion of the work (Gaunt, *Gender* 92–103; Krueger, *Women Readers* 35–39).

characters to distinguish themselves, courtly behavior including chivalry, *courtoisie*, and all the material trappings of the court, especially fine food, fine horses, fine linens and tapestries, fine armor, and fine clothing. Yet in the very act of creating this dual world, writers shifted the representational axis that formed the basis for their work. They began to use composition and description in a new way and for a different result, namely, the creation of a representational universe in which signification occurs with greater dynamism. In this new system, signifiers had meaning relative to their contexts and resisted the confines of the preexisting vestimentary code.

Kelly contends that Chrétien de Troyes was an author who had mastered the techniques of composition and description to such an extent that he was capable of using them to create a new expression (*Romances* 197–207). Kelly has documented, in his chapter on description in *The Romances of Chrétien de Troyes*, a movement in Chrétien's work from formal, static description, defined as an iteration of "conventional stereotypes like perfect human beauty or consummate ugliness, stages in combat, . . . the ceremony of hospitality, etc." (191), to "glimpses" of a more abstract type, such as Chrétien's description of Enide as beautiful despite the ragged state of her clothes (198) or the simultaneous self-destruction of Laudine's beauty and its reconstruction by Yvain (200). Kelly's assertions attest not only to Chrétien's mastery of the literary aesthetic specific to romance but also to a more general trend in representation. Delineating the particular way that romance writers used a seemingly restrictive process of artistic creation actually to generate new forms, he shows how these writers inscribed ambivalence into their works through description. However, although Kelly sometimes draws upon clothing descriptions to illustrate his points, he is not specifically concerned with the writers' use of clothing as a signifying system or their deviations from a vestimentary code. My goal, by contrast, is to elucidate a similar, even parallel, process to the one Kelly describes, but I am focusing on and attempting to account for the ways in which writers both used the existing, highly restrictive vestimentary code and exploited its limitations to create new meanings for existing forms. Following Kelly's documentation of this movement from an overly determined system toward a freer, more creative expression, I am documenting a shift in a particular aspect of the entire representational system of the period and am examining the use of clothing as a signifier to do so. This transition occurs in the very process of signification by which meaning is assigned to a certain form.

Symbols, Signs, and the Rise of Fashion

To demonstrate the shift in the process of signification, I have found it useful to borrow from the field of linguistics two opposing terms: *symbol* and *sign*. These two terms convey two different types of relationships between a signifier and its meaning. I am following both Saussure and Kristeva when I define these relationships in the following way: the symbol has a relationship to its meaning that is fixed and motivated, or more specifically, based on a resemblance of some sort, whereas the sign has an entirely arbitrary and contingent relationship to its meaning. My assertion is that a shift in mentality occurred in the twelfth century. Until this period, a mentality prevailed for which the symbol was the dominant model for the attribution of meaning in the world, but during the course of the century this mentality was at least challenged, if not replaced, by one whose model was the arbitrary nature of the sign and its contingent relationship to meaning. This transition in mentality is, in my view, a result of and a response to changing conditions in the material world, such as the encroachment of the merchant class upon the wealth of the nobility. These changes made necessary a shift in the attribution of meaning precisely because they themselves introduced arbitrariness and ambiguity into the social system of the day. I do not, however, mean to suggest that the sign as a linguistic phenomenon replaced the symbol in any absolute sense: I merely wish to use the distinction to illustrate a shift in mentality that became manifest in the artistic expression of the period. Moreover, as I will argue below, symbol and sign coexist as part of the clothing signifying system that derives from the vestimentary code of the twelfth century. A more detailed discussion of the properties of both the symbol and the sign will assist in making my point.

In her essay "Du symbole au signe," Julia Kristeva claims that the symbol predominated as the basis of medieval thought until the thirteenth century: "C'est une pratique sémiotique cosmogonique: ces éléments (les symboles) renvoient à une (des) transcendance(s) universelle(s), irreprésentable(s) et méconnaissable(s)" (26). Although I completely agree that the sign replaced the symbol as the dominant mode of thought during the Middle Ages, I would assert that this transition began not in the thirteenth century but in the twelfth. The evidence that I document throughout this study in the verse romances of the twelfth century forms the basis of my argument. However, despite our differing assignment of dates to the phenomenon, we are in agreement with regard to the mechanism by which it occurred. Kristeva is remarking upon more than a linguistic property: her contention concerns the very axis upon which meaning travels. Her assertion echoes that of Johan Huizinga when he tells us that "the Middle Ages never forgot that all things would be absurd if their meaning were exhausted in their function and their place in the phenomenal world, if by their essence they did not reach into a world beyond this" (201). Symbols are therefore signifiers that are motivated; that is, there is some inherent (or perceived inherent) relationship between the signifier and the signified. Saussure defines the symbol by its lack of total arbitrariness: "Il n'est pas vide; il y a un rudiment de lien naturel entre le signifiant et le signifié" (101).[15] To illustrate the motivated nature of the symbol, Arthur Asa Berger asserts that the symbol of a pair of scales to signify "justice" cannot be replaced by just any other symbol, such as a chariot (18). Kristeva calls symbols restrictive in nature because their meanings exist prior to their actual articulation (27). For example, in twelfth-century France, armor designated "knighthood," and had done so since before any single given piece of armor was worn or even made.

During the course of the Middle Ages, Kristeva maintains, the relationship between the signifying unit and the idea weakened, and the signifying unit "prend de plus en plus de 'matérialité' et va jusqu'à oublier son 'origine'" (28). This transformation, according to Kristeva,

> révèle une loi: l'unité signifiante n'est plus renvoyée à 'l'idée' qui se proliférait à travers elle dans son immensité; l'unité signifiante, par contre, devient opaque, s'identifie à elle-même, se 'matérialise,' et sa dimension verticale commence à perdre de l'intensité, et c'est sa possibilité d'articulation avec d'autres unités signifiantes qui s'accentue. . . . Cette possibilité de l'unité signifiante de s'articuler soit avec soi-même (donc de se répéter) soit avec d'autres, souvent opposées, substitue à une structure monovalente (la structure symbolique), une structure hétérovalente, déchirée, double. (29)

Moreover, in this system, as Saussure points out, the sign has meaning only in relation to other signs (117). Kristeva goes on to maintain that the sign essentially has three properties:

---

15. Charles Sanders Peirce attests, moreover, to the fact that symbols are based on habit, rather than upon innovation, and thus "do not enable us to add to our understanding even so much as a necessary consequent, unless by means of definite preformed habit" (251).

- Il ne réfère pas à une réalité unique et singulière, mais ÉVOQUE un ensemble d'images et d'idées associées. Il tend à se détacher du fond transcendantal qui le supporte (on peut dire qu'il est 'arbitraire') tout en restant expressif.
- Il est COMBINATOIRE et en cela CORRÉLATIF: son sens résulte de la combinatoire à laquelle il participe avec les autres signes.
- Il recèle un principe de TRANSFORMATION (dans son champ les structures s'engendrent et se transforment à l'infini). (35)

The distinction between the motivated symbol and the arbitrary sign may also be applied to clothing under the rubrics of *prefashion* and *fashion*. Clothing up until the late twelfth century would fall under the category of prefashion.[16] During this period, a person's dress was highly determined by his or her socioeconomic situation, and the available "looks" or styles were determined by economic, technological, and even political factors. The quality of a person's dress, then, was in direct correlation to that person's status, geographic location, and political situation. In this way, clothing before the late twelfth century was functionally a symbol because it had a motivated relationship with its meaning, the wearer's identity; it was monovalent, since any given article of clothing could refer only to a unique wearer's identity or status.

Most costume historians place the rise of fashion at some point in either the thirteenth or fourteenth century.[17] Anne Hollander defines fashion as "constant, perceptible fluctuations of visual design, created out of the combined forms of tailored dress and body" (90), and she claims that in the twelfth century, "fashion was not truly moving" (363). Malcolm Barnard claims that fashion explicitly requires "the possibility of moving between classes in order to exist" (59), which would place the advent of fashion well after the economic rise of the bourgeoisie.[18] Fred Davis describes fashion as highly context-dependent: "What some combination of clothes of a certain style emphasis 'means' will vary tremendously depending upon the identity

---

16. Sarah-Grace Heller discusses the impact that the Crusades in the late eleventh century had on the rise of fashion, arguing successfully that although this contact with the East surely inspired in the European noble imagination the desire to possess Eastern textiles and fashions, it does not appear that such fashions actually existed in Europe until the late twelfth or early thirteenth century; see her article "Fashion in French Crusade Literature."

17. Elizabeth Ewing is the exception to this rule, placing the advent of fashion in the middle of the twelfth century (18).

18. Hollander agrees that the rise of fashion coincides with "the rise of towns and the middle class, along with the consolidation of monarchical power" (362).

of the wearer, the occasion, the place, the company, and even something as vague and transient as the wearer's and the viewer's moods" (8).

This shifting of the relationship between the signifier and the signified, as Davis puts it, "recognizes the possibility of alternative, contradictory or obscure interpretations" (22). The clothing code in a fashion system corresponds to the attributes of the sign outlined above by Kristeva. Fashion provides heterovalent clothing, evoking a collection of ideas while remaining distant from any absolute reading; this clothing has a correlative meaning based on its interaction with other signs; and new styles are constantly articulated and transformed.[19] In fact, pushed to its extreme, fashion provides, as Baudrillard notes, signifiers empty of external meaning: the signifiers signify themselves.[20] The fashion to which Baudrillard refers is a distinctly modern one, at great odds with the burgeoning ambiguities introduced into the vestimentary code of the twelfth century: the shift toward a fashion system began in the twelfth century but did not manifest wholly for centuries to come.[21]

Sarah-Grace Heller, in her *Fashion in Medieval France*, convincingly argues for the existence of a fashion system operating in France in the thirteenth century. She bases this assertion upon ten criteria that she identifies as crucial to such a system, including factors such as the desire for newness; constant, systematic change; and individual expression within a framework of social imitation, as well as an emphasis on consumption, superficial changes, and a democratizing aspect (8–9). She asks: "The thirteenth-century ideal hero is repeatedly represented as an individual who strove for distinction in appearance. Is that not fashion?" (4). I would say so. Fashion, as she defines it, constitutes a criticism of the past and its tastes in favor of what is new, and while it is true that twelfth-century nobles certainly desired new, aesthetically pleasing

---

19. Davis points out that the couturiere Coco Chanel advised "her wealthy clients to dress 'as plainly as their maids' and to wear cheap costume jewelry" but to wear "real jewelry 'as if it were junk'" (63). This advice constitutes a "fashion statement" that is possible only in a system of signs for which the signifier-signified relationship has become unstable.

20. Baudrillard discusses fashion in general, that is, all types of fashion rather than uniquely vestimentary fashion, in *L'Echange symbolique* (129–52). He situates his discussion firmly within the context of modernity, claiming that only in the framework of the opposition between the "traditional" and the "modern" can fashion exist (135).

21. In Baudrillard's terms, twelfth-century France would be seen as part of "l'ordre primitif" because in such societies "l'ostentation des signes n'a jamais cet effet 'esthétique'" (*L'Echange* 136). Here, he is alluding to the modern experience of fashion as an aesthetic experience, whereas the ostentation of clothing in twelfth-century French society serves a social or ritual function. Exotic or expensive clothing affirms status, establishes identity, and provides the owner a means to reaffirm social ties through gifts. So, although there are surely aesthetic considerations to be made with regard to the desirability of garments, aristocratic clothing performs less of an aesthetic function than a ritual one.

clothes, they did so in the hopes of maintaining class distinction. So, while two of Heller's criteria are met (newness and pleasure), the remaining eight are not, at least not fully, during the twelfth century, as evidenced in literary texts.[22]

Fashion is therefore a system in which the symbolic nature of clothing that prevailed until the late twelfth century becomes destabilized and admits new possibilities of interpretation for individual clothing signifiers. Although the cases are certainly rare, the increasing wealth of the merchant class would allow some merchants to dress in clothing that had previously been worn only by the nobility, thereby destabilizing the symbolic meaning of "noble" for these articles of clothing. This opening up of the clothing system coincided with the changing material conditions in France during this period and could be taken as evidence for placing the very beginnings of the advent of fashion in the late twelfth century.[23] Although the main distinction between the clothing of the different classes was based primarily upon the varying quality of materials used to produce it, the twelfth century witnessed a practical, though not technical, innovation: people, particularly nobles, began to lace the sides of their garments to give the illusion of fitting (Ewing 18, Netherton 7). This modification of silhouette provides a glimpse of the fashion system that would fully articulate itself in later centuries. Thus, the destabilization of the clothing symbol at the more abstract level perfectly reflected this material announcement of the clothing sign that typifies fashion and its inherent arbitrariness.

Vestimentary Significance: The Meaning of Clothing

Without question, clothes have meaning, and this meaning is social in nature.[24] Barnard makes the claim, borrowed from Thomas Carlyle, that part of clothing's role or function is "to make society possible, to be part of

---

22. Heller elaborates on her ten criteria throughout *Fashion in Medieval France*, as well as exploring thoroughly the various theories about the date of the birth of fashion. Her book brings new light into the discussion and provides, I am convinced, at least a firm answer to when we can for certain discern the existence of a fashion system. My argument is that in the twelfth century, things were far murkier, less obvious; French society was on the verge, exhibiting some characteristics of the fashion system but not others. I also fully agree with Heller that it is through literary works of that period that we can most clearly make out the contours of change.

23. This conclusion is indeed the one that Ewing reaches when she places the rise of fashion in the middle of the twelfth century (18).

24. Burns, in her volume *Courtly Love Undressed*, attests to this social function even within the context of a literary universe, referring to the literary dressed body as the "sartorial body," one that arises from an understanding of clothing as "an active force in generating social bodies" (12).

the production and reproduction of relative power within a society" (48). A society's material culture is part of the mechanism by which behavior patterns are acquired and transmitted because intellectual and cultural features become embodied in artifacts, for our purposes, clothing, by imbuing these objects with symbolic meaning (Berger 9). Different modes of dressing within a society have such embedded meanings and, as Barnard points out, serve "to communicate membership of a cultural group both to those who are members of it and to those who are not" (56).

Social structures such as family, economy, polity, religion, and class make up the larger pattern of social organization that constitutes the social order, and associations of individuals with these structures are often made visible through that person's clothing (Roach and Eicher 2). As Roach and Eicher note: "As human beings within a society develop social selves, dress and adornment are intimately linked to their interacting with one another. These personal accouterments assist the individual in presenting his image and expressing himself. He can manipulate his appearance to fit his interpretation of a specific situation, adjusting to the variety of situations in which he finds himself" (2). During the process of socialization, an individual learns to read the various symbols of his or her society. Material objects, especially clothing and adornment items, carry messages and serve as the symbols of a given social setting, becoming the tangible means for exerting some degree of control over the social situation (187). The process of socialization is first and foremost the acquisition of a set of social norms, as well as the capacity for understanding and reproducing them. Behavior that varies considerably from society's norms is considered a deviance (188). A certain degree of deviation from the norm is tolerated by a society, but "there are limits beyond which idiosyncrasy will not be endured" (189).

Roach and Eicher outline ways in which clothing performs within societies, helping to define visually social roles, by differentiating the powerful from the weak, the provider from the receiver, the lord from the serf, and the leader from the follower (10). The apparent opposition inherent in this clothing function tends to derive from a garment's rarity. "Acquiring the most expensive clothing is often a way of achieving differentiating through rarity, which usually commands social admiration" (9). Conversely, a person's clothing may be deceptive (10), as when the increasing wealth of the merchant class over the course of the Middle Ages created opportunities for its members to attire themselves as nobles. Related to this first function are two other functions that clothing performs in a society: as a statement of social worth and as an indicator of economic status (12–13). Statements about social worth entail the use of symbols, a scarlet mantle lined with ermine, for example, and have obvious connections to economic status. "The elite maintain a monopoly on these symbols as long as they maintain a monopoly on wealth, for lack of economic resources prohibits lower classes from adopting adornment that could proclaim for them a social worth equal to that of the upper class" (12). Again, the implications for the nobility of twelfth-century France are clear: the merchants' encroachment upon the nobles' economic well-being and the latter's need to cling to an idealistic social role created the potential for play, or slippage, in the highly codified vestimentary system nobles embraced. Finally, Roach and Eicher write about two other functions of clothing that, unlike the habitual functions described above, are less frequent and more transitory in nature, noting the importance of clothing in certain social rituals (14). Coronations, weddings, funerals, investitures, and dubbing ceremonies fall into this category of function. They also affirm that all these categories are susceptible to subversion; a person's clothing choice is just as capable of disguising his or her identity or state of being as it is of reinforcing it (8).

Clothing has many functions in a society, but there are two main categories: expressive and instrumental (Roach and Eicher 6). Clothing is a visual signifier that divulges information about the person wearing the clothing—his or her beliefs, sentiments, status, rank, or place within the power structure. This would correspond to the expressive function of clothing. However, clothing may be used to fulfill certain goals as well. This is the case with ceremonial or occupational dress, both of which would be considered the instrumental function of clothing. Furthermore, these two functions may be simultaneous (6). We could also borrow a distinction from medieval rhetoric in which expressive dress would demonstrate a character's *ethos*, or the customary and habitual moods or states of mind. Instrumental dress, by contrast, being geared toward action, would allow expression of *pathos*, characterized by strong movements of emotions, thus transitory in nature. In this last case, it is clear that clothes "are associated with a complex of strong emotions and serve to channel strong emotions" (Cordwell and Schwartz 28).

Literary, or written, clothing deserves some special consideration. Roland Barthes, in his semiotic study of clothing, *Système de la mode*, talks of written clothing in terms of a translation of the real garment in which the author chooses the features of the garment he or she will represent. Literature uses the technique of description to transform a hidden object, whether real or imaginary, into language: thus, description makes this object exist (23). Unlike a visual representation of the garment or the experience of a real garment, the verbal representation limits the possibilities of perceiving the object (23–24). The language used to describe the clothing object singles out features or elements of the article of clothing for emphasis (25–26), and the audience's perceptions of any given literary clothing object are thus determined by the choices that the author has made in his or her description of the object. In literature, the article of clothing exists only through its representation: it is "porté par le langage, mais aussi il lui résiste, et c'est dans ce jeu qu'il se fait" (14). In this way, written clothing "est tout entier constitué en vue d'une signification" (18). Clearly, written clothing has the potential to mediate the material reality of the world and the imagined universe of the ideal. Equally clear is that the writers of twelfth-century French courtly literature are engaged in such a project.

2

MATERIAL MATTERS:
CLOTHING IN CHANGING CONTEXTS

THE TWELFTH CENTURY, WITH its great societal shifts, new literary expressions, and technical innovations and improvements, accordingly saw a heightened emphasis on personal adornment, particularly given the influx of luxurious fabrics from the East and the introduction of different modes of dress borrowed from Muslim societies. Nonetheless, change did not occur overnight, and the advent of fashion was, as Heller has shown, tempered by a nostalgia among the nobility to retain its position at the top of the social hierarchy.

Costume History

For the most part, twelfth-century French clothing possessed a stability of form inasmuch as each individual garment remained remarkably constant in terms of both cut and shape even across many variables, such as class. However, certain modifications, particularly those of a decorative nature, were beginning to appear. In medieval France, the layering of clothing was the norm. Men and women both wore several types of garments, some of which could be added or removed depending on climactic conditions, the formality of the occasion, or the class of the wearer.[1] Clothing vocabulary is notoriously difficult to translate, for two reasons. First, the terms no longer correspond to any modern clothing items, and the modern reader of medieval romance can be easily baffled by the terms, leading to a misreading of the text. Second, there is little possibility of costume historians identifying with perfect certainly what clothing terms in medieval texts, especially of the twelfth and thirteenth centuries, match up to what little visual evidence

---

1. Yvonne Deslandres asserts: "Il peut paraître étrange que nous ne puissions percevoir aucune différence entre les vêtements d'été et d'hiver; mais l'habitude étant toujours de superposer les robes les unes par-dessus des autres, on peut supposer que l'on supprimait une ou deux suivant la température" (101).

remains of clothing of the period.[2] The entire ensemble, or outfit, was referred to as a *robe*, unlike the modern French usage of the word (Goddard 198). The basic components of typical aristocratic male and female dress in the twelfth century were the same. The undergarment, or *chemise*, usually made of linen, was a loose tuniclike garment with long sleeves worn under all other garments.[3] The long *chainse*, most likely of wool or linen for everyday wear, tended to have fitted sleeves and often served as an outer garment on an informal occasion or as an intermediate layer under the *bliaut*, the outer gown, which was most often made of wool or silk and worn belted (Evans 5). One also wore a cloak (*chape* or *chasuble*) over the *bliaut* if weather necessitated it. The vast majority of outer clothing articles were woolen, despite the numerous passages in verse romance describing garments of the finest silk, and this discrepancy once again highlights to what extent the writers of romance were creating an idealized world for their audience. Men additionally wore *braies*, or britches.[4] In colder weather, men, and likely women, wore *chausses*, hose of tailored cloth worn over the feet and legs and under the shoes (Boucher 172). The garments of the period, according to Hollander, "show a fairly static simplicity of shape," differences obtaining mostly for utilitarian reasons (363). She further explains: "Sumptuous fabrics were worn by the rich, mean ones by the poor; but the

---

2. Further complicating the matter is that most visual evidence that dates from the twelfth century does not correspond to the vernacular tales recounted in the romances of the period. The vast majority of manuscript illumination of the second half of the century depicts biblical and liturgical figures rather than the laity. We must wait until manuscripts of the thirteenth century to witness images of the characters of twelfth-century romance, and very often this has meant that Chrétien's knights and ladies are presented in costume of the thirteenth century. There are, in fact, even more representations of the same narrative material that date from the fourteenth century, when fashion had taken a radical turn away from the more simple shapes of the late twelfth century. These late manuscript illuminations are beautiful and contribute visual aids to imagine the exploits of the characters of the romances, but they do very little to illuminate the actual vestimentary realities of the period in which Chrétien and Marie composed their tales.

3. Romaine Wolf-Bonvin reminds us that in Chrétien's *Perceval*, the hero, in his Welsh costume, wears a *chemise* of hemp (*chanvre*), whereas in Chrétien's *Cligés*, Alexandre arrives in Arthur's court wearing a *chemise* of silk (*soie*) ("Un vêtement" 392n2). These are, however, depictions of unusual characters, for Perceval is noble, and he should rightly be wearing a finer fabric as an undergarment, but here Chrétien is underlining the hero's rustic lifestyle; Alexandre, who is the son of the Eastern Emperor, is wearing a silk *chemise* to demonstrate his wealth and status, but also very likely because of his easy access to the silk production in Byzantium.

The universality of the *chemise* is noted by Hollander, who calls it "a voluminous white garment of extreme simplicity with little or no shaping and trimming" (159). She also remarks upon its symbolic importance, standing for "the humility of nakedness at a time when real nakedness was usually very well covered" (159).

4. For a discussion of *braies* as depicted in the romances of the twelfth and thirteenth century, see Burns, "Ladies Don't Wear *Braies*."

cut and fit of clothes was uniformly simple and unsophisticated for all classes and both sexes.[5] Wealth and rank were expressed in the nobility's clothing but no kind of aesthetic or stylistic superiority" (363). Piponnier and Mane echo her assertion but add that dramatic changes in types of fabrics and their decoration, influenced by access to the cloth goods of the Islamic world, were steadily transforming the appearance of aristocratic clothing (59).[6]

Although, in previous periods, men had sometimes worn short tunics, around the year 1140, most everyone, and not only royalty, began to wear long gowns (Pinasa 69).[7] The nobility further accentuated this lowering of the hemline by exaggerating certain features of their costume, such as long trains on cloaks and wide, draping sleeves on *bliauts* (Boucher 171, Evans 5, Pinasa 73). The sleeves of ladies' *bliauts* were sometimes so long that the hanging ends were knotted (Evans 7). The church generally disapproved of what it saw as an excessive consumption of goods, and many church fathers wrote to condemn the fashion; for example, Maurice de Sully writes: "Neis a femes deffent il qu'elles ne se fachent trop beles por leurs maris par leurs vesteures, car trop i a de luxure. Par ces paroles se devroient castier cil et celes qui ont leur orgeuleuses vesteures mi paries et entaillies et lor lons trains" (It is prohibited for women to make themselves too beautiful for their husbands with their clothing, for there is too much debauchery. With these words, they should be ashamed, those who wear prideful, fitted clothes cut from two colors of cloth with long trains).[8] Adding to the luxurious nature

---

5. I think Hollander's value judgment here is a bit too harsh, since she equates simplicity of cut with a lack of sophistication in design. We have no evidence that the garments of the period were perceived by those wearing them as "unsophisticated."

6. Burns has examined the prevalence of Islamic fabrics in the elaboration of a Western courtly identity among the nobility during this period. Her assertion is that, although twelfth-century Europeans experienced enmity with the Muslim East, they nonetheless constructed exquisite garments from their textiles, thereby introducing an Eastern element into what was the Western ideal of beauty. See in particular her chapter "Saracen Silk: Dolls, Idols, and Courtly Ladies," in her *Courtly Love Undressed*.

7. Enlart agrees with Pinasa's date, whereas Laver places the lengthening a decade earlier. "Une révolution se produisait, en effet, vers 1140, et la mode des vêtements longs pour les deux sexes semble être venue alors d'Orient, par l'intermédiaire des Normands de Sicile" (Enlart 31). "The tunic of the nobility, from about 1130 onwards, began to be made with a tight-fitting body and the long skirt to be slit up from the front to thigh-level and kept in place with a sword-belt" (Laver, *Costume* 31). François Boucher points out that the "short *bliaut*" of the early twelfth century was probably the descendant garment of the *gonelle* of the Carolingian period (171).

8. Bibliothèque de l'Arsenal, ms. fr., 2111, f. 35, as quoted in Bourgain (303). The Norman monk Ordericus Vitalis echoes his concern in condemning the "French" fashion among the young nobility (Bumke 138). Saint Bernard of Clairvaux, in a letter to the virgin Sophia, laments that women of the court adorn themselves so richly and so extravagantly while their souls are in peril; he claims emphatically that the superficial beauty of one's garments constitutes no replacement for the

of their clothing, the nobility often decorated the hems or edges of the sleeves with precious bands of embroidered cloth.[9] Essentially concurrent with these clothing trends was the tendency among ladies to lace the sides of their gown to accentuate their female shape. Elizabeth Ewing explains that around 1150, women's dresses became tight fitting and appeared waisted, although "there was as yet no cutting to form the waist and no separation of bodice and skirt, but the lacing created the first closely defined waistline in modern dress history. Buttons and other fasteners did not yet exist, so lacing was the obvious way to achieve this effect" (18). Robin Netherton asserts that in the absence of certain construction technologies, such as the set-in sleeve, a necessary component of "truly form-fitting clothing," lacings along the side seams of the torso are the most likely explanation for the fitted shape of the dress (7). Netherton also points to the lack of conclusive evidence that this technique was universal, reminding us that there are relatively few examples of visible lacings in the artwork of the period (7). Perhaps the twelfth-century trend in lacing, which later disappeared, was limited to the nobility, much as was the "French" fashion of using great lengths of fabric.

The courtly literature that constitutes the subject of this study concerns itself almost exclusively with the nobility and often royalty, and therefore, the vast majority of the clothing that it describes or mentions belongs to noble characters. Although aristocratic dress was characterized, for the most part, not by different articles or cut of clothing, but rather by the materials used to produce the garment, the exception to this rule was the mantle, which was often fur lined. Only persons of a certain status possessed mantles, and these items were, it is believed, ceremonial garments, worn on occasions of some importance. Commoners wore cloaks, *chapes*, for warmth and protection, as did aristocrats when they were wearing their everyday clothing. Although many of the garments worn by members of the aristocracy were lined with fur, the type of fur used carried meaning.[10] Ermine has associations with

---

real beauty of the soul (174–77). Serlon of Séez, Radbode of Noyon, Milon of Térouane, and Pierre le Chantre also speak out against the excessive use of cloth and adornment (Bourgain 300–303).

9. Camille Enlart tells us: "On appelait *orfrois* ou *orfrais* . . . des galons brodés et généralement larges; ils pouvaient avoir jusqu'à 20, 30, 50 centimètres de largeur. Sur un galon de soie ou de drap d'or ou d'argent, on faisait à l'aiguille des dessins d'ornement . . . L'Orient a fourni aux occidentaux une grande quantité de galons tissés de fil d'or et de soie à dessins variés autant d'élégants" (235).

10. Enlart notes that the most coveted furs required trade with often distant foreign locales, attesting also to the fact that this was a developing trend in the twelfth century: "La mode [d'apporter] ces fourrures se développa beaucoup au XIIe siècle, avec les progrès du commerce international. On se mit à l'importer d'Allemagne, de Norvège et même de Russie et de Sibérie" (229).

royalty and, in fact, was typically only worn on state occasions (Evans 10). The wearing of highly embroidered silks, such as samite, was reserved for ceremonial occasions, as well (10). The fine fabrics obtained through trade with the East were among the most prized for use in the construction of clothing for the nobility, but even nobles must have worn woolen garments every day, for the climate would have required it. The nobles would have had their clothing made of the finest wool, produced in northern France and in Flanders, areas whose economies owed much of their development and expansion to the booming cloth trade.

The Economy of Cloth

The economic situation in twelfth-century France was one of transition. Growth in the economy was the result of a number of factors, involving many social classes: changing aesthetic considerations among the princely class, the expansion of the merchant economy, and the increase of the number of laborers and the improvement of their techniques and equipment. The advances in technology of the twelfth century had a tremendous impact on the rapidly developing economy, producing surpluses of goods for less labor, and, according to Rondo Cameron, the "largest and most ubiquitous industry was no doubt the manufacture of cloth" (68).[11] Certain areas in Europe, such as Flanders, northern Italy, Tuscany, southern and eastern England, and southern France, specialized in the manufacture of cloth.[12] The cloth production of these regions included wool of different types and quality; linen (especially in France); and silk and cotton, whose production was limited to Italy and Muslim Spain (Cameron 69). From the eleventh to the thirteenth centuries, Europe went from being primarily an importer to becoming an exporter as well, and cloth was vital to this

---

11. Roland Barthes notes the primacy of technological factors in determining dress when he claims that "la structure du vêtement réel ne peut être que technologique; les unités de cette structure ne peuvent être que les traces diverses des actes de fabrication, leurs fins accomplies, matérialisées" (*Système* 15).

12. Cameron notes that these areas had begun to specialize in textiles as early as the eleventh century (68–69). Pirenne confirms that the Italians of Lucca were manufacturing silk by the twelfth century, although their raw materials came from abroad, and that the manufacture of cloth was creating great wealth in the towns of Ghent, Bruges, Ypres, Lille, Douai, and Arras (33–36). Bloch situates the cloth centers in Flanders, Picardy, Bourges, Languedoc, and Lombardy (1: 113). Duby accentuates that the expanding cloth trade of the mid-twelfth century required a more specialized work force and affirms that this kind of specialization is possible only in large towns (*Guerriers* 266–69).

new status (Bloch 1: 113). The new ability to export cloth resulted from both increases in population and new agricultural technologies, especially in plowing, which yielded bigger and more frequent harvests and provided sustenance for more weavers, dyers, and cloth shearers than before (1: 113). The increase in the number of workers accompanied several technical innovations in the production of cloth that dramatically increased productivity at the beginning of the twelfth century: the horizontal treadle loom, replacing other, simpler looms; the spinning wheel, replacing the distaff; and the water-powered fulling mill (Cameron 69).

In addition to the technological advances being made in Europe, the Crusades figured prominently in the growth of the European economy. The main outcome of the supposedly religious wars was, in fact, commercial, that is, "a new culture and material prosperity, a vastly extended knowledge, a well-formed and far-reaching ambition" (Beazley 119). Besides occasioning the revival of economic exchanges, which had declined since antiquity, the Crusades enhanced the development of international communications, strengthened royal power, and facilitated the emergence of a new social class of merchants and artisans (Boucher 178). Economic growth produced an increasing awareness among the nobles of their clothing (Duby, *Guerriers* 262).[13] Duby explains this phenomenon well: "Dans l'espèce de paix qu'instaura l'établissement de la féodalité et que raffermit progressivement le renforcement désormais à l'extension des besoins des grandes maisons seigneuriales, à l'élévation progressive du niveau de la vie qu'on y menait, à l'aisance que procurait, à ceux qui exploitaient le droit de ban, l'accroissement constant des revenus, fondé lui-même sur l'expansion de la production rurale" (*Guerriers* 262). The French aristocracy thus found itself increasingly confronted with new types of expenditures.

The Crusades had also brought Europeans into contact with exotic civilizations rich in gold, marble, silk, and ivory through expeditions to Spain, southern Italy, and the Holy Lands and had expanded French tastes for luxury and better living conditions (Contamine et al. 154).[14] Deslandres observes: "La société du douzième siècle s'arrache petit à petit à une vie

---

13. Françoise Piponnier and Perrine Mane maintain that "le culte du paraître . . . s'inscrit dans l'idéal de largesse cultivé par la classe chevaleresque" (73).

14. Alison Lurie elaborates: "The crusaders who went to fight in the Holy Land . . . [brought] back to Europe a selection of exotic styles that became the rage of aristocratic Christendom: the Saracen turban, the pointed shoes of the Turks and the Jewish steeple headdress. The Crusades also introduced new colors such as azure and lilac, whose names preserve their Persian origin" (88–89).

Jacques Anquetil explains that the patterns and motifs of Eastern fabrics influenced not only European tastes in cloth but also designs used in many other decorative arts in Europe (22).

étroitement liée à la nécessité quotidienne" (101). The desire among nobles to display their wealth to the greatest extent that their means allowed spurred the further development of the merchant economy: "Sovereigns, prelates, the aristocracy, and, to some extent, the wealthier strata of the population required various sorts of articles and merchandise that could not be produced locally and thus had to be imported from other and at times distant places. Not only luxurious garments and stuffs, fine tableware, and other rarities to satisfy the governing elite's need for prestige, but also more ordinary merchandise was often furnished by the merchants who plied the waterways and the land routes" (Gurevich 243). The increased volume in trade required certain measures to improve the conditions in which it took place. The twelfth century saw the construction of many bridges (Bloch 1: 112). Moreover, trade between southern and northern Europe had become a reality, primarily because the Alpine mountain passes had been made safer.[15] Feudal lords had reduced the risk of bandits and improved the roads, religious brotherhoods had organized relay stations and rescue services, and professional companies of carters and muleteers provided transport facilities for traveling merchants (Cameron 65). Kings and princes were interested in commerce not only because it provided them with the goods they required to demonstrate their status, but also because it was a source of prosperity for them. In addition to levying tolls and duties on the mercantile activity facilitated by improved roads and bridges, they came to understand "l'importance vitale qui s'attache pour [eux] à la libre circulation des ordres et des armées" (Bloch 1: 112).

Of crucial importance to the emerging European economy were the merchant fairs of the Champagne region in France. Cameron explains:

> The fairs of Champagne emerged in the twelfth century as the most important meeting place in Europe for merchants from north and south. Under the protection of the counts of Champagne, who provided merchandising facilities and special commercial courts as well as protection on the road for traveling merchants, the fairs rotated almost continuously throughout the year among the four towns of Provins, Troyes, Lagny, and Bas-sur-Aube. Located roughly midway between Europe's two most highly developed

---

15. The Alps had presented a tremendous obstacle to trade in medieval Europe, especially as a result of avalanches, wild animals, a lack of maps, and the necessity of using pack animals (Mackay 131).

> economic regions, northern Italy and the Low Countries, they
> served as meeting ground and place of business for merchants from
> each; but they also played a role in the trade of northern Germany
> with southern France and the Iberian peninsula. The commer-
> cial practices and techniques that developed in these towns—for
> example, the "letters of fairs" and other credit instruments, and
> the precedents of their commercial courts—exercised an influence
> far broader and longer lasting than the fairs themselves. Even after
> their decline as commodity trading centers, they continued for
> many years to serve as financial centers. (65)

These huge commercial events, almost a year-round phenomenon, did a great deal to fuel the development of the European economy, and it is particularly interesting that one of the major categories of goods traded at the fairs was cloth and other goods necessary for the manufacture of luxury clothing.[16] It is perhaps no coincidence that Chrétien de Troyes, the major trendsetter in twelfth-century French literature and whose clothing signify-ing system is one of the most highly developed examples that we have, was so closely associated with the court of Champagne. This court benefited from its close proximity to the fairs and its protection of their trade practices, in terms both of economic gain and of access to luxury cloth and other rare and highly prized vestimentary materials. At these fairs, north met south, or, in terms of the clothing constantly represented in courtly literature, fur met silk, allowing also for east to meet west as the styles and materials from the east came to define the courtly dress of the western aristocracy. The situa-tion was ripe for the expansion of the potential of clothing, both materially and representationally.

Raw Materials

The itinerant merchants, by building up trade networks with faraway cultures, incorporated foreign threads into the very fabric of everyday feu-dal life, as well as into its imagination. The new connections established as

---

16. Peter Spufford notes the importance of the fairs for banking, and especially interna-tional banking, since their trade was greatly facilitated with the advent of the bill of exchange, first as a notarized *instrumentum ex causa cambii*, some of which survive from the twelfth century, recording transactions between Genoa (where banking in Europe first arose) and the Champagne fairs (xxxi).

the result of the Crusades and the increased safety of passage bore the fruits of new raw materials for the manufacture and embellishment of clothing in France. The thick, massive forests of northern Europe and Russia provided great amounts of fur, some very valuable, such as sable, miniver, and ermine (Abbott 5). Vair and gris, also furs of Baltic origin, were made from the hides of squirrels; vair was made from whole squirrels and derived its name from the variation in color, unlike gris, which was made only from the gray back of the winter skins of the animals whence it gets its name (Veale 228). Russian furs, especially ermine, were more expensive, and therefore more desirable, than local furs, and the aristocracy monopolized these imported furs throughout the medieval period (Abbott 7). Scandinavian and Russian furs were "ceremonial wares, an insignia of wealth and standing" (Postan and Miller 169). Ermine had a strong association with the ideals of the nobility, for it was believed that the animal, rather than spoil its winter white coat, would kill itself; the animal's action echoed the bravery, virtue, and rarity to which the royalty aspired (Abbott 8). In courtly circles, a veritable "fur vocabulary," in Abbott's terms, grew up in which "'fur signs' were the highest expressions in a socioeconomic code" (5).

Fur may have been the most desirable lining for a garment belonging to an aristocrat, but silk was the fabric of choice. Unlike woolen fabrics, whose production was, for the most part, if not local, then of not so distant provenance, silk had exotic origins. Moreover, the fabric possessed aesthetic qualities unparalleled by "lesser" fabrics: "The special magic of silk stems from its interaction with light. . . . When light plays on a piece of silk, the weave appears, in turn, to glisten, change color, become moiré, lustrous, or matte. Silk is capable of such infinite metamorphosis that no adjective can describe it exactly" (Anquetil 7).

Silk's luminosity and rareness proved to be far more than the nobility of the twelfth century could resist.[17] The Crusaders had discovered new *soieries* whose products possessed a richness coupled with brilliant color and a high degree of ornamentation, and whose fineness seduced Europeans (Pinasa 67). Commercial relations with the Middle East expanded rapidly, conveying to Europe such exquisite fabrics as *cendal, paile, siglaton, osterin,* and samite (Pinasa 67).[18] In addition to this commercial activity with the Levant, by the end of the twelfth century, the Italians had begun to

---

17. Heller has examined the draw of luminosity and how light had become, by the early thirteenth century, a major feature of a glamorous image, in her essay "Light as Glamour."

18. *Cendal* was a lightweight silk similar to our modern taffeta, often red (Pinasa 67), and it was often used to line garments of silk or wool, as well as for making accessories and cushions

import raw silk from Asia for weaving. The Italian silk manufacture of the Middle Ages was first concentrated in Sicily (Muthesius, "Sicilian Silks" 165–66), where the invading Normans developed the craft both artistically and technically (Anquetil 24). At the end of the twelfth century sericulture and fine-figured silk weaving expanded to mainland Italy, particularly to Lucca (25). The Italians were expert dyers, often importing fabric from other places to finish it, particularly fine wool from Flanders and raw silk from the East (Bourquelot 212). Italian-finished cloths found their way to the rest of Europe through the intermediary of Venetian and Genoese traders who traveled with their goods to the merchant fairs (Anquetil 29–32). The Venetians had also cornered the import market for Eastern dyestuffs (Leix, "Medieval Dye Markets" 326) such as brazilwood (or sappan), indigo, and lacca (Leix, "Trade Routes" 317), while the Genoese practically held a monopoly over the importation of alum, the most important mordant for the dye trade (320). Woolen cloth from northern France and Flanders began to be exported to the East through the port of Genoa by the second half of the twelfth century (Pirenne 144).

The expansion of the cloth trade created a greater need for dyestuffs, for, with the exception of linen and hemp, almost all cloth was dyed. The most common dyes of medieval Europe were derived from local, usually vegetal, products, but some of the most desirable dyes, the ones used to color the most exquisite fabrics of the day, were produced from resources found as far away as India. However, although some Eastern dyes were

---

(Piponnier and Mane 20). It is also believed to be a mixed silk, woven with other fibers to create more suppleness (Ditchfield 402).

Paile, sometimes referred to simply as imperial (according to Wingate), was a brocaded silk from Alexandria (Pinasa 67), which may have been striped. Robert Irwin, in his *Le Monde islamique*, argues that, in fact, some fabrics that carry the designation "d'Alexandrie" were not actually produced in that city but transported through its port on its way to Europe (159).

Siglaton was a "rich, heavy damask silk, usually ornately brocaded and often embroidered in gold" (Munro 23), produced throughout the Middle East, and used for garments of the highest luxury (Pinasa 67). It was later produced widely in Muslim Spain (Irwin 161).

Osterin was a purple silk from Byzantium, which had inherited the secret of the costly purple dye used for this fabric from the classical world (Pinasa 67). By the twelfth century, however, the availability of murex was diminishing if not exhausted throughout the region (Pastoureau, *Petit livre* 34); thus it is possible that references to this fabric in texts of the period rely upon a suspension of disbelief among their audiences in favor of a nostalgic view of what was actually available.

Samite was a weft-faced compound twill (Muthesius, "Silk" 343), woven in such a way as to create a pattern, often with gold or silver thread, and it was sometimes used as a base for embroidery. For a full discussion of medieval samite, see Anna Muthesius's chapter "From Seed to Samite: Aspects of Byzantine Silk Production," in her *Studies in Byzantine and Islamic Silk Weaving*. I thank Elena House for help with this description of samite.

in use in the northern parts of Europe, most of the wools were colored with native dyes (Leix,"Trade Routes" 321). Woad and madder were the most common dyes and came from northwest Europe (Postan and Miller 634). Woad, a blue dye also used as a base for other colors, was the most prevalent in the Middle Ages (Crowfoot, Pritchard, and Staniland 19). To increase color saturation with woad, dyers would draw the cloth through the dye bath multiple times: several times to achieve black, fewer to achieve blue, and still fewer to achieve green (Neuburger 338). Madder typically produced a warm brick-red color, although it could also produce peach, yellow, violet, brown, and tan, as well as boosting other colors such as green and blue (Crowfoot, Pritchard, and Staniland 200). Woad and madder were often used together to yield colors such as violet, sanguine, and burnet (Postan and Miller 634). The two other sources of red dye in the Middle Ages were not available in Europe and had to be imported from the East, at considerable cost: kermes, or cochineal, which produces a scarlet color and was used to dye only the finest of fabrics, and brazilwood (Crowfoot, Pritchard, and Staniland 200).[19] Other important dyes were weld, saffron, safflower, orseille, indigo, and lichen purple (Neuburger 338). Wold was also cultivated in Europe and, used alone, produced a yellow color that was not very much in demand, but when combined with woad, it yielded a desirable green color (Postan and Miller 634). To achieve a richness in color commensurate with the quality of a fabric such as silk, one needed expensive dyes, prized for the brilliance of color they achieve. The intense red color deriving from kermes, also called grain or scarlet, replaced purple as the royal color during the Middle Ages.[20] "L'écarlate adopte volontiers un rouge intense . . . à laquelle la théorie médicale des humeurs et de leurs correspondances attribue des qualités prophylactiques. Chargée de signification, écarlate devient l'insigne du pouvoir féodal" (Piponnier and Mane 72–73). Accordingly, the mantles given to knights on the occasion of their dubbing were cut from scarlet (73).

---

19. Although fabrics dyed with kermes are most often silks, John H. Munro points out that the "woolen scarlet was incontestably the most renowned luxury textile manufactured in medieval Europe, even if rivaled and often surpassed in value by oriental and Italian silks" (Harte and Ponting 14).

20. The recipe for imperial purple obtained from murex was lost to the West during the Middle Ages, and kermes, which was as difficult and costly to obtain, replaced it as the dye of choice, producing a red of a brilliance without equal. As Michel Pastoureau points out: "Pour l'oeil médiéval, l'éclat d'un objet (son aspect mat ou brillant) prime sur sa coloration: un rouge franc sera perçu comme plus proche d'un bleu lumineux que d'un rouge délavé. Un rouge vif est toujours un marqué de puissance chez les laïcs comme chez les ecclésiastiques" (*Petit livre* 35).

The Gift Economy

The ritualized gift typified by the dubbing ceremony holds a special position in the organization of feudal society.[21] In the twelfth century, at the same time that the mercantile economy was rapidly expanding, a different form of exchange, among the members of the nobility, was prevalent and even preferred—the gift economy. Feudal society was based on a system of reciprocal relations between persons of different social classes, and one of the most important means for solidifying these ties was gifts, and in particular, gifts of clothing, armor, or cloth: "Between equals or near-equals, cordial relationships were created and affirmed by the exchange of gifts. Between individuals or groups of differing status, the disparity of the exchanges both articulated and defined the direction and degree of subordination" (Geary 173).

Under feudalism, a vassal swore homage to a lord, who gave his protection in return, and often a gift from the vassal to the lord accompanied this exchange. "The goal of gift-giving was not the acquisition of commodities but the establishment of bonds between giver and receiver, bonds that had to be reaffirmed at some point by a countergift" (Geary 173). Following this initial gift, it behooved the lord to provide many gifts for his vassals. Indeed, "le seul vrai maître était celui qui avait donné" (Bloch 1: 251). Moreover, lords' "autorité était à la mesure de leur largesse, vertu majeure des dirigeants, indispensable" (Duby, *Trois ordres* 192). These feudal lords expressed their largess by hosting great feasts and through gifts of clothing:

> Être riche au XIIe siècle . . . obligeait . . . à donner . . . à ses amis, à les accueillir nombreux, à étendre aussi largement que possible la maisonnée, à [*les*] *parer*. . . Les cours, au centre de la seigneurie banale furent donc . . . des lieux d'accueil largement ouverts à tout venant; la plus grande gloire du maître était d'y distribuer les plaisirs, et ses largesses répandaient les plaisirs de la vie parmi ses hôtes, permanents et temporaires, comme parmi ses serviteurs (*Guerriers* 261–62; emphasis mine).

They also expressed their generosity less directly, namely in the hosting of tournaments, which often marked a significant social event, such as the marriage of a knight. Preparation for tournaments necessitated a tremendous

---

21. In fact, this attitude toward gifts is not confined to twelfth-century France; it is, as Marcel Mauss tells us, common in "archaic" societies for people to regard gifts as crucial markers of lines of mutual obligation (65).

expenditure and distributed wealth to the industries involved in equipping knights and providing entertainment. The lord paid for all the activities involved in tournaments, which, as Duby has noted, rarely if ever increased the monetary fortune of the host. Great lords

> combattaient sans cesse; leurs fils, dans les tournois, jouaient à combattre, et cette activité coûtait beaucoup plus qu'elle ne rapportait. Elle faisait couler très abondamment les deniers des mains des princes, les répandant parmi les petits chevaliers, parmi les éleveurs de chevaux, les fabricants d'armures, parmi tous les trafiquants et les amuseurs attirés par la foire très animée qui environnait chaque tournoi. C'était maintenant, par un complet retournement, la principale fonction économique de la guerre: non plus ajouter aux ressources de l'aristocratie, mais la pousser à dépenser davantage. (*Guerriers* 257)

All members of the aristocracy, including knights, needed to demonstrate largess, primarily because it most clearly distinguished them from other classes, whose concerns over money were greater. For knights, who had the military means to procure whatever they desired, and routinely did so, this need to demonstrate generosity was particularly strong. For members of this warrior class, as Bloch notes, "le gain est légitime. A une condition toutefois: qu'il soit promptement et libéralement dépensé. . . . A laisser couler entre ses doigts la fortune vite acquise, vite perdue, le noble croyait s'affirmer sa supériorité envers des classes moins confiantes dans l'avenir ou plus soucieuses de la calculer" (2: 44).

However, the ruling class did not perceive largess as an absolute social obligation. As is the case with the modern notion of charity, the nobles determined when, where, what, and to whom to give.[22] The privileged class had what Duby calls "des attitudes mentales qui jadis avaient été celles des rois," resulting in its members' refusal to engage in any form of exchange of wealth to which they had not freely consented (*Guerriers* 190). Moreover, the aristocracy refused "toute prestation qu'elle n'a pas consentie et n'accepte de se dépouiller de ses biens que par des dons gratuits et par des générosités mutuelles" (190). It is perhaps this attitude toward the distribution of wealth that kept the other classes worried about their future affluence. Yet the circulation

---

22. For a discussion of how during the twelfth century samite's dissemination was controlled through Byzantine imperial gift practices for the purposes of creating allegiances and bonds, see my forthcoming article "Superlative Silk: Samite and the Grail."

of luxury items surely constituted a source of further anxiety for the ruling class, since these gifts not only pleased the recipients but also helped to construct new social identities for them. As E. Jane Burns notes, "Clothing passed from the nobility to jongleurs, knights, or paupers marks the ruling elite as generous while also making recipients of aristocratic dress more courtly than their lineage or occupation would otherwise indicate" (*Courtly Love* 29). It is precisely because of the portability and exchangeability of clothing that it has the potential to create confusion by blurring demarcations of class, rank, and role (30). Largess expressed through clothing gifts thus served both to solidify social bonds and to ignite culture anxieties among the ruling elite by disrupting the continuity of the vestimentary code.

Although clothing gifts tend to be normative in their literary expression, primarily because of their important societal function as the material manifestation of social ties, there exists a more complicated interpretation of such clothing gifts, as evidenced by the gift of a scarlet mantle on the occasion of a knight's dubbing, to make my point. This expensive gift of clothing to newly dubbed knights usually accompanies a gift of armor, armor being the symbol of knighthood. This double gift, however, problematizes the straightforward symbolism of the act, in that it conveys the social necessity of conferring as much status as possible to knights, given their diminished role in society as a result of the movement from wartime to a more peaceful period. Knights, typically the younger sons of aristocratic families, possessing few if any land rights and therefore unlikely to marry, were, in fact, socially inferior to the lords to whom they swore their oaths of fealty. The combined gift of armor, the necessary accouterment for battle, and a mantle, the appropriate dress for a noble at court, confers both function and status upon the knight. Yet it is also an indication of the knight's need, indeed his lack, in his original situation. The double gift is analogous to what Umberto Eco refers to as a "surplus of expression" (*Theory* 270). In using a double signifier to confer status on its knights, twelfth-century French society has increased the informational possibilities of the message of the clothing gift. "The message has in effect become a source of further and unpredictable information, so that it is now semantically ambiguous" (270).

Play in the System: Consequences of the Expanding Economy

The expanding merchant economy certainly provided the nobility with the goods that it required, but this economy also had its drawbacks. Itinerant merchants themselves represented a threat to the established order of the day since they tended to be strangers, culturally, religiously, and ethnically, heralding often from far-away lands and cultures (Reyserson 2–4). Bourquelot, in his seminal study on the fairs of Champagne, cites the extensive networks of mercantile activity that were established by the twelfth century and finds evidence of the presence of merchants from every part of Europe, from Scandinavia, and from the Orient at the fairs (133ff.). Reyserson also notes that even merchants who were not trading at a great distance from their own homes were perceived as strangers, because they did not participate in the "archetypical tripartite vision of medieval society: those who fought, those who prayed, and those who worked" (2). The increase of mercantile activity threatened the very fabric of feudal society because it defied the traditional social organization and rejected the values of the ruling class. Not only did its values conflict with those of the gift economy, but the peace required for its flourishing also had a destabilizing effect on the traditional military role that had defined the gentry's previous social superiority. For centuries, the landed nobility had passed their lands to eldest sons, and the other sons had preserved their nobility through chivalry, that is, by being knights. But war is a costly endeavor, and many nobles were exhausting their wealth in elaborate displays, involving, for example, clothing, gifts, and huge communal meals.[23] These ever-increasing expenditures necessary for preserving social status required many among the nobility to turn to credit (Kellogg, "Economic and Social Tensions" 15). The end of the twelfth century saw a financial crisis among the nobility caused by its increased indebtedness (15). Many baronial families began to mortgage their lands and villages to pay for the various goods and services required by their status: providing fiefs, dowries, and expenses for crusades or pilgrimages, as well as personal spending on clothing and the like (16). Moreover, the nobles had a powerful disdain toward any source of revenue that did not derive from their function as landholders. Their station prevented them from engaging in trade or in any other vocation, and thus they were unable to relieve themselves of the burden of debt. The commercial economy that developed during this period increasingly favored the merchant class, whose ethics did not place such a restriction upon their gainful activities.[24] The wealth of

---

23. The excesses of the nobility, inspired by a taste for the exotic through the exposure afforded by the Crusades, are charmingly described in Kraemer-Raine (26–27).

24. According to Beazley, medieval commercial practices were actually "superior to the ancient commercial activity in claiming greater privileges for the trader, in giving more attention to

many nobles was therefore becoming ever more unstable and, with a heavy reliance on credit, abstract.

The nobility placed a premium on the ability to distinguish social rank immediately from a person's dress, and according to Barnard, clothing constructs "visual identities for the different classes and thus . . . naturalize[s] the inequalities of wealth and power" (103–4).[25] The desire of nobles to maintain their absolute position in society gave rise both to the need to dress as well as their means afforded, and sometimes beyond those means, and later to the proliferation of sumptuary laws.[26] Sumptuary laws governed the consumption of luxury items and were often used as an attempt to control which classes wore which kinds of clothing, thereby preserving class distinctions.[27] Barnard claims that, in fact, sumptuary laws represent a governmental effort to "fix the meaning of . . . clothing," by deciding which clothing components were appropriate to particular social classes (75). The laws were also occasionally used "as a means of inducing people to save money" (Roach and Eicher 296), as well as a way to protect local industries from unfair competition from abroad (Deslandres 177). There are essentially no records of sumptuary laws in twelfth-century France, but laws governing the consumption of fine goods, including clothing items, would begin to appear early in the next century.[28] Alan Hunt defines sumptuary laws as

---

freedom of trade intercourse, in undertaking more daring and speculative operations, and in devoting greater energy to the discovery of new markets" (119).

25. In medieval Europe, dressing above one's station, as the newly wealthy merchants were beginning to be able to do, was viewed as an illegitimate action, to use Peter Corrigan's term: "Clearly, the underlying assumption is that clothing *ought* to tell us something about the social world—we read it as if it did, hence the danger of illegitimately arrogated apparel in a world of rigid class differences" (437).

26. Elizabeth B. Hurlock explains the situation well: "In a feudal society where the lines of demarcation between classes was strictly drawn, the nobility displayed its superiority by abstaining from any form of productive labor. But as trade and commerce increased, and as the towns became the centers of wealth, the feudal lords found competition in the wealthy middle class, and, as a consequence were forced to set a new standard of differentiation[,] . . . conspicuous expenditure of money" (Roach and Eicher 295).

27. The ruling class was concerned uniquely with the usurpation of their status by classes just under their own. Deslandres points out that no sumptuary law ever had to stipulate that a peasant should not wear gold brocade, because his economic situation prevented such an acquisition and because such a garment would present an impediment to his everyday activities (177).

28. There is, however, a record of an edict handed down by Philippe–Auguste to his soldiers, prohibiting them from wearing "le vair, l'hermine et le petitgris" (Lériget 73). Bumke reminds us that the French king and Henry II of England were, at that time, 1188, preparing to set off for the crusade and that they "drew up a military code, which among other things, prohibited the crusaders from wearing costly fabrics during the expeditions" (129). Philippe–Auguste's reasons appear to have little to do with preservation of class distinctions and more to do with practical travel considerations.

a response among the ruling class to increasing uncertainty about the reliability of appearances:

> When economic change disrupts a "static" system of social relations emulation becomes an increasingly available strategy by which people lower in the social hierarchy attempt to realize their aspirations towards higher status by modifying their behavior, their dress and the kinds of goods they purchase. At the same time it becomes even more significant for the economically weakened nobility to resist these changes that express themselves in the frequently voiced anxiety about the difficulty of distinguishing between different categories of persons. (25)

In twelfth-century France, the increasing wealth of the merchant class, along with the indebtedness among the aristocracy, was beginning to create such a crisis. The codified system that had grown up naturally from technological, economic, and social factors was being called into question by new situations. The nobles wished to preserve the system in which their social status and financial situation were identical, but for many among them this was no longer the case. In the same way that medieval authors looked to antiquity as, in Roland Barthes's words, "une matière absolue qui est le trésor antique, source d'autorité" (*Aventure* 104), society looked to what remained of an absolute vestimentary system, and the symbols of wealth and status, such as fur and silk, which visually alluded to the secular authority of the nobility. Nobles wanted their dress to communicate clearly and unambiguously their socioeconomic status, but the absolute relationship between their status and monetary reality was rapidly changing. A system that had once been symbolic and thus motivated (because symbols have a relationship to what they symbolize, just as the medieval mind saw words as having an inherent meaning divinely ordained and derived) was suddenly encountering a system of arbitrary signs.[29]

The first true sumptuary law in post-Roman France seems to have appeared in 1229: "Une loi de 1229 défend aux comtes et barons de donner plus de deux livrées par an aux personnes de leur suite. Les écuyers domestiques ne pourront porter de vêtements dont le prix excède sept sous l'aune" (Giraudias 52).

29. The ultimate expression of the arbitrary system in clothing is fashion in the modern sense of the word, and although there are differing opinions as to when the rise of fashion occurs, only Ewing dates it before the thirteenth century. Her argument is based on the advent of lacing in the twelfth-century *bliaut*, which she considers to be a significant enough alteration of appearance to constitute fashion (18).

The introduction of arbitrariness, however contained, necessitated measures to preserve the integrity of the previous symbolic system. The play in the system of appearances echoes the play in the representational system: both are moving from static values toward a more dynamic form in much the same way that the economy was becoming ever more dynamic. The evidence of this play is perhaps never clearer than in the mechanics of the transition from a vestimentary code to a fully developed signifying system of clothing and in the transition from absolute meaning to contingent meaning for the clothing signifier.

Nobles, threatened by changes in the material world, looked to the writers of romance to entertain them and regale them with stories that glorified all that they treasured and believed themselves to embody. To illustrate his sympathy for the threatened nobility, the narrator of *Jaufre* suspends his tale for forty lines to deliver a diatribe condemning those who would wrongly appropriate the appearance of nobility, particularly since these usurpers do not adopt noble values:[30]

> Qe nu puesc esser tan jausens
> Can ne vei tan d'avol maneira,
> C'us fils de calqe camareira
> O de calqe vilan bastart
> Qe sera vengutz d'autra part,
> Can aura diners amassatz
> E es ben vestitz e causatz,
> Cuja tot la meilor valer.
> . . . .
> Aisi avols hom ben vestitz
> Es bels defor e dins poristz,
> E tut farsit de malvestat,

---

30. The romance of *Jaufre* is an Occitan work written in the south of France, dating most likely from the early thirteenth century. For the dating of the poem, see in particular Rita Lejeune's "La date du roman de *Jaufre*," her "A propos de la datation de *Jaufré*," and Paul Rémy's "A propos de la datation du roman de *Jaufre*." Although the romance postdates the primary period under consideration in this study, it is useful for inclusion for several reasons. First, it has been firmly established among scholars that the author of *Jaufre* was highly influenced, both in style and content, by the writers of romance in the north of France at the end of the twelfth century; see, for example, Tony Hunt's "*Texte* and *Prétexte*," Emmanuèle Baumgartner's "Le Défi du 'chevalier rouge,'" and Jean–Charles Huchet's "*Jaufre* et le Graal." Moreover, the *Jaufre* poet makes use of the same clothing signifying system discernable in the romances of his northern counterparts of the twelfth century.

Car aisin sun plen e enflat
Qe no lur pot dedins caber,
E fan lu deforas parer.

(vss. 2568–83, 2603–8)

[I really cannot be happy when I see so many lowborn people, when the son of a chambermaid or of some peasant bastard who comes from somewhere else—once he has gathered a little money and is well dressed with good shoes—thinks he is equal to the best of men. . . . A low but well-dressed man is handsome on the outside but is rotten on the inside and stuffed with dishonesty. They are so full and inflated with it that they cannot contain it inside, and it shows up on the outside.]

The writers fulfilled the desire of their patrons and audience but, true to the societal function of art, inscribed their works with the very changes that the nobles so feared. The mediation between a world of flux and the stability of the imagined past is readily apparent in the writers' treatment of clothing. They carry out their project by using clothing in a variety of ways and for a variety of ends through the development and elaboration of a dynamic signifying system that borrows its form from the absolute symbolism to which the nobles were accustomed while incorporating the ambiguity, ambivalence, and arbitrariness of the changing material world around them. The clothing system functions at three different levels in the text: writers elaborate character identity and states of being through descriptions of clothing; clothing interacts with the plot, sometimes motivating or precipitating events; and clothing contributes to the overall narrative structure of many romances. In every instance, however, the writers call upon their audience to interpret clothing signifiers in light of these signifiers' specific narrative contexts, in keeping with the aesthetic of *conjointure*; in light of the transition in the representational system from symbol to sign, and in light of the material reality that ultimately the nobles could no longer ignore or deny.

3

DRESSING UP THE CHARACTER:
THE ELUCIDATION OF CHARACTERS THROUGH CLOTHING

IN A LITERARY TEXT, and arguably within all human societies, the primary function of clothing resides in the establishment of identity. This identity is a venture between the individual and his or her society. Mary Ellen Roach and Joanne Bubolz Eicher explain the importance of clothing and other vestimentary items for this process of identification: "As human beings within a society develop social selves, dress and adornment are intimately linked to their interacting with one another. These personal accouterments assist the individual in presenting his image and expressing himself" (2). In twelfth-century France, a person's appearance was believed to be an especially clear indicator of that person's identity, since society placed a premium on the absolute conflation between appearance and reality. This ideal so predominated the thinking of the time that a veritable cult of appearance had established itself among the upper classes. Piponnier and Mane remind us that this kind of attention to appearance was part of the ideal of largess, meaning that those who had wealth flaunted it (73). The wealthy surrounded themselves and their entourages with every luxury they could afford and made gifts to those less fortunate. For a long time, the nobles had been the wealthiest members of society, their means beyond the grasp of any other class, but increasingly during the twelfth century their absolute domination of society was being put into question by the enrichment of the merchant class. Accordingly, nobles had for a long while been able to afford to dress themselves better, indeed to manipulate their appearance with greater ease, than any other class. Their initial financial ability to demand luxury goods from far away is ironically the very means by which the merchant class was increasing its own wealth: the trade of luxury items was making rich those who conveyed merchandise. Understanding that the ability to transform appearance through apparel opens up the possibility for appropriation of a different identity, nobles must have become wary of any manipulation of appearance beyond their immediate control, sensing its capacity to undermine their own status. This fear explains their need to stabilize the vestimentary code and to create the illusion of the immutability of the code.

This desire for an absolute vestimentary code conflicts with the desire of writers inasmuch as rigidity limits creativity. I do not mean to suggest that restraint precludes imagination, just that too much limitation inhibits the ways in which creativity may be expressed. If creativity is defined as the capacity to invent new meanings, then a symbolic code can never be fully creative, because it bases itself on predetermined meanings that do not expand. The writers of romance in the twelfth century certainly used the vestimentary code, but they also pushed it to its limit and sometimes even transcended it. In their romances, they often set up the code to resemble its function in society, but they then used clothing to surpass and subvert the code. One of the primary uses of vestimentary imagery is for the development or elucidation of characters. A short discussion of the changing conception of character will be useful in providing both an analogy for and a better understanding of the ways in which the writers of the day were moving away from fixed, static conventions, and toward a more dynamic representation.

The literature that preceded the rise of romance, as well as the other literary genres of the period, tended to conceive of characters as "types." The convention of types is a representational system that values the normative sociocultural role of stereotyped characters, instead of the elaboration of individual personalities. The characterization of these types is immutable and fixed; they are symbols with absolute and non-negotiable meaning. Although character types certainly exist in the romances, they do not dominate them, and they tend to be less important characters. Rather, in their elaboration of characters, the writers of romance often diverge from the highly conventional descriptions emblematic of those of character types and favor a more fluid system of representation that incorporates the more ambivalent and ambiguous property of signification. This divergence in descriptive practices necessarily, even purposefully, introduces dynamism into the art and gives rise to individualism in character development. One of the primary loci of this disturbance in the system lies in the description and depiction of characters' clothing. Here again, there is a discernible movement in the representational system from a primarily static technique of description toward one that invites, even requires, interpretation. Like the characters who wear it, clothing is beginning to change from a set of stable absolute symbols to a system of contingent signs that must be understood in context.

Description

The art of description figures prominently for the medieval author of romance. Chrétien de Troyes and his contemporaries fill their texts with descriptions of characters, often including references to or descriptions of their clothing as well. The most obvious purpose of such descriptions is of course, as Alice Colby attests, to provide readers with a "clear picture of a person" (99). Colby also notes that portraits of characters, descriptions of some length that tend to relate the physical attributes of the character to his or her moral qualities, are highly conventional in romance (99), defining a portrait as a description of a character composed of at least twenty lines of verse and providing both physical and moral attributes (4–5). This conventionality has its origins in Horatian rhetoric, in which *descriptio* involves the elaboration of types that stress the general rather than the individual (Kelly, *Art* 53).

When writers of romance wish to represent characters who belong to the high nobility—and almost all the principal characters of such works fall into this category—they rely on certain vestimentary features that they describe in a very conventional manner. For the most part, the description extends only to the outer garments of a character's outfit, that is, the *bliaut* and the mantle, generally described with the use of superlatives. In most cases, the *bliaut* is made of fine fabrics of exotic origins, and silk predominates. Additionally, the silk is often of a heavily decorated type, such as samite. The most common colors for these garments, if mentioned, are scarlet, green, or blue. Authors often describe in detail the mantle, a ceremonial garment designating high rank. Mantles, more often than not, have fur linings, the most precious being ermine.

Renaut de Bâgé, in his *Bel Inconnu*, provides a number of rather lengthy and highly conventional descriptions of clothing, some of which are part of character portraits that involve physical and moral features in addition to the clothing of a character.[1] Conventionality in these descriptions does not in any way imply that they are identical, for the details do vary, lending texture and richness to the text. The description of Blonde Esmerée as she appears for the first time in the text provides a fairly elaborate but very formally

---

1. In *Textus*, Romaine Wolf-Bonvin analyzes Renaut de Bâgé's extentive use of female portraiture, calling the work "une longue série de portraits féminins, car la quête se déroule dans un monde où évoluent des demoiselles de plus en plus parées (149)."

typical example of conventional clothing description. Renaut begins with the outermost garment, her mantle:

> D'une vert popre estoit vestue;
> onques miundre ne fu veüe.
> Molt estoit riches ses mantials:
> deus sebelins ot as tasials;
> la pene fu et bonne et fine
> et si estoit de blanc ermine.
>
> (vss. 3279–84)

> [She was dressed in green silk; no better had ever been seen. Her mantle was very rich: it had two sables as tassels; its white ermine lining was good and fine.]

Blonde Esmerée is a queen, and it is therefore fitting that she wear a mantle. The fabric of her outfit is superlative and rare: *porpre* is a type of imported silk usually produced in the Levant.[2] The ornamentation and lining of her mantle are costly furs, and the ermine underlines her status as a royal personage. The description continues its evocation of exotic embellishment with its depiction of the truly extraordinary clasps on her mantle:

> Les ataces qui furent mises
> furent faites de maintes guises.
> Molt par faisoient a proisier:
> nes puet on ronpre ne trencier;
> ensi les ovra une fee
> en l'Ille de la Mer Betee.
>
> (vss. 3285–90)

> [The clasps that were upon it were intricately made; they were very worthy of praise and could not be broken or cut, so well they had been wrought by a fairy on the Island of Mer Betee.]

Not only are the clasps finely worked pieces of artistry, but they are also marvelous in nature, made by a fairy, with distant origins—the Dead Sea.

---

2. The term *porpre* during this period is in fact a reference not to the fabric's color but rather to the type of fabric itself.

If the ermine trim and sable trim on her mantle left any doubts as to the rank and importance of this character, the rarity of the clasps makes her status apparent. The description of her *bliaut* reiterates and reinforces the royal imagery:

> De cel drap dont li mantials fu
> fu li blials qu'ele ot vestu.
> Molt estoit ciers et bien ovrés;
> d'un ermine fu tos forrés.
> Plus de cinc onces d'or sans faille
> avoit entor le kieveçaille;
> as puins en ot plus de quatre onces.
> Par tot avoit asis jagonsses
> et autres pieres de vertu
> qui furent deseur l'or batu.
>
> (vss. 3291–3300)

[The *bliaut* she wore was made from the same cloth as her mantle. It was very expensive and well made and was fully lined with ermine. More than five ounces of gold encircled the neck, and more than four ounces were around the wrists. All over, hyacinths and other stones of value had been set into the forged gold.]

The *bliaut*'s description echoes that of the mantle: the *bliaut* is made of the same luxurious fabric with the same lining of royal fur, and the trim of the *bliaut* receives as much elaboration as the trim of the mantle. Blonde Esmerée's clothing accurately reflects her nobility. Moreover, their description is perfectly balanced, suggesting that she possesses the moral quality of balance and harmony among parts. Arthur will later recognize her merit and status when he honors her request that he bless her marriage to Guinglain.

Other clothing descriptions in *Bel Inconnu* tend to concentrate on a character's mantle or his or her *bliaut*, but not both. When Blanches Mains first appears in the story, Renaut describes only her mantle:[3]

---

3. Before launching into the description of her clothing, Renaut describes the lady's face, emphasizing the contrast between the whiteness of her skin and the redness of her lips. Wolf-Bonvin discusses this color contrast in terms of the richness of its lexical fields and symbolic meanings and associations dating from antiquity on, an analysis she continues with later descriptions of Blaches Mains in black and white (*Textus* 163–74).

> Ele estoit d'un samit vestue;
> onques si bele n'ot sous nue.
> La pene en fu molt bien ouvree,
> d'ermine tote es[che]keree;
> molt sont bien fait li eschekier;
> li orles fist molt a pris[ier].
>
> (vss. 2245–50)

> [She was dressed in a samite; never was one so beautiful seen under heaven. The edging was very beautifully fashioned from checkered ermine; so well was the checkering executed that the border was very worthy of praise.]

He specifies the fabric as samite, even the finest samite, a costly silk, usually heavily decorated with gold and obtained from the Levant or Muslim Spain. The mantle's ermine trim of northern provenance and the quality of the work in the creation of the checkered design are both indicative of the royalty of the garment's wearer. In this single garment, the cultural east meets west, and the geographic north meets south, all to be assembled with great care and purpose in the center of the imagined chivalric world—the Arthurian domain. This rather short description very efficiently communicates Blanches Mains' status and situates her at the very heart of chivalry. Later, when Guinglain returns to Blanches Mains and finds her riding out for a hunt, the text indicates that she has removed her mantle because of the heat—"Son mantiel osta por le caut" (vs. 3967)—but goes into a short description of her *bliaut*:

> ele avoit vestu un bliaut
> ki tos estoit a or batus.
> Plus rices dras ne fu veüs;
> ovrés estoit et bien et bel.
>
> (vss. 3968–71)

> [She had donned a *bliaut* that was made entirely of forged gold. A more rich fabric has never been seen; it was well and beautifully fashioned.]

This fabric, like the one used for her mantle, is exquisite and rare. The cloth, with its use of gold in the weave, could be a brocade or a samite, both of which are imported fabrics. Regardless of the origins of the fabric, which remain unclear from the description, its quality and rarity befit a queen.

The mantle was the only specifically noble garment of the twelfth century, and there are three additional exceptional mantles that appear in *Bel Inconnu*. To reconcile with Guinglain, Blanches Mains sends him the gift of a beautiful mantle made of two different exquisite fabrics, a Persian *osterin* and a *diaspre*, and lined with two different costly furs, Hungarian miniver and ermine.[4] Later, Blonde Esmerée goes into Arthur's court for the first time wearing a mantle of Middle Eastern cloth upon which all the wild beasts on land and from the sea are depicted in gold embroidery.[5] Both

4. Une robe aporte molt biele
partie de deus dras divers:
de soie d'un osterin pers
et d'un diaspre bon et biel.
La pene qui fu el mantiel
refu molt de rice partie,
de rice vair de vers Hungrie;
l'autre d'ermine bon et fin,
ki estoit d'un rice osterin,
et li vairs el diaspe estoit.
Un molt rice seble i avoit
dont li mantials estoit orlés.
Molt estoit li dras bien ouvrés
de coi estoit fais li mantials.
Ja mar querrés deus dras plus bials
que cil de cele reube estoit,
molt bien andoi s'entravenoient.

(vss. 4230–46)

[She was carrying a beautiful robe made of two different fabrics: one of a Persian *osterin* silk, the other a good and beautiful *diaspre*. The lining of the mantle was made of very rich parts, one a rich miniver from Hungary, the other a good and fine ermine that lined the rich *osterin*, and the vair lined the *diaspre*. The mantle was adorned with a very rich sable. The fabric from which the mantle was made was highly worked. Never were there seen two fabrics more beautiful than those from which the robe was made, and the two went together perfectly.]

5. Illueques se fait atorner
de chiere reube d'outre mer
qui tant estoit et biele et riche
qu'en tot le mont n'ot cele bisse—
caucatri, lupart, ne lion,
ne serpent volant, ne dragon,
n'alerion, ne escramor,
ne papejai, ne espapemor,
ne nesune bieste sauvage
qui soit en mer ne en bocage
que ne fust a fin or portraite.
Molt estoit la roube bien faite!

these garments are exceptional. Guinglain's mantle is carefully designed to achieve a balance and harmony of disparate but luxurious parts, while Blonde Esmerée's mantle is nothing less than a marvel. Despite the truly extraordinary quality of these garments, their descriptions remain conventional because they in no way challenge assumptions. The superlative, the hyperbolic, and even the marvelous are standard features of medieval descriptions. Reginald Abbott makes it clear that the audience expected to be dazzled by such elaboration (9).

However, the third remaining description of a mantle does call convention into question. When Blanches Mains comes to pay a midnight visit to Guinglain, she comes dressed in a magnificent mantle:

> Sans guimple estoit eschevelee
> et d'un mantiel fu afublee
> d'un vert samit o riche hermine.
> Molt estoit bele la meschine!
> Les ataces de son mantiel
> de fin or furent li tasiel.

> El mantiel ot pene de sable
> qui molt fu bone et avenable.
> Li orles estoit de pantine:
> (Ço est une beste mairine;
> plus souef flaire que canele.
> Ainc ne fist Dius beste si biele.
> Dalés le mer paist la rachine
> et porte si grant medechine,
> qui sor lui l'a ne crient venin
> tant le boive soir ne matin.
> Mius vaut que conter ne porroie.)
> Et d'une çainture de soie
> a or broudee tot entor
> si s'en estoit çainte a un tor
> molt cointement la damoissele.

(vss. 5143–69)

[There she had herself adorned with a costly robe from overseas that was so beautiful and rich that in all the world there was no beast—crocodile, leopard, or lion, flying serpent or dragon, eagle or *escramor*, popinjay or *espapemor*, or any other wild beast whether in the sea or forest that was not depicted there in pure gold. The robe was beautifully made! The mantle had a sable lining that was very good and went well with it. The trim was of pantine (this is a sea creature which gives off a scent nicer than cinnamon. God never made a beast so beautiful. It eats the herbs by the sea and has such medicinal effects that he who wears it need fear no venom drunk day or night. I cannot tell you how much it is worth.) And a silk *ceinture* embroidered with gold all the way around, the maiden tied around her waist to beautiful effect.]

Desus sa teste le tenoit;
l'orlé les la face portoit:
li sebelins, qui noirs estoit,
les le blanc vis molt avenoit.

(vss. 2395–2404)

[Without a wimple, her hair was loose, and she was dressed in a mantle of green samite lined with fine ermine. The young lady was very beautiful! The tassels on the laces of her mantle were of fine gold. She held it [the hood] over her head; she wore the border around her face: the sable, which was black, accented well the white of her face.]

Once again Renaut dresses a character in a samite mantle lined with ermine and trimmed in sable, with clasps of the finest gold. Thus far the description is as conventional as anything we have seen, and it draws a parallel between the beauty of the garment and the beauty of the lady, also a convention in romance. But, in the lines that follow, an unanticipated, even shocking, element of the description emerges:

N'avoit vestu fors sa chemisse,
qui plus estoit blance a devise
que n'est la nois quis ciet sor branche.
Molt estoit la cemisse blance
mais encore est la cars molt plus
que la chemisse de desus.
Les gambes vit: blances estoient,
qui un petit aparissoient.
La cemisse brunete estoit
envers les janbe[s] qu'il veoit.

(vss. 2405–14)

[She had only donned her *chemise*, which was more white than the hazel flower sitting on its branch. The *chemise* was very white but the flesh beneath the *chemise* was far whiter. He saw her legs: white they were, the little that showed. The *chemise* seemed dark brown compared with the legs he saw.]

Blanches Mains is wearing nothing but her *chemise* under this stylized, ceremonial garment! The mantle, the ultimate symbol of wealth and status, is being sexualized by the suggestive nature of the description of this lady in her *chemise*. There is little doubt that a well-crafted mantle of luxurious, pleasing materials has a seductive quality, but seldom is that seductiveness extended into an explicitly sexual content. The total contrast between the outermost garment, particularly one used primarily on distinctly public occasions, and the garment that is essentially equated with nudity in the twelfth century creates an unusually dynamic description.[6] Moreover, the image of this scene marks Guinglain, for he has recurring dreams about it. Blanches Mains is herself a highly unconventional character, but this description of her clothing gives her character even more interest, precisely because it challenges the audience's assumptions about how a lady should dress. She becomes more vibrant, more alive, thereby surpassing her rival, Blonde Esmerée, in the minds of both the audience and the hero. In this way, Renaut uses clothing not only to develop the character of Blanches Mains but also to enhance the dynamism of the work as a whole.[7]

The descriptions of clothing in *Bel Inconnu* serve a greater narrative function, but most are nonetheless highly conventional in form and placement, with the notable exception of Blanches Mains' ensemble in her midnight visit to Guinglain. This dynamic description bears witness to the existence of the kind of play in the representational system that is characteristic of and necessary for the slow transition from an absolute symbolism to a more fluid signifying system. In this particular case, the public symbols of wealth and status—the individual features of the mantle along with the mantle itself—merge with the symbol of nudity, that is, the *chemise*, to form a dynamic image that is highly context dependent. Were Blanches Mains to wear this costume in public, she would no doubt look ridiculous and possibly incur some degree of scorn. The two symbols would negate each other. Instead, she wears her unusual ensemble to seduce a knight, and it works, because of the juxtaposition

---

6. A similar description occurs in Chrétien's *Chevalier de la charrete*, in which Guenevere comes dressed for her tryst with Lancelot in a pure white *chemise* directly under a luxurous mantle of fine scarlet cloth and marmot fur (vss. 4574–82). For an analysis of Chrétien's scene, see my article "What Was Arthur Wearing?" Like the image of Blanches Mains in her *chemise* and mantle, this image of Guenevere is clearly sexualized, especially since she is on the verge of committing adultery with Lancelot.

7. Commenting upon the many female outfits presented throughout the text, Wolf-Bonvin writes: "La galerie de portraits féminins présents dans le *Bel Inconnu* n'a donc rien d'insignifiant. En marquant une pause dans le récit entre passé et future, ils effectuent une mise au point où sont visualisés les lignes de forces du moment, concentrées en une sorte de résumé virtuel. Placés au seuil des épisodes marquants, ils annoncent les directions de lecture antérieurement à toute avancée de la narration" (*Textus* 209).

of symbols in the particular context. Her outfit requires interpretation, which Renaut supplies: his description takes on an increasingly suggestive tone, evoking her body and bare legs, to leave no doubt that this description is meant to sexualize the wearer of the strange outfit. Throughout the text of *Bel Inconnu*, Renaut uses conventional clothing descriptions to demonstrate the nobility of his characters, sometimes pushing his descriptions toward the marvelous, but in the description of Blanches Mains' nighttime visit, he introduces so much vestimentary contrast that he must provide supplemental imagery to assist the reader in interpreting the textual ambivalence.

Similarly, the *Enéas* poet, in two parallel descriptions of the lady warrior Camille, inscribes textual ambivalence with regard to her gender.[8] The contrasting image of Camille, first dressed in elegant feminine attire and later fully armed for battle, is not simultaneously achieved as is Blanches Mains' description, but must evolve over the course of the romance. The poet describes Camille in great detail when she makes her first appearance in the romance, explaining that she has a dual nature. She is both king and queen, pursuing typically masculine activities by day and being attended by women by night (vss. 3977–81). Although the poet prepares his audience for the later depiction of her fully armed, he first describes her physically in her feminine aspect, thereby easing his audience toward the image of her as a knight. In this initial description, the poet emphasizes her extreme beauty and lovely clothing. Both her *bliaut* and mantle are made of *porpre*, and the mantle's lining is in a checkered design using ermine and red martin, indicating her wealth and status. However, certain details of the two garments indicate marvelous origins:

> la porpre fu a or broudee,
> par grant entante fu ovree:
> trois faees serors la firent,
> an une chanbre la tisserent;
> chascune d'els s'i essaia
> et son savoir i demonstra
> et firent i poissons marages,
> oissiaus volanz, bestes salvages.
>
> (vss. 4011–20)

---

8. Of interest is the fact that the name Camille is nongendered in Old French, which further adds to the gender ambivalence of this character. She is clearly of the female sex, sex being a physical trait, but her gender, that is her socially assigned role, is less clear.

[The *porpre* was embroidered with gold, worked with fine expertise: three fairy sisters made it, in a room they wove it; each one of them tried to demonstrate her mastery in it, and depicted sea fish, flying birds, and savage beasts upon it.]

The fabric from which this outfit is cut provides yet another example of an already exotic fabric, *porpre*, elevated to the level of a marvel through the mystical craft of the design. In a friendly competition to do the best work, fairy sisters depicted a bestiary of animals upon the fine fabric. While the designs on the fabric of the *bliaut* have been carried out by otherworldly creatures, the trim of her mantle is actually made from a magical creature:

> li orles fu mervoilles biaus
> et fu de gorges d'un oisiaus
> ki sollent pondre al fonz de mer
> et sor l'onde sollent cover;
> cent toises covent an parfont;
> de si chaude nature sont
> que, se desus lor les ardoient;
> bien fu orlez de ces oisiaus,
> desi qu'a terre li mantiaus.
>
> (vss. 4035–44)

[The border was marvelously beautiful, made from the throat of a bird that likes to lay its eggs at the bottom of the sea and brood them on the waves; they brood them sometimes at a hundred fathoms deep; their nature is so hot that if they sit on them, they will burn them with their heat. Of these, her mantle was handsomely bordered to the ground.]

The exotic rarity of her clothing perfectly reflects Camille's quality as an extraordinary personage, but there is, as yet, no firm indication of her femininity, since neither the cloth nor the marvelous embroidery indicates gender in any way. An earlier quatrain of the description introduces the expressly feminine quality of her image:

> Vestue an fu estroitement
> dessus fu ceinte cointement

d'une sozceinte a or broudee;
menuëment ert botonee.

(vss. 4007–10)

[She was attractively dressed with a tightly cinched overbelt embroidered with gold; and she was skillfully laced into her gown.]

In keeping with the style at the time of the writing of this romance, Camille wears her dress tightly laced at the sides. The fitted shape of her *bliaut* combined with the intricately embroidered and decorated sash accentuates the shape of her body, and the poet makes sure that the shapeliness of her body is visible when he specifies that she leaves her mantle open to reveal her right side: "Ele an ot antroverz les pans, / qu li parut le destre flans" (She had slightly opened the side, which allowed her right side to be seen) (vss. 4045–46). In this initial and rather lengthy description of Camille, the poet clearly asserts both Camille's social rank and her femininity, but Camille's uniqueness goes well beyond any trappings of wealth, status, and beauty. She is also a female knight. The full articulation of her personal and vestimentary fortitude occurs almost three thousand lines later, as Turnus comes upon her:

Iluec a Camille trovee
ou el l'atendoit tote armee;
. . . .
et el fu bien aparoillie
. . . .
Apoiee fu sor sa lance;
a son col avoit son escu;
o bocle d'or d'ivoire fu,
et la guige an estoit d'orfois.
Ses haubers ert blans come nois
et ses hiaumes luisanz et clers,
de fin or ert toz par carters;
la coife del hauberc fu faite
en tel maniere qu'ele ot traite
sa bloie crine de defors
que el li covri tot lo cors.

(vss. 6907–8, 6914, 6922–32)

> [He found Camille there, where she awaited him fully armed . . . and she was well attired. . . . She was leaning on her lance; at her neck was her shield with an ivory-and-gold shield-boss and a grip made of orphrey. Her hauberk was white like the hazel flower and her helmet was glittering and bright, made with fine gold in all the quarters. The headpiece of the hauberk had been made so that she could pull her blond hair through to the outside, and it covered her whole body.]

The lovely, exquisitely attired woman who dazzles with her beauty and unusual clothing is thus transformed into a fully armed knight, ready for battle. Moreover, in the same way that, in the first description, the poet alludes to Camille's masculinity even as he gives a distinctly feminine description of her, here he accommodates her femininity with the specially made hauberk that allows her long hair to flow while he shows her in her most masculine aspect. This image completes the description of Camille begun much earlier when the poet informs us of her vocation, and the two depictions become one extended, dynamic description. Taken as one description, the image focuses on clothing as a means to embed Camille's gender ambivalence into her textual representation.

Both the depiction of Blanches Mains and that of Camille inscribe some sort of ambivalence into the textual representation of character through contradictory vestimentary imagery: in Blanches Mains' case, it calls sexual imagery into question, whereas in Camille's case, it is gender ambivalence. The first time the character Enide appears in the text of *Erec et Enide*, Chrétien introduces ambiguity with regard to social class in her description. Although Enide's family has been reduced to poverty, the family is noble, and Chrétien beautifully depicts the tension between her outer poverty and her inner nobility through a very unconventional and nearly shocking description of her clothing. The diminished economic condition of certain members of the nobility in the second half of the twelfth century makes Enide's situation quite believable, and in her portrait, Chrétien represents this social reality with artistry: he shows her reduced state rather than simply relating it, while evoking her absolute beauty and nobility. That she is poorly dressed creates a dramatic contrast with her social rank:

> et sa fille, qui fu vestue
> d'une chemise par panz lee,

deliee, blanche et ridee.
Un blanc cheinse ot vestu desus;
n'avoit robe ne mains ne plus,
et tant estoit li chainses viez
que as costez estoit perciez.
Povre estoit la robe dehors,
mes desoz estoit biax li cors.

(vss. 402–10)

[As did her daughter who was dressed in a *chemise* of wide cloth, fine (threadbare), white, and creased (wrinkled).[9] She wore over it a white *chainse*; she had no other clothes. And so old was the *chainse* that it was worn through at the sides. Poor were the clothes on the outside, but the body beneath was beautiful.]

Over her worn *chemise*, Enide wears but a tattered *chainse*. The *chainse* is a dress normally worn on very informal occasions and in the home, but in this case, Enide's family is receiving one of Arthur's knights (and a king's son) into their home. The lack of a *bliaut* to cover her *chainse*, especially in circumstances that merit it, clearly indicates the family's poverty. Enide is inappropriately dressed, and this fact creates a great deal of tension in the text.[10] This discord between Enide's state of dress and her social status, like the discrepancy between the two parts of Blanches Mains' outfit and the contrast between Camille's image as a woman and as a knight, inscribe vestimentary ambivalence into the text.[11] For the noble audience hearing of

---

9. The precise meaning of "deliee" here is a matter of some dispute. David Staines translates it as "threadbare" to emphasize the poor condition of it, but most other translators have chosen to translate it as "fine," emphasizing instead that the garment at one point, like the family's fortune, was in much better shape. I have included both readings here.

Again, "ridee" has posed problems for translators, many of whom translate it as "pleated." To my knowledge, a pleated *chemise* was not common or practical, and I therefore prefer a reading that incorporates instead the notion of a well-worn and wrinkled garment to one that would give Enide's *chemise* a more exotic association.

10. Kelly points out that once Enide receives the queen's gift of clothing, she must spend the rest of the romance acquiring the attributes of wife, princess, and queen ("Art" 198–99). Although at first Enide's lack is material and her attributes as noble sufficient, once the queen has dressed her, the situation is reversed. She must then grow into her clothes.

11. Interestingly, Erec arrives at Enide's father house also inappropriately dressed for his task. At the beginning of the romance, he sets out with the queen dressed in courtly attire (vss. 95–104). His manner of dress becomes inappropriate when a knight's dwarf slaps the handmaiden of the queen and Erec must avenge her. He regrets his lack of armor because it prevents him from completing his task right away. Erec's inappropriate dress prefigures Enide's.

Enide's plight, however, the instability of her situation was surely dramatic; the nobles threatened by the enrichment of the merchant class could have easily imagined themselves in a similar situation, whether such a possibility was remote or not. Fortunately for both the heroine and her family, Erec decides to marry her, thereby restoring wealth to his in-laws.[12] This development undoubtedly allayed the fears and unease that the unconventional initial portrait of Enide caused the audience to experience. Nonetheless, the description had its effect, and although Chrétien reassures his listeners and readers and reaffirms their status, he has forced them to face a material reality. Moreover, Enide's portrait is nothing less than a subversion of the vestimentary code of the period. Regardless of what Chrétien does for these characters later in the text, he has made a fissure in the wall of the impermeable representational world and has paved the way for other transgressions to follow.

Later, in his *Conte du Graal*, or *Perceval*, Chrétien again uses a contradictory vestimentary image, but inverts it. Whereas Enide makes her entrance into the text dressed beneath her noble station, when we see Blancheflor for the first time, she is dressed well beyond her current means. This first image of Blancheflor, the lady who becomes Perceval's love, as Douglas Kelly puts it, "contrasts person [again, represented through clothing] with dwelling" ("Art" 205). The first view we have of Blancheflor in her besieged castle communicates a strangely contradictory image:

> Ses mantiax fu, et ses blïaus,
> D'une porpre noire, estelee
> D'or, et n'estoit mie pelee
> La penne qui d'ermine fu;
> D'un sebelin noir et chenu,
> Qui n'estoit trop lons ne trop lez,
> Fu li mantiax au col orlez.
>
> (vss. 1798–84)

[Her mantle and her *bliaut* were of black *porpre*, starred with gold, and the fur lining, which was of ermine, was not the least bit worn;

---

12. Wolf-Bonvin argues that Enide's tattered state of dress should be understood as an exemplification of the corrupt and degraded texts that Chrétien says he will restore through his *molt bele conjointure*, just as Erec will restore status and wealth to Enide's family, and that, at the conclusion of the romance, when the tale has been restored to its full glory through Chrétien's artistry, Erec's coronation robe should be read as the textual emblem of Chrétien's success (*Textus* 13).

the mantle's collar was adorned with a black, thick sable that was neither too long nor too wide.]

This description of the lady's clothing seems wildly disconnected from the physical reality of her present situation: she and her people are on the verge of starvation, but Blancheflor is dressed like the wealthiest of queens. Reginald Abbott examines this passage in detail, placing it in the historical and cultural setting necessary for interpretation of the meaning that this luxurious garment would have carried for Chrétien's twelfth-century audience: "Blancheflor's robe is brand new and an exact length to suit her. Newness and exact fit are here characteristics of garments lined with a fur (ermine) used conservatively even by those (royalty) with every right (duty) to wear it and the means to acquire it. Blancheflor is the ruler of a city besieged" (9). Abbott notes that despite the siege of the lady's castle, she still manages to find the means to procure for herself the ermine fur whose origins are as far away as Russia (9). The fact that her tailored garment was made just for her, according to Abbott, confirms that it was not "a royal hand-me-down or second-hand garment" (9). This costume is of the utmost splendor: "When Perceval meets Blancheflor, she is attired in a robe befitting the highest royal personage at a ceremonial occasion, a robe of great price and rarity, exactly tailored to fit her, and brand new. . . . For the medieval reader, this is the stuff of legend" (9). Abbott goes on to claim that the hyperbolic nature of Blancheflor's clothing in this description is part and parcel of Chrétien's need to dazzle his aristocratic audience, presumably themselves dressed in fine clothing, with a show of bravura bordering on one-upmanship (9). He does provide ample and convincing evidence that Blancheflor's robe is at best an unlikely historical garment, if not completely impossible, given the lady's current situation.[13] However, the implication of Blancheflor's dress may be extended much further than Abbott is willing to take it.

Kelly remarks that Blancheflor's description is highly conventional in and of itself, but that it contrasts greatly with the current state of her dwelling and affairs ("Art" 205). He asserts that this seemingly incongruous description is actually necessary for the plot because Blancheflor's beauty is what inspires Perceval to perform his precocious defeat of her enemy, thereby liberating her city (205). In other words, Perceval's hyperbolic

---

13. His evidence is based on trade records, royal inventories, and commissions of actual royal garments during the twelfth century and beyond.

performance on the battlefield requires Blancheflor's hyperbolic beauty, and a major component of her beauty is her clothing. Blancheflor is, at this point in the text, an idealized woman, and her clothing is more than symbolic: it is instrumental. The splendor of her dress helps to accomplish her goal of liberating her castle. The seductive power of such an ideally and beautifully adorned woman assures her success in engaging Perceval to champion her cause.

Abbott contends that he and Kelly disagree on the interpretation of Blancheflor's robe (14–15n12), but, in fact, their arguments are not contradictory. Abbott suggests that the perfectly unrealistic quality of the garment's existence in such circumstances pushes the limits of credibility and that the noble audience is pleased by the garment's very unlikelihood and hyperbolic rarity. Kelly argues that Blancheflor's beauty, a prominent feature of which is this extraordinary garment, inspires Perceval to perform an equally extraordinary feat that no one before him could accomplish, even with many men. Both arguments point to the exceptional quality of the garment and its unique ability to please and inspire. In short, the garment is an unattainable ideal and carries with it the full seductive appeal of such a rare and exquisite object. The description of Blancheflor's dress in its specific narrative context provides an example of a more dynamic type of description so that what would have otherwise been a pause in the narrative actually creates tension, through such obvious contrast, and moves the action forward. The highly symbolic nature of the garment that Abbott characterizes as denoting nothing short of the highest level of royalty is problematized by the surroundings in which the wearer finds herself. Inserted into this scene of destitution is a character of extreme beauty, unscathed by the war around her, whose clothing's symbolism is potent but out of place. The French aristocrats of the twelfth century certainly could have seen themselves in this portrait. The economic climate in which they found themselves increasingly favored the merchants, whose social status did not preclude them from profiting from trade, just as the siege of Blancheflor's castle was more favorable to her enemies than to her. Chrétien accounts for the changing system in this description, calling it into question through what could be viewed as the utter absurdity of Blancheflor's dress (which mirrors his status-conscious noble audience), but he ultimately reasserts the value of her vestimentary display by allowing Perceval, once inspired by her beauty, to defeat her enemies. Chrétien leads the aristocracy toward accepting the changing economic situation around them by inscribing its fluctuating valences in his romances in an inoffensive, even pleasing, way.[14] Here, then, Chrétien places a dress whose symbolic value is absolute into an incongruous setting and reestablishes the order of the system around his play. He has once again subverted the vestimentary code of the period and then reassured his audience of its efficacy. Through the agency of his hero, Chrétien restores Blancheflor to her prior station as lady of her domain, and with this change in her situation, her lavish dress becomes once again appropriate. He has nonetheless forced his noble audience to face an undesirable material reality: their position is subject to outside threats. Moreover, their capacity to imagine themselves unequivocally as the heroes of society through the mediation of romance is no longer without threat. The play in the system requires the audience to interpret more than the clothing sign: it requires the nobles to reinterpret their own world.

Identity and Disguise

In addition to using clothing effectively as class markers within a literary text, the writers of twelfth-century romance capitalize on the identificatory role of clothing in ways other than description, and often make mention of clothing as a type of shorthand to indicate a character's class affiliation in very few words while still lending richness and detail to the text. The vestimentary code of twelfth-century France was a code by which individuals associated themselves with a faction of society, such as a certain class, rank, role, economic situation, and so on.[15] Perhaps the most extreme example of identification of characters uniquely in their social roles occurs in the *Roman de Thèbes*. The poet of this romance has a propensity for depicting knights through a synecdochic representation, most often referring to them as "shields." At one point, however, the author extends his synecdoche and refers to knights by naming other parts of their equipment as well. The poet describes the knights that Capaneüs brings with him into battle:

---

14. Judith Kellogg argues this point in her article "Economic and Social Tensions Reflected in the Romances of Chrétien de Troyes." Her argument centers specifically on economic considerations, which sometimes involve clothing but often not.

15. Roach and Eicher point to the expressive quality of clothing, which can express affiliations with social groups and the values and standards belonging to them. Clothing "divulges something about each human being—his beliefs, his sentiments, his status and rank, his place within the power structure" (6).

> Tant bel houme ot en sa compaingne
> tant bon escu de l'or d'Espaingne
> tant bon hauberc menu maillié
> tant entreseing bien entaillié
>
> (vss. 4781–84)

[So many great men he had in his company, so many good shields of Spanish gold, so many good hauberks finely mailed, so many well-engraved insignia.]

The knights in this passage have no individualized identities, and the poet makes no effort to humanize them. The principal characters of his romance are all noble, and most are royal. The knights who make up the two warring brothers' armies are necessary for the narrative, but their identities are not. Their narrative role is limited, as is their social role, to that of warriors, and the most visible part of that role has much less to do with their humanity than with their ability to operate their equipment. This hyperassociation between the knights and their social role obscures their personal identities and underlines clothing's innate capacity to reveal and conceal simultaneously. Here, the armor clearly and unequivocally reveals the social identity of its wearers but conceals their personal identity in order to overemphasize and even equate them with their social role.

The use of clothing to represent a person's high status within society is apparent in several passages in the corpus of verse romance of the period.[16] In Chrétien's *Cligés*, Arthur's court recognizes simply by their appearance that Alexandre and the twelve counts and princes accompanying him are the sons of kings:

> Ne cuident pas que il ne soient
> Tuit de contes et de roi fil,

---

16. In twelfth-century romance, characters of less than noble lineage are somewhat rare, but they do exist. Occasionally, writers of romance take care to provide a short description of them that often includes references to their clothes. One such case occurs in *Yvain* when Calogrenant tells of meeting a hideous "vilain" during his travels. In addition to his grisly physical features, the hunchback is dressed very oddly: "vestuz de robe si estrange / qu'il n'i avoit ne lin ne lange, / einz ot a son col atachiez / deus cuirs de novel escorchiez, / ou de deus tors ou de deus bués" (dressed in an outfit so strange that it was made of neither wool or linen, but he wore, attached to his neck, two newly skinned hides from either two bulls or two cows) (vss. 307–11). The "barbaric" image that Chrétien gives his audience of this less than noble character contrasts greatly with his descriptions of his noble characters and their dress.

Et por voir si estoient il.
Molt par sont bel et de lor aage,
Gent et bien fet, de lonc corssage;
Et les robes que il vestoient
D'un drap et d'une taille estoient,
D'un sanblant et d'une color.

(vss. 316–23)

[They did not doubt that they were all sons of counts and kings, and in truth they were. They were very handsome and in their prime, noble, well built and tall; and the clothes they wore were of the same cloth and size, the same aspect and color.]

Not only does the court easily recognize the worth of the young men immediately upon seeing them, understanding that they are sons of kings or counts and that they are young and strong, but it also understands that they themselves are all as "cut from the same cloth," as are their clothes. These young men have the appearance of nobility and the attributes to match. This particular instance demonstrates to what extent clothing is linked to status and social identity in this period.

Likewise, in *Amadas et Ydoine*, the young man who passes by to bring news of the tournament is well-dressed, and as a result the news that he bears has greater authority than it would were he dressed less well.[17] He is first described as simply "mult bien atourné" (very well attired) (vs. 4051), but then:

Si tost com Amadas le voit,
A son atour bien aperçoit
Et as letres qu'il voit porter
Qu'il est de court et a l'aler.

(vss. 4059–62)

[As soon as Amadas saw him, and saw how he was dressed, as well as the letters he carried, he knew he was of the court and going there, too.]

---

17. Wolf-Bonvin devotes a chapter of her *Textus* to the discussion and analysis of the poet's use of clothing in *Amadas et Ydoine* (227–95), but for my purposes, the example cited clearly demonstrates a common feature of romance with regard to identification of character through clothes.

Once Amadas addresses the page, who looks at the one speaking to him, the page, in turn, realizes that the former is not a "borjois" but a knight. The text specifically states that it is upon seeing Amadas that the page realizes with whom he is speaking. The two recognize each other's status by their clothing.

While the quality of one's clothing in the twelfth century made it possible to identify a person's social class, it is also instrumental in the expression of individual identity. Quentin Bell points out that clothing is an important part of a person's identity, "as though the fabric were indeed a natural extension of the body, or even the soul" (19). Anne Hollander posits that a garment's main function is "to contribute to the making of a self-conscious individual image" (xiv). Burns points to the "sartorial body," which emerges from a conception of "clothes as an active force in generating social bodies" (*Courtly* 12). Individuality is a new phenomenon for the twelfth century, just beginning to manifest itself, and as Michel Pastoureau, in his *Figures et couleurs*, argues, "Le douzième siècle est le siècle de l'émergence de l'identité" (54).[18] Furthermore, romance is the literary genre in medieval France that first sees the rise of the individual.[19] Marc Bloch asserts that "la nouvelle littérature tendait à réintégrer l'individuel et invitait les auditeurs à méditer sur leur moi" (1: 169). The expression of individual identity also manifests in vestimentary ways: characters are often recognized as individuals on the basis of their clothing. Conversely, characters who wear unfamiliar clothing often go unrecognized.[20] Moreover, characters who are nude or not

---

18. R. W. Southern, writing about the changing values in the monasteries in the twelfth century, asserts that the period saw the rise of "a new emphasis on personal experience, an appeal to the individual conscience, a delving into the roots of the inner life" (228).

19. David Staines, in his introduction to his translation of Chrétien's romances, makes the following assertion: "Traditionally, the epic and chronicle depict a nation; their characters are the embodiment of national destiny; their ultimate concern is the nation itself. By contrast, the romance depicts the individual. . . . The romances of Chrétien distance the individuals from their society, allow them their own identities, and examine their understanding of both themselves and their world." Staines is writing specifically about Chrétien, and whereas Chrétien's depiction of his characters may very well be exemplary with regard to their expressed individuality, Chrétien's contemporaries certainly created and articulated individualized characters. Indeed, Robert W. Hanning sees the emergence of the concept of the individual in the twelfth century as a major driving force behind the literary production of the day and asserts that the chivalric romance "offered a literary form in which to work out the implications of individuality" (3).

20. In fact, in romance, disguise virtually always works, demonstrating once again to what extent the vestimentary code places a premium on the perfect conflation of substance and appearance.

dressed in their normal attire defy recognition altogether.[21] The writers of twelfth-century romance represent the vestimentary code as immutable in a very peculiar way. Because their imagined society makes a complete and direct association between appearance and being, a character's use of disguise is foolproof in the romances. So dependent is the society upon clothing signifiers to establish identity, and so absolute its identifying power, that disguise always works. It never seems to occur to the characters deceived by disguise that this kind of manipulation of signifiers is even possible. Significantly, therefore, the omnipotence of the vestimentary code is most clearly visible through the subversion of it.

Thus far, my discussion has centered primarily upon the capacity of clothing to reveal something about the wearer, but its tremendous power to conceal is equally remarkable. What is fascinating about the signifying system in twelfth-century romance is that concealment by clothing is just as firmly based upon knowledge of the code as is reading clothing for revelation. It is explicitly because the community knows the code that individual members can understand and reproduce it. In other words, clothes have meaning that everyone in society is capable of deciphering because the entire group is in agreement on what that meaning is. This correspondence, however, is threatened by the possibility of disguise, which is the conscious and intentional manipulation of the code in order to subvert it. In the fictive universe of romance, characters who can reconfigure the code in this way have a clear advantage over their fellow characters. The fact of disguise, while in every way a *real* possibility, always seems to take the other characters completely by surprise, as if they cannot bring themselves to admit the potential of clothing to conceal. For the vast majority of characters, it is inconceivable that someone's appearance does not reflect reality. This denial of possibility once again gives evidence of the prevailing fear among the aristocracy of the disruption of the code, whether vestimentary or otherwise.

In romance, characters are clearly able to disguise themselves by wearing clothes that do not associate them with their normal identities. For example, when, in Béroul, Tristan puts on the clothing of a leper, the other

---

21. In Chrétien's *Chevalier au lion*, maidens have a difficult time recognizing Yvain, because he is nude and therefore not dressed in the manner in which they are accustomed to seeing him. The text asserts that were he dressed as he normally was, the ladies would recognize him quickly: "mes molt le regarda einçois / que rien nule sor lui veïst / qui reconuistre li feïst; / si l'avoit ele tant veü / que tost l'eüst reconeü / se il fust de si riche ator / com il avoit esté maint jor" (But she looked at him long and hard before she saw on his body any indication that would allow her to recognize him. She had in fact so often seen him that she would have recognized him quickly if he had been dressed as magnificently as he had been many days) (vss. 2890–96).

characters, except those who previously knew what he was intending to do, do not recognize him. Béroul describes his costume:

> Tristran, li suens amis, ne fine,
> Vestu se fu de mainte guise;
> Il fu en legne, sanz chemise;
> De let burel furent les cotes
> Et a quarreaus furent ses botes.
> Une chape de burel lee
> Out fait tailler, tote enfumee.
> Affublez se fu forment bien,
> Malade senble plus que rien;
> Et nequeden si ot s'espee
> Entor ses flans estroit noee.
>
> (vss. 3566–76)

[Tristan, her beloved friend, was not idle, but made himself a good disguise; it was in wool, without a *chemise*, his *cote* of ugly burel (brown coarse cloth) and his boots were made from patches.[22] A tattered rank cloak (*chape*) of ugly burel he had made. His disguise was marvelous, and he looked more diseased than anything; nonetheless, he also had his sword tightly girded around his waist.]

Tristan dresses himself in the poorest of attire, and he appears to be truly ill. Throughout the day, he begs the people who know him, including his uncle, to give him their clothing. Not only does he appear before them, but he also has lengthy verbal exchange with them. Yet not a single one of them recognizes him, and no one even seems to suspect, despite Yseut's oath that only the leper and her husband have ever been "entre [s]es cuisses" (vs. 4203), that the leper could possibly be Tristan in disguise. Rather, they accept his identity as it is presented sartorially. Later, during the joust that precedes the oath, Tristan comes disguised to participate:

> Cote, sele, destrier et targe
> Out couvert d'une noire sarge,

---

22. This image of Tristan, not only dressed in extremely rough and poor attire, but also especially without the benefit of a *chemise*, the undergarment that could have offered a bit of barrier between his skin and the cheap wool, provokes pity, yet serves also to show us to what lengths Yseut's lover will go to please her.

> Son vis out covert d'un noir voil.
> Tot out covert et chief et poil.
> A sa lance ot l'enseigne mise
> Que la bele li ot tramise.
>
> (vss. 3999–4004)

[He had covered his *cote*, saddle, warhorse, and shield with black serge, his face concealed with a black veil. He had completely covered his head and hair. On his lance he had attached the insignia that his lady had sent him.]

The black serge covers Tristan's identity so well that Girlet takes him to be the bewitched Black Knight of the Mountain, and as a result, no one will fight him (vs. 4016). In these cases, Tristan manipulates the code—he does not in any way *change* it—but transgresses it. He uses the vast normative and symbolic capital of the vestimentary code already in place in society perhaps in an unorthodox way, but his use does not alter either its normative or its symbolic power. He simply uses it to his own ends.

Like Tristan, other characters use the concealing potential of clothing for their own strategic purposes. In *Cligés*, Alexandre devises a plan to gain access to the castle of the traitorous Count Angrés. He and his men will don the armor of the count's fallen men to enter the castle without resistance and then to take revenge by capturing or killing those inside. The plan works marvelously:

> Les escuz as morz vont seisir
> Si se metent an tel ator.
> Et as desfanses de la tor
> Les genz del chastel monté furent,
> Et les escuz bien reconurent,
> Et cuident que de lor gent soient,
> Car de l'aguet ne s'apansoient,
> Qui desoz les escuz se ceuvre.
> Et li portiers les portes oevre,
> Si les a dedanz reçeüz.
> De c'est gabez et deçeüz,
> Car de rien ne les areisone,
> Ne uns de cez mot ne li sone.
>
> (vss. 1830–42)

[They (the Greeks) will take the shields of the dead and put on their equipment. The people of the castle had gone up into the donjons of the castle, and they easily recognized the shields, believing them to be of their own men, for they did not foresee the trap that the shields hid behind them. And the porter opened the doors and let them enter. He is taken in by their ruse for he does not address a word to them and none of them speaks a word to him.]

Here again, there is never any questioning of appearances by the other characters; they assume the absolute impenetrability of the code. Because they recognize the armor, the knights inside believe they know the identity of the wearers.[23]

The cases cited above are very representative of the effectiveness of disguise in twelfth-century romance. The authors create imagined societies in which the vestimentary code is absolute for the vast majority of characters. Only a select few of the characters have access to the possibility of manipulating the clothing signifiers that make up the system. These characters tend to be the protagonists of the romance and the characters whose point of view the author most often assumes. The author thus sets his protagonists apart from the rest of society and invites the audience into this exclusive group. Certainly, this position of exclusivity appeals to the members of the audience and makes them more sympathetic toward the protagonists and narrator. However, the author's use of disguise as a means to subvert the vestimentary code is completely obvious and explicit in these cases.

Progressive Manipulation of the Code

In other instances, there is a less blatant but still discernible manipulation of the a code, at three distinct levels of manipulation: duplication of the code but with new conventions, contextual or community changes that result in the necessity to interpret rather than simply read signifiers, and the absence of a code. The duplication of the code with changed conventions means that members of a particular linguistic community use different signifiers than

---

23. Armor, as I will discuss in more detail later, is ideally suited for the concealment of identity, and this material property is exploited for purposes of disguise throughout the period that armor was worn and in all the literary genres of the period. What is interesting for this study is the fact that, except on rare occasions like the one discussed, none of the characters acknowledge this capacity. See also Lacy, "On Armor and Identity."

those normally used to communicate the same meaning.[24] An example of this phenomenon would be if two or more teenagers began to use the word *bad* to mean "good." They might even invent a new word that has the same meaning as an existing word in their language. The process of signification is the same, but they have substituted one convention for another, one signifier for another. Alteration of the signification process involves changes that occur at levels besides that of the signifier. These changes may take place at the level of the linguistic community or of the context. In this case, the meaning of a signifier is dependent upon with whom a speaker is conversing or in what environment the conversation is taking place. This first type of alteration to the signifying process is at the base of the insignia of such entities as secret societies; for example, an article of clothing or a piece of jewelry that has no meaning for the society at large will have a very specific meaning to a group within that society. Context-dependent signification occurs when signifiers have multiple meanings that vary according to the context in which they are used.[25] The meaning of a white cotton-blend overgarment changes according to the setting in which it is worn: it means "chef" in a restaurant, "doctor" in a hospital, "pharmacist" in a drugstore, and so on. Finally, the manipulations of a code can become so extensive, so overwhelming to that code, that it transcends itself to become a signifying system that, in Jonathan Culler's words, "can produce meaning instead of merely refer to meanings that already exist" (20). In this kind of system, the meaning of a signifier is understandable only through an interpretive process that may vary from one situation to another.[26] It calls for more than the reading of symbols and more than the reading of signs in a specific context or community: it calls for the capacity to create meaning. In vestimentary terms, we may think of this system as parallel to a personal style in dress or, on a larger scale, the couturier's creation before it has become the fashion and therefore codified.

My first discussion of code manipulation centers upon the duplication of the code with different conventions, and as noted above, this sort of alteration represents the first position on the continuum of progressive manipulation. Instances in which characters duplicate the form of the existing socially

24. I am borrowing the term "linguistic community" from the field of linguistics. Dubois et al. define the term in the following way: "Un groupe d'êtres humains utilisant la même langue ou le même dialecte à un moment donné et pouvant communiquer entre eux. . . . Elle se subdivise en de nombreuses autres communautés linguistiques inférieures. Tout individu appartenant à la communauté peut évidemment appartenir en même temps à plusieurs groupements linguistiques." (96)

25. The discussion of context-based signifiers will continue in Chapter 4.

26. This dependence of the sign upon the interpretive process is underlined by Peirce, who writes: "The whole purpose of a sign is that it shall be interpreted in another sign, and its whole purport lies in the special character which it imparts to that interpretation" (247).

accepted vestimentary code and create new conventions tend to involve a recognition device. In both major French accounts of the Tristan legend of the twelfth century, those by Béroul and by Thomas, Yseut gives Tristan a ring so that she can positively identify him or his messenger (Béroul vss. 2707–32, Thomas vss. 2454–63); examining each of these instances in turn will illustrate code manipulation by duplication with new conventions. The use of a ring in these two romances to indicate and mark identity is formally similar to common practices of the day by which holders of an ecclesiastical or legal office wore an emblem of their position so that everyone could recognize their social role.[27] The vestimentary item is invested with powerful and unequivocal symbolism that extends throughout society. In Tristan and Yseut's case, the ring has little or no meaning, certainly no precise meaning, for society: it is a private symbol. The process by which the ring has meaning, however, is an exact duplication of the process by which signifiers take on meaning for a society. For both, a community agrees upon the referent and its meaning. Tristan and Yseut's ring represents a language that only the two of them speak. They maintain the code but change its conventions.

In Thomas's account, the ailing Tristan sends Kaherdin, disguised as a cloth merchant, to speak with Yseut. They know that if he does not disguise himself, he will not be allowed to speak with her. His disguise works, preventing anyone from recognizing him. Moreover, he gains an audience with the queen by insisting that she would certainly not want to miss out on the fine cloth that he has to show her. It is significant that he takes the disguise of a cloth merchant, for this costume makes it perfectly clear that Kaherdin, working on Tristan's behalf, has a special ability to manipulate cloth for his own means. In this instance, Kaherdin peddles cloth in three ways. First, he pretends to make his living from its trade; second, he uses the cloth of his disguise to conceal his identity and enter the city forbidden to him and to Tristan; and, last, he employs it as a ruse to speak with the sequestered Yseut. In this scene Kaherdin is the ultimate manifestation of the play in the system. As a merchant, he is the most potent agent for change; as a man who handles cloth, he is the provider of the most obvious means to alter appearance; and as a disguised man, he has used the vestimentary code and subverted it. Kaherdin's disguise is so complete and effective that even Yseut does not at first recognize him. But Tristan has sent Kaherdin with

---

27. As mentioned in Chapter 1, I am using as broad a definition of clothing as possible, one that includes jewelry, armor, and any other items of adornment, since all these items figure as part of the vestimentary code of the day. Additionally and crucially for the current discussion, these vestimentary items are part and parcel of a character's identity.

the ring, the agreed-upon recognition device, and when he shows it to the queen, she immediately understands the situation. The ring has a powerful meaning, and it is a sign that requires further action. Upon seeing it, Yseut must reinterpret appearances, reevaluate the situation, and read beyond the normative and symbolic meaning of Kaherdin's disguise as a cloth merchant. Only when she performs this interpretation can she see his true identity and his purpose for being there. The ring's power is nonetheless a private one: no one outside the limited community of Tristan, Yseut, and Kaherdin is capable of deciphering its special meaning.

Whereas the type of duplication of the vestimentary code that I have been describing represents the first position on a continuum of movement away from an impenetrable code, the middle position, by which the code is altered by changes in either linguistic community or context, contains a greater number of possibilities. This increased flexibility exists because, rather than simply changing the conventions of the existing code to create a new one, alterations to the process of signification occur at the middle position. One such alteration is the changing of the community. As we have seen, a code exists when the members of a linguistic community agree upon meaning, that is, on the relationship between the referent and what it signifies. We saw that in both Tristan romances, both Tristan and Yseut agree upon the meaning of the ring. There are cases in which a vestimentary item allows recognition even though the wearer is not part of the community, and I will examine three examples that illustrate just this kind of signification process. One such instance occurs in *Milun*, one of Marie's *lais*.[28] The knight Milun conceives a son with a lady promised to another man, and when the child is born, his parents send him to be raised by a distant relative. Much later, when the boy has reached manhood, Milun goes out in search of him in the region where his relative lives. The two encounter each other on a battlefield, and Milun recognizes his son because of a ring he wears, a ring that Milun and the lady had sent with their infant son long ago. This ring has just as much meaning as Tristan and Yseut's ring, for it too occasions recognition, but in this case, it has meaning for only one of the two involved in the recognition episode. The son cannot participate in the interpretation of the ring as a sign of parentage; he may only be an observer. The code remains indecipherable to him because he is not included in the linguistic community that agreed upon its meaning.

---

28. See also Van Vleck on the use of textile in this *lai* (45–47).

The second instance of exclusive linguistic communities that I will examine occurs in the romance *Guillaume d'Angleterre*. King Guillaume's twin sons are parted from their father and mother as infants and are adopted by two merchants. Before their abduction, the king ripped out the sides of his coat in order to swaddle them. Although much later the two pieces of cloth will be the emblem by which the king definitively determines his sons' true identity, the adoptive fathers do not read these signifiers in this way. In fact, they mistakenly take them to be indicators of their adoptive sons' low birth. The twin sons also remain unaware both of their true origins and of the importance and significance of the pieces of cloth. Only Guillaume (and possibly his wife, although we are not explicitly told of her awareness) is capable of reading the pieces of cloth cut from his old coat as emblems of his lost sons' identities. The linguistic community in this case is quite possibly a single person, but this person is tremendously important, and his capacity to read the pieces of cloth as signifiers of the sons' true identity is crucial for the romance. He is the only character capable of carrying out the process of signification that occasions the process of identification for the sons.

Finally, *Erec et Enide* offers a particularly interesting example of alteration of the linguistic community with regard to clothing. In this particular case, the specialized linguistic community consists of Enide's family, Erec, and at least Guenevere, if not Arthur's entire court. During the passages in which Erec first meets Enide's family and in which Erec makes arrangements to marry Enide and provide for her family (vss. 387–546, 1310–94), both Erec and Enide's father are adamant that Enide continue to wear her ragged attire until the appropriate occasion arise and the worthy dresser arrive. The family and Erec are in complete agreement in this attitude. Moreover, they all interpret Enide's current clothing to mean the same things: Enide's personal worth demands that a truly extraordinary person dress her; the right person to dress her has not yet come along; and as of yet no one worthy of dressing her has offered. Once Erec brings Enide to Arthur's court, he finds the worthy Guenevere willing and able to dress Enide in nothing less than the queen's own new and exquisite *bliaut* and mantle (vss. 1563–1652). Whereas Guenevere explicitly states to Erec that he has followed the right and proper course in bringing Enide in her ragged attire to court ("Molt avez bien fait: / droiz est que de mes robes ait" [You have done very well; it is right that she have one of my robes] [vss. 15763–64]) and then dresses her in a lively and elaborate scene, many people in Enide's town were baffled by first Enide's father's then Erec's refusals to allow anyone to provide better clothes for the maiden.[29] Enide's cousin explains: "'Molt grant honte / sera a vos, plus qu'a autrui, / se cist sires an mainne o lui / vostre niece si povremant / atornee de vestement'" ("Great shame will be yours, more than anyone else's, if this knight takes with him your niece so poorly dressed") (vss. 1344–48). These detractors misunderstand the attitude of Erec and Enide's father because they simply do not belong to the community of people who can attach the one correct meaning to Enide's attire. They attach an entirely different meaning to the garments: that it is disgraceful and dishonorable to take Enide to Arthur's court thus dressed when, in fact, according to the community in question, it is exactly the right path to pursue. This example clearly shows how a single vestimentary item in these romances may be read differently by different linguistic communities, and it demonstrates to what extent the writers of romance are calling into question the larger, monolithic vestimentary code of their society. Multiple possible meanings of a single vestimentary signifier introduce ambiguity into the code, thereby defying the absolutism and constraints of the code that the audience of romance would have preferred to remain constant and unproblematic.

The last position within code manipulation is the absence or transcendence of the code. To illustrate this extreme position I will draw upon a remarkable example of code subversion from Chrétien's *Chevalier de la charrete*, or *Lancelot*, that involves Lancelot's armor, the tournament at Nouaz.[30] A short discussion of armor and its identificatory power will be useful. With regard to this vestimentary code, armor is a special case, both in terms of its material type and with regard to its capacity for symbolism. While the quality of the clothing that a knight wears may identify him as having that particular social role and rank, the heraldic design depicted on his armor can identify him individually.[31] At the same time that the members of society

---

29. The author spends close to a hundred lines describing the dressing scene in which Guenevere not only gives Enide one of her own magnificent gowns and beautiful mantles, but also oversees the "making" of the new Enide (vss. 1567–1652). Guenevere sees to it that silk ribbons and gold clasps adorn the gown and mantle and then urges Enide to cast away her old ensemble. Enide's transformation from impoverished maiden into a proper lady of the court, which directly precedes her marriage to Erec, is thus made material in the changing of her clothes.

30. Matilda Tomaryn Bruckner has thoroughly and beautifully analyzed this complex and important scene, and my discussion of it owes a great deal to her expert reading of it in *Shaping Romance* (61–77).

31. Lacy points to an unusual scene in romance: in the Gauvain section of *Perceval*, Arthur's nephew is believed by onlookers to be not a knight, but a merchant, because he has two shields ("On Armor" 368). This bizarre reading by the others suggests that it is impossible to identify properly when the code is violated, or in Lacy's terms, when identification is at odds with identity.

were being mobilized to identify with certain factions and groups within the society, on the battlefield, the knights had every reason to keep their individual identities clearly visible (Pastoureau, *Armorial* 54). Ideally, knights in battle *need* to distinguish among themselves, although sometimes they cannot; they *need* to identify their enemies and allies in order to fight the right opponents. Pastoureau points to innovations in the armor of the twelfth century as the driving force behind the development of heraldry (55). With the development of the nosepiece, which covered a good part of the face, recognition by normal means became impossible, and to compensate for this effect, the knights began to paint emblems upon their shields.[32] The armor of knights communicates their social role and status, but the emblems on their shields are nothing less than markers of individual identity.

The romances of the twelfth century are replete with references to heraldry. The reliance of knights upon heraldic designs to identify one another is clearly portrayed in Chrétien's *Lancelot*, when several knights who are no longer participating in the tournament at Nouaz identify the knights on the field for the queen and her ladies:[33]

> Antr'ax dïent: "Veez vos or
> celui a cele bande d'or?
> par mi cel escu de bernic?
> C'est Gouvernauz de Roberdic.
> Et veez vos celui aprés
> qui an son escu pres a pres
> a mise une aigle et un dragon?
> C'est li filz le roi d'Arragon
> qui venuz est an ceste terre
> por pris et por encor conquerre.
>
> (vss. 5773–82)

---

[32]. "Nous connaissons la cause principale [de l'apparition des armoiries en Europe occidentale]: le développement du haubert et du casque rendant peu à peu les combattants méconnaissables, ceux-ci prennent l'habitude de faire peindre sur la grande surface de leur bouclier des figures servant à se reconnaître au coeur de la mêlée; on peut parler d'armoiries à partir du moment où le même personnage fait constamment usage de la même figure" (Pastoureau, *Armorial* 89).

[33]. Krueger has analyzed the tournament scene in terms of a double subversion of feminine desire under the guise of Guenevere's complete dominance over Lancelot and his performance on the battlefield. First, when the seneschal's wife frees Lancelot from his prison on condition that he return and give her all his love, it is a promise she knows he cannot keep. Second, the ladies of Nouaz are frustrated that none can marry the best knight, subverting entirely their original intention for holding the tournament (*Women Readers* 62–63).

[Among themselves they said: "Do you now see the one with gold band across a red shield? That's Governal of Roberdic. And do you see the one after who has a shield on which he has placed an eagle and a dragon side by side? That's the son of the king of Aragon who came to this country to win esteem and glory.]

This naming of knights by their coats of arms continues for another forty lines or so, providing ample evidence of how important emblems on armor are for recognition. Heraldry is a symbolic system that resolves the identity ambiguity of armor that conceals the face of the wearer, but it is not an immutable system. Armor, even emblazoned, often hides identity rather than revealing it. Knights are, in fact, one of the more problematic entities from the standpoint both of society and of the vestimentary system. Their armor lends itself extremely well and quite often to disguise, whether intentional or not, and to manipulation. For society, knights are perhaps the most visible vestige of ancestral glory, that of the *bellatores*, and are the very emblem of it. Yet they also embody the paradoxes of the vestimentary code. The very attire that makes them knights has all the potential to undermine its absolute meaning, its identificatory power. Armor is thus the internal flaw of the code, in that it invites disguise and therefore ambiguity. The symbolism of a coat of arms can never be absolute, even though the nobility is most invested in its absolutism.

The naming scene cited above is also important for the narrative because the knights' ability to name the others is compromised by the appearance of Lancelot, who is incognito.[34] This most accomplished of knights arrives to participate in the tournament wearing borrowed armor that none of the others is capable of recognizing.[35] Lancelot's winning performance on the field baffles the company of knights, for they cannot imagine who this knight in unfamiliar armor might be. The queen, on the other hand, looks beyond Lancelot's outer trappings and sees her knight through his deeds rather than through his clothing. As Matilda Tomaryn Bruckner has remarked, the queen "acts first, in order to reveal Lancelot's identity by concealing it from

---

34. Bruckner remarks that the tournament itself is not recounted to us directly (except for forty-two verses) but rather through the eyes of observers: "Rather than offer us direct description of fighting, the narrator multiplies the spectacle through the varying and contradictory perspectives of heralds, damsels, Queen, and knights, combatants and non-combatants (including Gauvain) who witness and evaluate what they see. The enumeration of and description of the best knights' shields, which imitates the second day of the tournament, exemplifies this tendency to see the tournament as an object of contemplation" (*Shaping* 63).

35. The herald, of course, has recognized Lancelot by having seen the knight in his miserable lodging the night before, so without his armor.

everyone else" (*Shaping* 74). In fact, the queen verifies his identity through instructions to do his worst, then his best, which is exactly what determines his actions on the battlefield. Bruckner suggests even that the queen "recognizes Lancelot through a slight delay before a brilliant performance — the pattern typical of Lancelot and Lancelot alone throughout the romance — her immediate recognition is nevertheless subject to caution," since she has, after all, been subject to the false signs of his death earlier in the romance (*Shaping* 76). She devises her test to confirm his identity whose "form itself indicates how well the Queen has read Lancelot's character (and the previous events of the romance)" (76). Guenevere has made the heraldic code obsolete through her skillful imagining and arrives at a new way of discerning identity, one that is ambiguous: at once verbal (through the intermediary of the damsel who understands nothing of what she is communicating) and silent (between the two lovers) and behavioral, involving her perception of his patterned actions and his obedience through his acts to her requests.

Chrétien has very clearly set forth the heraldic signifying system; with the voice of his characters he demonstrates how heraldic recognition works. However, the poet simultaneously subverts the system as he develops it. Lancelot, known by every person present at the tournament, knowable to everyone by his deeds, remains unknown to all but one observer. Chrétien showcases the identificatory power of clothing, and here, armor, only then to show its breaking point. The heraldic system is a strictly symbolic system, and it breaks down with Lancelot's introduction of ambiguity into it. Lancelot's presence requires more interpretation than simply looking to his armor to identify him. His identity is discernible only when other information is taken into consideration. The queen recognizes him because she has *interpreted* his identity rather than simply read it. In this case, Chrétien clearly demonstrates his capacity to manipulate a symbolic code, the heraldic code, until it transcends its limits and becomes a system in which meaning is created.

To posit that this play, this capacity to move beyond the limits of the code, is unique to the representational universe would be to make a false claim. It is precisely because this slippage exists in the system used by the society that the writers of romance in the twelfth century could exploit it so fully in their works. Codes are problematic in nature for the very reason that the meaning of their signifiers is an invention. Jonathan Culler explains the paradoxical nature of semiotic systems:

> The very energy employed in the proliferation and naturalization of signs — the desire to make everything signify and yet to make

all those meanings inherent and intrinsic—finally undermines the meaning accorded to objects. These two processes which seek in opposite ways to affirm meaning, by creating and naturalizing it, contribute to what becomes, in effect, a self-contained activity. Absorbing and undermining the two contributory forces, the process of signification becomes an autonomous play of meaning. (40)

The writers of romance inscribe this play into their literary works because it is real, because it is true. The nobles, cling as they might to the code and the notions from which the code derives, cannot deny that there is play in the system. However, the romances provide them with a safe environment in which to explore the intrinsic contradictions in the system. In each romance, the noble heroes and heroines triumph, despite the introduction of ambiguity, ambivalence, and arbitrariness by the writers. The romances have challenged the clothing conventions to which the nobles are accustomed and then reassured the nobles that even with widespread manipulation of the vestimentary code by others, they still retain their place at the top of society. Additionally, the writers have produced rich works of high artistic merit, evidenced by their transcendence of both the vestimentary code and the rigid convention of character elaboration, and they have still pleased their audience. Their use of clothing in such an inventive and creative way has been crucial to their accomplishment of the dual goal of challenging and pleasing. The writers have dressed their characters with their artistic goals in mind, and, indeed, the clothes have made them who they are.

CLOTHING ACTS AND THE MOVEMENT FROM CODE TO SIGNIFYING SYSTEM

CLOTHING ACTS ARE THOSE actions taken by characters to alter the appearance of themselves or others. Appearance was extremely important to the twelfth-century French nobility insofar as it provided the strongest and a very stable indicator of identity, both personal and social, both within society and in its literary expression.[1] Therefore, clothing acts are a seemingly natural place for writers to inscribe ambiguity, ambivalence, or arbitrariness into their texts, since these acts specifically and inherently involve the modification of appearance. That a character chooses to make alterations to his, her, or another's appearance, and thus to that person's social and personal identity, attests to the existence of the very possibility of such changes. Varying one's or another's appearance, then, becomes a mechanism of transformation in a much larger sense. The fact that romance so often portrays characters in the process of changing clothes confirms both the capacity for evolution of these characters and the openness of the representational system to the introduction of more fluidity. In much the same way that the characters become, in changing clothes, manipulators of appearance, writers of romance become experts in manipulation of the vestimentary code.

This transformation may be viewed as occurring in a progressive fashion, although I do not mean to suggest that this progression was absolute in any sense. In fact, adherence to the code occurs throughout the romances of the period; however, it does not prohibit the writers from using it in different ways and for different purposes. Their manipulation of convention is apparent alongside their more standard use of it. Writers use the code as a resource to portray features of their characters quickly and to provide important details for the plot efficiently; it serves them as a sort of shorthand.

---

1. This situation is not unique to twelfth-century society, the near absolutism of the concordance of appearance to identity is beginning to wane. In the following centuries, clothing would still be relied upon to make indications about social and class identity, but the fixity of such a system could no longer be taken for granted.

However, romances boast many examples of considerable adjustments to the code, some so substantial that the code is forced into transforming into a true signifying system capable of generating new meanings rather than simply reiterating previously established ones.[2] This chapter focuses upon modifications to convention that involve alterations to the contexts in which the clothing signifiers occur.

Clothing acts are especially interesting for tracking code manipulation, first, because these acts already invite, if not force, a questioning of the absolute and motivated meaning of the signifier and, second, because they have a particular relation to narrative context: they are acts rather than descriptions. As such, they introduce the clothing signifier into the plot of the romance. Clothing becomes performative rather than simply descriptive, and, accordingly, the vestimentary code is pushed into the action as well. Moreover, because clothing acts are actions taken by characters, they may be considered in terms of the character's motivation. Often, a character's purpose for performing an act involving clothing is not realized. In such cases, we must look further and consider the act in different contexts to grasp its meaning for the narrative.

Gifts of Clothing

In twelfth-century France, gifts, whether of clothing or not, solidified and reified social ties and therefore performed a crucial function. Both in the society at large and in its literary expression, gifts remained symbolic acts, motivated by society's need for internal organization and a system of interrelations among social classes. Clearly, gifts are the currency of the gift economy to which the nobility clung during this period. Lester K. Little explains that "in a gift economy, goods and services are exchanged without having specific, calculated values assigned to them. Prestige, power, honor, and wealth are all expressed in the spontaneous giving of gifts; and more than just expressed: these attributes are attained and maintained through largess" (4). So important was this form of structuration to twelfth-century French society that the entrepreneurs of the merchant class, once they met

---

2. This definition of a signifying system—as a system "which can produce meaning instead of merely refer to meanings that already exist"—comes from Culler and his discussion of the limits of a code (20). This distinction is basic to the one that I make throughout this study between the vestimentary code and the clothing signifying system. See also my discussion in Chapter 1.

with a certain degree of affluence, themselves began to emulate the nobility's penchant for largess (8). It is therefore not surprising that in literature, gifts would continue to be important for the establishment of social ties. The stakes seem to be too great to risk society's well-being by questioning or problematizing the gift economy too rigorously. Accordingly, throughout the romances, the act of giving clothing for the most part upholds the conventions of the vestimentary code. In fact, the movement charted in Chapter 2 from a symbolic language toward a system of more freely interpretable signs is largely, although not completely, absent with regard to the gift of clothing. Nonetheless, a discussion of clothing gifts is useful in that it provides striking evidence that writers of twelfth-century romance extensively used the standard vestimentary paradigm alongside their manipulation or subversion of it.

There are numerous examples of clothing gifts in twelfth-century verse romance that demonstrate aristocratic largess.[3] In *Cligés*, when Alexandre sets off from Greece to prove himself in the Arthurian court, he asks his father for a number of supplies, but, in particular, he asks for "dras de soie" so that he may show his largess by richly providing for his retinue (vss. 140–45). In honor of Erec's wedding, Arthur gives gifts of clothing to the minstrels who regaled the court (*Erec* vss. 2055–64). In *Lanval*, once his encounter with the mystical lady has changed the hero's fortune for the better, he shares his wealth, bestowing gifts of clothes upon jongleurs (vs. 211). Jaufré gives out gifts of luxurious clothes upon his return as lord to Brunissen's land (*Jaufre* vss. 10800–10821). Finally, upon his father's death, Erec distributes clothes to the poor and to priests to honor the solemn occasion (*Erec* vss. 6474–84). All of these clothing gifts establish or reaffirm social ties among groups of people, particularly between lord and vassal or between social superior and inferior. The gifts highlight the importance of sharing wealth on state occasions or in prosperous times. They also reflect the social practices of bestowing gifts during periods of changing status, as in the cases of Alexandre, Erec, and Jaufré, as well as the immediate redistribution of wealth after acquisition, as in the case of Lanval.

The dubbing of a knight provides a highly codified occasion of clothing gifts, especially but not limited to the gift of armor. Guigemar receives armor from the king he serves once he is of age (*Guigemar* vss. 43–50), and Amadas has his father beg the duke to make him a knight and give him armor (*Amadas* vss. 1312–28). Arthur dubs Jaufré and gives him a warhorse

3. A detailed discussion of the social function of largess appears in Chapter 2.

and a suit of armor (*Jaufre* vss. 634–48). These gifts of armor not only solidify the bonds between lord and knight; they also provide the knight with the equipment necessary to perform his new role. Thus, the gift of armor upon dubbing has more than interpersonal value: it is a transformational device for the recipient. A knight is defined and identified by his armor. Therefore, this gift has far more than the power to bind one man to another in the context of a gift economy: it actually transforms a regular man into a knight, bestowing status, rank, and role upon another human being. Not only does a lord give the new knight a suit of armor, but he also provides him rich clothing items. Whereas these articles of clothing do not have the same value as armor in terms of establishing a knight in his new social role, they facilitate his ability to perform the other duties of his new status—his appearance at court. One way in which romance often differs from epic is in its placing an equal emphasis upon a knight's behavior at court and upon his behavior on the battlefield.[4] The fact that romance would depict gifts of fine, courtly clothing alongside gifts of armor is therefore perfectly in keeping with the new values of the romance genre. In the universe of the courtly romance, the one gift indeed necessitates the other.

Piponnier and Mane remark that a common clothing gift at dubbing might be a scarlet mantle (33), but there are references to other items as well. For example, in honor of Erec's wedding, Arthur dubs one hundred knights and gives each of them a "robe vaire / de riche paisle d'Alixandre, / chascuns tel com il la volt prandre / a son voloir, a sa devise" (an outfit in vair and rich Alexandrian silk, each one taking the one he wants, according to his desire and taste) (*Erec* vss. 1966–69). And later, at Erec's coronation, Arthur dubs more than four hundred knights, giving them, the texts states, the clothes necessary to improve their appearance at court:

> Ot adobez li rois Artus
> .IIII. cenz chevaliers et plus,
> toz filz de contes et de rois;
> chevax dona a chascun trois
> et robes a chascun trois peire,
> por ce que sa corz mialz apeire.

---

4. By this I do not mean to suggest that no behavior in court is depicted in epic, nor do I mean to suggest that the line between epic and romance conventions is so clearly drawn as to be unproblematic. Quite the contrary, the lines do often blur, but I speak here of a general tendency in romance to value a knight's behavior at court, or in courtly situations with the opposite sex, to a similar extent that it values his accomplishments of feats on the battlefield or on adventures.

> *Molt fu li rois puissanz et larges:*
> ne dona pas mantiax de sarges,
> ne de conins ne de brunetes,
> mes de samiz et d'erminetes,
> de veir antier et de dïapres,
> listez d'orfois roides et aspres.
>
> (vss. 6599–6610; emphasis mine)

[King Arthur had dubbed four hundred knights and more, all sons of counts and kings: he gave to each three horses and three (pairs of) robes, so that his court would look better. The king was very powerful and generous: he did not give mantles of serge, nor of rabbit, nor of dark brown wool, but of samite and ermine, and whole vair and *diaspre*, bordered with stiff and rough orphrey.]

The text goes on to explain how much more generous Arthur's offerings at this event are than those of Alexander or Caesar (vss. 6612–23). This favorable comparison with great rulers of history asserts Arthur's superiority over them, for, as we have seen, largess is the mark of a great ruler. There is nonetheless a great benefit to Arthur himself as he bestows such luxurious gifts to the new knights of his court: his becomes the most resplendent court in memory. His free and expansive expression of his largess augments the renown of his court and establishes him as the greatest ruler ever to live. These examples of Arthur's generosity demonstrate very clearly that largess is a mutually beneficial exchange by which the knight enjoys material gain while the lord garners intangible but nonetheless considerable return.

There are other equally compelling examples of Arthur's reaping intangible benefit from his expression of largess. Toward the end of *Jaufre*, Arthur decides to replace the clothing that was destroyed during the episode in which the knights removed all their garments to cushion his fall at the beginning of the romance (vss. 10064–10110). His decision results from the queen's complaint to the enchanter knight that the latter could never make up for the harm his earlier actions have caused her. Arthur is attempting to make reparations even though he is not the cause of the harm; his responsibility stems, rather, from his perhaps too ardent desire for adventures (to which the enchanter claims to be responding) as well as the fact that the damage has occurred in his court. At any rate, his replacement of his court's clothing is lavish, going well beyond what was expected of him.

> E aqui meseus li borzes
> An fait cargar tut demanes
> .v. carres trastoz de cendatz,
> E .v. de samitz orfresatz,
> E .x. dels milhors draps de grana
> Que crestian ni crestiana
> Anc en neguna terra vi,
> E .xx. clagueron n'attressi
> De vertz e de rics cisclatons,
> E de palis ben fais e bons,
> E enaissi sun s'en intrat
> El palais, on an descargat.
>
> (vss. 10079–90)

[And at once the townsmen filled the whole order with five carts full of *cendal*, and five carts of orphrey-embellished samite, and ten of the best scarlets that any Christian man or woman had ever seen in any land, and twenty more of green and rich *siglatons*, and well-made and good silks. And they came thus into the palace and unloaded it.]

We learn that there has never been at any court so much of these rich fabrics sewn into clothing; the narrator says that to describe it fully would become tedious (vss. 10097–10110). Clearly, Arthur is using the excuse of replacing the worn-out clothes (since it defies verisimilitude that his fall onto the pile of them could have destroyed them) to grandly demonstrate his largess. Moreover, he offers his gift to anyone, regardless of whether their clothes were used in the pile or not. This degree of generosity is indeed exemplary and extends into the realm of hyperbole.[5] Only a king of Arthur's standing could either afford such largess or be expected to make gifts of this magnitude. And while ostensibly he is replacing clothing ruined in the process of saving him, his motivation is the restoration of peace and order in his court as well as its trust. His gift, then, does as much for his own benefit as for its recipients.

The preceding examples attest to the predominance of seigneurial largess within the literary expression of the period. Yet, as discussed above,

---

5. In fact this romance's propensity for hyperbole is well noted, and scholars have tended to view it as evidence of a satirical or parodical treatment of typical Arthurian themes and motifs. See Caroline Jewers's "The Name of the Ruse and the Round Table"; Veronica Fraser's "Humour and Satire in the Romance of *Jaufre*"; and Suzanne Fleishman's "*Jaufre* or Chivalry Askew."

these gifts certainly do not occur without repercussions: texts also relate the rewards of a character's largess. One example of this occurs in *Thèbes* when the people of Thebes grieve the loss of Ates and remember him primarily for his largess (vss. 6312–25). This example shows clearly that largess is an inherent and essential trait of a good leader, but it also makes clear that gifts are not forgotten or taken for granted. In fact, as Little notes, in a gift economy, "the act of giving is less free than the connotation of 'giving' suggests, because one gift obliges the recipient to make a counter-gift," and furthermore, "the failure of a recipient to reciprocate properly can lead to the rupture of the social ties involved" (4). Reciprocation may, however, as Marcel Mauss informs us, take many forms other than a similar countergift (151): "De plus, ce qu'ils échangent, ce n'est pas exclusivement des biens et des richesses, des meubles et des immeubles, des choses utiles économiquement. Ce sont avant tout des politesses, des festins, des rites, des services militaires, des femmes, des enfants, des danses, des fêtes, des foires dont le marché n'est qu'un des moments et où la circulation des richesses n'est qu'un des termes d'un contrat beaucoup plus général et beaucoup plus permanent" (151).

The exchange of gifts, then, may be imagined in a more abstract way, rather than in uniquely material terms. For example, the lord who dubs a knight and gives him a gift of armor may expect his gift to be reciprocated by the knight's service and protection, that is, by the use of the armor. In the example from *Thèbes*, the outpouring of grief for Ates is a type of reciprocation for the many gifts that he has given over the years. In *Erec et Enide*, Erec's offer to dress his future in-laws richly (vss. 1324–36) is a particularly good example of the rewards of generosity. Enide's father allows Erec to wear his own beautiful armor to participate in the sparrowhawk episode, and the text emphasizes that the armor fits Erec extremely well (vss. 763–72). Erec repays Enide's father's generosity by the promise of fine clothing, thereby returning in kind but to a much greater extent the gift of armor. By having the expensive cloth sent from his own home, he is doing much more than simply reciprocating a gift: he is providing Enide's family the means to integrate seamlessly into his own.

In Chrétien's *Le Chevalier au lion*, or *Yvain*, there is a fascinating example of past largess inspiring a similar response: the recipients of Lunete's repeated and consistent gift-giving take pity upon her state of undress as she is being led to the stake. What distinguishes this example is that their pity, evoked in a similar way to his people's grief for Ates, mobilizes them into action, an action that constitutes the exact reciprocation of the clothing gifts she has so often given them. For her "crime" of having convinced

Laudine to marry Yvain, Lunete is being taken to be burned at the stake "trestoute nue en sa chemise" (completely nude in her *chemise*) (vs. 4316). However, the other ladies realize that Lunete has been too harshly judged, and they remember that she has provided them with beautiful clothes to wear: "Par son consoil nos revestoit / Ma dame de ses robes veires" (By her counsel, my lady gave us her vair robes to wear) (vss. 4360–61). Finally, they decide to send a set of clothes, including a mantle with which to cover herself (vss. 4368–73), effectively reducing her shame. Therefore, Lunete's past generosity toward these ladies inspires in them the desire to offer help to Lunete when she needs it. Furthermore, they assist her by providing clothes to her in kind. In this last case, the reciprocal nature of feudal society is in clear evidence. Lunete, when in a position of some power, gives gifts of clothing to those less fortunate, but once her fortune changes, the former beneficiaries of her generosity assume the role of provider and clothe her.

Gifts of clothing are not always limited to the expression of a lord's largess; sometimes they occur for other reasons and with other effects. Three categories of nonlargess gifts deserve brief mention here: restorative gifts, identificatory gifts, and love gifts. In all three of these classes, the act of giving clothing is reciprocated by a counter act of some sort and is thus similar in effect to gifts that characterize a lord's largess. Further, there is certainly some overlap among these categories, including the category of largess. Restorative gifts of clothing are often the main mechanism by which a character's former status or health is restored. For example, in *Amadas et Ydoine*, the innkeeper provides Amadas, who is recovering from love-induced madness, with everything he needs to resume his knightly activities. The text twice articulates the innkeeper's provision. First, Ydoine tells him that his host "Li trouvera tout son desir, / Cevaus et dras a grant honor, / Armes, harnois et bel atour" (will find him all he desires, horses and honorable silks, arms, and fine equipment) (vss. 3888–90). A second list occurs about a hundred lines later, this time somewhat extended: "Robes li trouvera et dras / Fres et noviaus et vair et gris, / Et armes et cevaus de pris / Et, se lui plaist, autre harnois" (He will find robes and fresh and new silk and vair and gris, and arms and prized horses, and if it pleases him, another harness) (vss. 4014–17). It is through these gifts, symbols of the care accorded to Amadas, that he is able to heal. The wife of Meleagant's seneschal gives Lancelot her husband's new red armor so that he may continue on his way and participate in the tournament, on the condition that he give her his love once he returns (*Lancelot* vss. 5495–5511). Each of them obtains something in this exchange: the lady is promised Lancelot as lover, and Lancelot can anonymously demonstrate his prowess at the tourney. Once more, it is the woman's concern, symbolized in the gift of armor, that Lancelot is capable of attending the tournament. In *Erec et Enide*, King Evrain replaces Erec's worn armor when he encounters him in the woods (vss. 5627–45), and this replacement of Erec's armor by a king himself reflects the queen's replacing of Enide's worn dress earlier. In all these cases, the clothing gift is crucial for the rehabilitation of the affected knight and for his restoration to his former capacities.

Identificatory gifts are those by which a character's identity is either established or enhanced by a gift of clothing. Often this establishment of identity comes at a long interval from the giving, but the counter act is almost always the restoration of a lost person to a former interpersonal relationship. In *Fresne* the mother's wrapping her daughter in a beautiful and unique cloth (a piece of sumptuous silk brought back personally from Constantinople by the child's father) in addition to attaching a ring that reveals her daughter's nobility to a band around her arm, ensures that later in the text, upon seeing the cloth in the possession of the daughter, the mother will recognize her.[6] In *Guigemar* the two lovers devise clothing markers by which to remain faithful to one another after they are separated. She ties a knot in the hem of his shirt that only she knows how to untie, while he places a belt around her that only he knows how to unfasten (vss. 557–75). Although the purpose of these devices is that the two may refuse to love anyone who cannot release them, the knot and the belt also provide a means for the lovers to recognize each other at the *lai*'s end.[7] In these cases, the gift of clothing unequivocally establishes the identity of the recipient in the eyes of the giver. Clothing becomes an important mark of identity, one that is even more potent than physical attributes inasmuch as it is equivalent to personal identity. In *Le Bel Inconnu* Guinglain spends the first half of the romance completely unaware of his own identity, the situation from which the romance derives its name. Blanches Mains reveals his identity to him, however, once he liberates the Desolate City. She moreover tells him that

---

6. Whalen, in his excellent study on memory in the *Lais*, highlights the scene of the passing along of the textile and ring and its textual repetition multiple times within the short *lai* as crucial for assuring the remembrance of past events, as well as the capacity of the mother to recognize her child at such a great temporal delay (84–86).

7. Bruckner has argued that "the process of recognition requires all the resources of sense perception, the special trials of magic objects, the faculties of reason and memory, and the crowning movement of the whole process—the transformation of action into discourse, *récit*" (*Shaping* 169).

his mother is the one who gave him his armor and sent him to be one of Arthur's knights: "Vostre mere vos adoba, / au roi Artus vos envoia" (Your mother dubbed you, sent you to King Arthur) (vss. 4973–74). Guinglain's mother, therefore, gave him the identity of a knight without revealing to him his real, personal identity. Through the utilization of his armor and his ambition to be one of Arthur's knights, though, Guinglain eventually arrives at the place where he can learn of his origins. His armor, then, leads him to his personal identity. The mother's act is, like the acts of Frêne's mother and those of the lovers in *Guigemar*, a device of delayed recognition that allows for long periods of time to pass before recognition occurs. In contrast to the other acts, however, that of Guinglain's mother is not answered with her own recognition of her son, but rather leads her son along the path that will take him toward self-knowledge.

Gifts of clothing are often markers of love. Ydoine gives Amadas tokens of her love: "Par drüerie li envoie / une enseigne de fine soie / bien ouvree d'oevre soutil / et une mance de cainsil / et une çainture a armer" (For affection, she sent him an insignia of fine silk, well and subtly worked and a linen sleeve and a belt to arm himself) (*Amadas* vss. 1355–59). While he travels, she sends him other clothing tokens that communicate her love for him and her devotion to him: "Aniaus, çaintures, guimples, mances / De cainsil ridees et blances" (rings, belts, wimples, sleeves of pleated white linen) (vss. 1467–68). In Marie's *Eliduc*, the king's daughter sends Eliduc her ring and her belt. This act not only demonstrates her love for him; she claims that it also grants him possession of her: "Por ceo li enveiat l'anel / et la ceinturë autresi / que de son cors l'aveit seisi" (She sent to him the ring and the belt as well because she had granted him possession of her body) (vss. 510–12). They function as a synecdoche for the lady, and her action ultimately precipitates the free expression of love between the two, prefiguring his later physical possession of her. Their mutual but unexpressed love is already torturing the two separately but remains hidden from each other. The lady's gift and her inquiring about it later bring the love into the open and allow the two to become lovers. This gift's effects are very similar to the effects of Guenevere's gift to Alexandre in *Cligés* (vss. 1141–82). The queen gives Alexandre a *chemise* into which Soredamors, Alexandre's unconfessed love, has sewn, in one seam, a golden thread, and in the other, one of her own golden-colored hairs. It is significant both that the queen's gift comes in the form of a vestimentary object, additionally so because Soredamors made the *chemise* herself, and that Alexandre's beloved is physically present in the gift through the hair sewn in its seam. Soredamors's hair also functions here as a material substitution for her.[8] Hair is not simply an adorning element (hair being the part of the body that we most readily may alter for aesthetic purposes): it is a tiny physical piece of Soredamors herself. The poet describes the hair as being more beautiful, and thus more valuable, than the gold strand that is sewn into the other seam of the *chemise* (vs. 1548–50). Yet the burgeoning love between Alexandre and Soredamors shows most clearly the hair's true worth. The queen uses the *chemise* with its hair as a means to coax the two would-be lovers into a confession of their mutual love, despite their best attempts to hide it from the world as well as from each other. Finally, clothing gifts made to bring about the love of a character are not always successful. In *Guigemar* Mériaduc, although he takes good care of the lady he imprisons by dressing her well, never receives the love he desires from her (vss. 714–18). The lady's refusal to return his affections, of course, results from the fact that she loves Guigemar, but Mériaduc is also attempting to force her love. His attitude toward her is clear from the first moment he encounters her: he seizes her by her clothes and brings her, willing or not, to his castle, where he refuses to let her leave. His clothing gifts are not powerful enough to counteract the violence he has shown her at their initial encounter, nor do they in any way assist him in solving the riddle of the belt.

All the clothing gifts discussed thus far have conformed to conventional uses of the vestimentary code of twelfth-century France. Nevertheless, the tendency among romance writers to uphold the vestimentary paradigm where gifts are concerned does not exclude some striking code manipulation. Béroul's *Tristan* offers a set of remarkable examples of significant and masterful reshaping of both the concept of largess and the clothing code. These examples are clustered around a central feature of the fragment of the romance: the attempts by the two lovers to exculpate themselves and restore themselves to their former status after the period of exile in the forest, both the initial steps taken toward reconciliation with Marc and the oath-swearing episode at Mal Pas.

On the first of these occasions, Yseut receives two remarkable gifts of clothing. The first, from the hermit Ogrin, facilitates the reconciliation between Marc and the queen. While Yseut and Tristan have lived in exile, hard times have destroyed their clothes: "Lor dras ronpent, rains

---

8. Lacy has asserted that her hair "serves not only as a symbol and reminder of Alexandre's and Soredamors's love but as the actual instrument by which it was discovered and encouraged by the queen" (*Craft* 83).

les decirent" (Their clothes were falling apart, destroyed by the branches) (vs. 1647). For the appeasement that he is arranging, Ogrin goes to purchase costly materials to be made into lovely clothes for Yseut, thereby replacing the courtly clothes that have become ragged throughout the years of exile.

> Assés achate ver et gris,
> Dras de soie et de porpre bis,
> Escarlates et blanc chainsil,
> . . . .
> Ogrins l'ermite tant achate
> Et tant acroit et tant barate
> Pailes, vairs et gris et hermine
> Que richement vest la roïne.
>
> (vss. 2735–37, 2741–44)

[After having bought vair and gris, silk cloth and dark *porpre*, scarlets and white linen . . . Ogrin the hermit bought, acquired, and bartered so much silk, vair, gris, and ermine that the queen was richly attired.]

Yseut is, in fact, reconciled with Marc, and through the mediation of the religious hermit, the representative of the church, she may once again wear the luxurious clothes befitting her status as queen.[9] Later, Dinas makes a gift of clothing to Yseut, "un garnement / Que bien valoit cent mars d'argent, / Un riche paile fait d'orfrois" (a garment that was well worth a hundred marks of silver,[10] a rich silk made of orphrey) (vss. 2985–87). This time, Yseut does not keep the gift but offers it in turn to the church (vs. 2990). Her action is in keeping with the medieval tradition of making gifts to churches. As Piponnier and Mane note: "Dans la hiérarchie des dons, les croyances médiévales placent au premier rang ceux faits à Dieu, c'est-à-dire

---

9. Heller had noted that Ogrin is perhaps France's first recorded stylist, having done the shopping for Yseut; this is important not only because she could not take the risk to be seen out of hiding but also because it prevents her from entering into the mercantile economy, dealing with money, merchants, and transactions, all of which is beneath her station (*Fashion* 149). Interestingly, there is no mention of a monetary value, perhaps further protecting the lovers from mercantile activity, perhaps insulating Ogrin's portrait from it slightly.

10. Since Béroul wrote in the Anglo-Norman dialect, it is likely that he also wrote in Norman England, and it would thus follow that the mark he refers to here is, in fact, the English mark, or sterling. This monetary unit was one of the most stable in Europe at the time, a sort of "gold standard," suitable to evoke the costliness of a queen's garment.

à ses représentants sur la terre, églises, abbayes ou couvents. Les puissants offrent aux cathédrales et églises qu'ils patronnent ou aux chapelles de pèlerinage qu'ils visitent des ornements liturgiques dont la somptuosité reflète la qualité du donateur" (34). Yseut's gift to the church, then, establishes her as a good Christian, which certainly contradicts the image of her as a traitorous adulteress, but it also answers the gift she has received from Ogrin. In a sense, she is repaying him for his generosity through an act of charity. Moreover, the author is careful to state the high monetary value of the garment, thereby making an assertion about Yseut's social rank.

These episodes regarding Yseut's clothes serve as a contrast to Tristan's situation. Once the couple turn themselves over to Ogrin in the hopes of reconciliation with Marc, Tristan also returns to Marc's land. Tristan, unlike the resplendent Yseut, is dressed to protect himself: "Souz son bliaut ot son hauberc; / Quar grant poor avoit de soi, / Por ce qu'il out mesfait au roi" (Under his *bliaut* he had his hauberk, for he was sore afraid for himself because he had done wrong to the king) (vss. 2772–74). He fears for his safety even as Yseut is regaled and her return celebrated. Moreover, whereas Yseut receives the gift from Dinas that allows her to make a costly and extravagant gift to the church, Tristan later conceals his identity, dressing as a leper, and begs for fine clothing from passersby. The disparate treatment that each of the two characters receives is analogous to the way in which they are dressed and receive clothing. Tristan's status remains as uncertain as that of a beggar, while Yseut's social rank is reasserted through lavish clothing gifts.[11]

In fact, and at first glance perhaps curiously, Tristan earlier refuses to accept Marc's gift of riches and furs (vss. 2919–26). Tristan has come with Yseut to ask for Marc's pardon, but the king, on the advice of his barons, will not grant his pardon to Tristan, although, as a worried uncle, he offers him some material means to assist him. Tristan rejects the gift specifically in response to Marc's refusal to pardon him. The gift is insulting to Tristan, who prefers to make his fortune with another king at war than to accept a handout from Marc. Without Marc's pardon,

---

11. Kelly asserts that Yseut's rank is never really in question at any point in the romance. He, in fact, asserts that the apparent disparities between her attire and her station at certain points, as when she goes to be burned at the stake dressed in a magnificent court gown and later when she is reduced to wearing rags during her exile, are "so obvious, or would have been to Béroul's audience prepared to fix its attention on the obvious, that they required no authorial elucidation" ("Senpres" 131). Kelly also explains that though "Iseut's clothes may change from episode to episode, . . . it does not change the fact that she is queen and does deserve the clothing, surroundings, treatment that are her due and that we know to be her due whether she has them or not" (140).

the gift is devoid of all meaning, thus absurd. Tristan, whom Béroul consistently characterizes as a noble knight, is bound by duty to refuse such a gift. What is curious about Tristan's negative response to Marc's offer is that later, during the Mal Pas episode, he begs fine clothing from passersby, including King Arthur and, significantly, Marc. Why does Tristan accept a handout of clothing from Marc and others at this point when he rebuffed it on the previous occasion? Two factors must be considered in order to interpret his attitude and actions. First, Tristan is disguised as a leper, and no one recognizes him; he thus assumes a different identity. Had he accepted Marc's previous offer of clothing, he would have been accepting charity as himself. This charity would have confirmed, publicized, and moreover officialized Tristan's diminished status, the very status that he is desperately seeking to restore. The anonymity that the disguise affords Tristan at Mal Pas is precisely what allows him to accept charity without bringing shame to his name.

The second point to consider, although related to the first, is more far reaching and specifically concerns the covert nature of his acquisition of clothing at Mal Pas. Throughout Béroul's account, Tristan and Yseut have been illicit, and therefore hidden, lovers. To conceal their love, they have become masters of deceit and experts at covert maneuvers. Furthermore, because they must consistently deny and reject their love in public, the lovers have to value most what is veiled: their love. Once the love potion wears off during their exile in the forest, both lovers lament their degraded material conditions and desire a return to the former splendor of their lives at court (vss. 2160–2220). It is in this context that they decide to attempt a reconciliation with Marc, who responds to their plea by accepting Yseut back but refuses to allow Tristan to return. Tristan must, at this point, find other, stealthy means to restore himself to the material and vestimentary wealth that he previously enjoyed. Tristan had to reject the clothing that Marc offered because, as a handout, it contained no possibility of restoring his name. The episode at Mal Pas, however, of which Tristan's disguise as a leper is an integral and crucial part, provides a perfect opportunity for true reinstatement of both Tristan's and Yseut's place at court. Yseut's oath is contingent upon Tristan's appearance as a leper and exculpates them both, but his disguise also allows him clandestinely to acquire the vestimentary trappings of his prior, and soon to be recovered, status. His successful begging, then, answers Marc's offer of clothing, which is devoid of restitution. Tristan refuses the offer, preferring instead to take what is to his mind rightfully his through hidden means.

Tristan is not the only one among Béroul's characters to refuse a gift of clothing from a king. Arthur himself offers to make Yseut's servant a knight and give him knightly accouterments (vss. 3528–30). Perinis is alternately described as Yseut's "mesagier," her "meschin," and her "vaslez." His role during the separation of the two lovers is significant because he delivers messages from one to the other, as well as the message to Arthur from Yseut asking him to witness her oath. Arthur's motivation for making his offer to Perinis is to demonstrate both the respect he has for Yseut and the fact that he is quite impressed by the squire. Perinis, however, considers it unnecessary, if not entirely inappropriate. Since Perinis's sole mission is to assure Arthur's presence at the oath, Arthur's offer represents more than is needed; moreover, the lovers will be best served by Perinis's continuation as their messenger and by Arthur's bearing witness. It is likely that Perinis feels that Arthur's offer, if accepted, would be inconsistent with the rules of chivalry; he is, after all, in the service of someone else, thus not in a position to swear fealty to Arthur. In any case, Perinis's refusal is crucial for the text because of his role as Tristan and Yseut's messenger. Arthur's offer, then, attests to Perinis's suitability for knighthood, but his refusal confirms it. This refused clothing gift must be understood in light of the circumstances that determine Perinis's behavior; in any other context, his refusal remains inexplicable. Clearly, Béroul requires his readers to interpret even clothing gifts in consideration of their contexts, propelling the convention of largess into the signifying system that is emerging from the vestimentary code.

Tristan; Yseut; and even Perinis, their agent, are very sophisticated manipulators of appearance: it is precisely this ability that allows them to instill enough doubt in Marc's mind so that he can never fully and resolutely believe in their guilt.[12] Their modification of appearance is moreover accompanied by a highly developed ability to deploy the vestimentary code, especially the process of gift-giving. These two characters possess an impressive facility in choosing the context that will best accomplish their

---

12. Marc is, in fact, given to the misinterpretation of signs, as Lacy has noted ("Deception" 35). Lacy also records that even Tristan and Yseut are not immune to the misinterpretation of signs, for they misread Marc's message to them when he leaves his sword, ring, and glove with them as they sleep in the forest, taking them to mean that he is angry and will return to kill them (35). This lapse in their ability to interpret the signs that Marc leaves does not, however, detract from their ability to manipulate the code for their own purposes. Rather, it shows them in a very human light. Moreover, Corbellari proposes that the fact that the characters can so easily misread the codes suggests that the meanings of these symbols have become murky, unstable, and thus ambiguous, leading the protagonists down "fausses pistes interprétatives, destinées . . . à égarer un lecteur trop prompt à voir des symboles là où règne le réel" (163–64).

desires. In the same way that Yseut chooses the best possible location, that is, geographic context, for her oath in order for it to be beyond question, Tristan chooses the best social context to obtain the physical trappings, that is, noble clothing, of reconciliation with Marc and restoration of his former status as knight. Once Tristan has obtained these articles of clothing, Yseut's oath, dependent upon his disguise, makes official and overt the vestimentary emblems and covert restoration that Tristan has procured through begging. Tristan and Yseut effectively choose a context by which the meaning they desire to convey will be attached to the form of their actions. They alter the context of their clothing acts in order to create different meanings than otherwise would be possible. Of course, the author, Béroul, is ultimately behind their genius; it is his own agility in manipulating the vestimentary code that he demonstrates through his characters' acts.

With regard to the convention of vestimentary gifts as portrayed in the romances of the twelfth century, two opposing tendencies are discernable. The first and most common is to represent the convention of largess in a highly normative way, emulating actual social practices. This tendency surely derives from a need, felt even among those who shaped the art of the period, to preserve and resist questioning such an important feature of the fabric of their society. Therefore, in romance, as in society, gifts from social superior to inferior solidify bonds and structure society. Clothing gifts also perform other functions within the romances, but these are as conventional and normative as the tokens of largess: restorative gifts, identificatory gifts, and love gifts. The other tendency, embraced primarily by Béroul, represents nonetheless an important breach of an almost sacrosanct convention: his characters play freely with the system in order to serve their own needs and fulfill their desires. This feature of Béroul's romance is truly revolutionary even though it falls within the larger context of sweeping code manipulations and subversions as practiced by his contemporaries. These code transgressions are particularly apparent in the depictions by romance writers of the clothing acts of dressing and undressing.

Dressing and Undressing in Context

The very acts of dressing and undressing alter a character's appearance; they are, after all, transformations of appearance. It is therefore quite natural that this kind of act depicted in romance would provide numerous examples of manipulations of the vestimentary code. In addition to alterations of the code within character descriptions, code modifications may also include changes to the context in which a clothing reference occurs. These alterations mediate the connection between form and meaning, and, in some cases, allow for the creation of additional meanings for a unique form. It is precisely this kind of manipulation of a code that allows expansion into a fully developed signifying system in which not only do signifiers have an arbitrary relationship to their meaning, in the sense of a sign-oriented mentality, but also new, often multiple, meanings for old forms become possible.

I am using the term *context* to refer to a broad group of situations. Context may include any or all of the following overlapping levels: character elucidation, theme, plot, and narrative. The first of these situations, character elucidation, involves clothing acts that are best understood as providing important information about such character traits as personality, inner being, or development. In *Perceval* the hero's final scene involves a significant disarming act: Perceval removes his arms after the pilgrims admonish him for wearing his armor on Good Friday (vss. 6217–6518). Perceval's motivation for disarming is to remove from himself the shame of having become entirely self-absorbed and mindlessly devoted to the Arthurian realm, but the meaning of his act is much broader and deeper. His removal of arms reminds us of his late mother's wish that he never wear armor, never become a knight, and his two uncles' wish that he fulfill his destiny with them rather than through the emptiness of Arthurian chivalry. His act of disarming functionally erases his status as a knight and restores his status as a family member.[13] Perceval enters the text with his first encounter with knights; he leaves the text with his renunciation of the incomplete and imperfect Arthurian knighthood. Not only does Perceval's final disarming act close the narrative thread opened by his movement away from his mother and her family's values through his departure and initial arming, but it also clearly shows that Perceval's character has, through a series of actions that shape his character in the eyes of the world around him, come full circle as he finally understands that his own character can only be truly and completely realized in the context of his own identity as a member of

---

13. In fact, his final disarming inversely reflects his initial arming. This first arming, as Lénat points out and calls typical for the period, is a completely secular affair (198–99). Lénat makes clear that "la chevalerie, qui n'est pas née du christianisme, est jalouse de conserver sa nature première et tend à rejeter tout ce qui pourrait la contraindre ou l'altérer" (195). Considering the opposing natures and goals of "chevalerie" and "clergie," it is not surprising that Perceval must so definitively choose between the two.

his family rather than as a knight of the Round Table. His final clothing act has far more meaning than that of a standard disarming. Perceval is not disarming himself as he steps away from a battlefield; he is laying aside knighthood, at least in the terms in which the Arthurian realm imagines it. His act, then, signifies this renunciation and represents a defining, if not *the* defining, moment of his life.

Clothing acts that must be interpreted in thematic context are those acts that advance the theme of a romance. In *Jaufre*, for example, a major theme is the need to question appearances.[14] After King Arthur arms himself to fight the mysterious and enormous bird, he learns that the bird is nothing more than an enchanter wishing to bring Arthur an adventure (vss. 9867–82). Arthur's arming himself is a clothing act whose meaning is understandable only if we consider the theme of faulty appearances, because the act, we quickly learn, is without any real purpose, since there is never any real danger to the king or anyone else. Just as in the opening sequence about the enchanter's transformation into a beast who kidnaps Arthur for a while (vss. 226–484), the encounter with the bird results only from the enchanter's desire to provide Arthur with an adventure. Throughout *Jaufre* appearances can be confusing and tricksters abound, and this scene demonstrates the importance of questioning those appearances. Arthur's arming himself suggests that even the king needs to protect himself against this sort of visual confusion. The "danger" seems in fact to be simply the risk of falling prey to these false appearances or misinterpreting an appearance, as happens later in the text in a similar danger-free arming scene. When Jaufré and Brunissen's people are journeying home, Fada comes to meet them to thank them, with a feast and gifts, for rescuing her (vss. 10360–73). At her approach, however, Jaufré and Melian are afraid that she means mischief, so they arm themselves. Fada even taunts the knights for their inability to understand her purpose in coming into their camp. In both these examples, however, falling

---

14. This discrepancy between appearance and reality has been analyzed by Suzanne Fleishman as a larger, socially based one through which the conventions of romance provide one vision of knighthood, whereas the social reality was much less stable. She asserts that this discrepancy is the precise origin of the irony and parody of *Jaufre*: "If adventure is not being carried out properly, if one of its essential ingredients—the fantastic—surfaces only in distorted form, if the hero continually encounters situations in which his values and behavior are at odds with his surroundings and where antagonists seem to ignore the rules of the game, then clearly this suggests something about the viability of knightly ethos informing chivalric romance" (104). She concludes that the "creator of *Jaufre* was a skilled practitioner in his genre, a conscious craftsman who assumed the task of underscoring the gap between a disjointed social reality and anachronistic idealization of it that formed the stuff of conventional Arthurian romance" (129).

prey to appearances also presents no real danger, for Arthur appreciates the adventure and Jaufré and Melian receive only good-natured teasing from Fada. Also in both instances, the ostensible motivation for arming oneself is protection, but each scene ultimately serves to articulate and highlight a major theme of the romance — the necessity of questioning appearances.

The functional emptiness of a knight's arming himself may also communicate much more than the necessity of more closely evaluating appearances. Arthur's insistence in *Perceval* that Gauvain wear his armor to coax Perceval to return with him to Arthur's court (vss. 4348–4500) results in an arming act whose purpose is to demonstrate a tremendous lack in the Arthurian chivalric realm. After Sagremor and Keu are each defeated by Perceval, Gauvain decides that he should like to approach this young knight (who is contemplating the drops of blood in the snow) in a nonthreatening manner, by going unarmed to speak with him and ask him to come to court rather than going to fight with him. Keu quickly insults Gauvain by subtly accusing him of cowardice. Gauvain explains that he is simply trying to approach this man in a human fashion, but Arthur urges him to wear his armor.

> "Ore i alés, niez, dist li rois,
> Que molt avez dit que cortois.
> S'estre puet, si l'en amenez,
> Mais totes vos armes portez
> Car desarmez n'irez vos pas."
>
> (vss. 4413–17)

> ["Go ahead then nephew, said the king, for you have spoken very courteously. If you are able, bring him back, but wear all your arms, for unarmed, you will not go."]

Here, Arthur is saying to his nephew, "Go, and be as courteous as you wish, but be a knight first. Wear your armor." Gauvain does as his uncle wishes and wears his armor, but he addresses Perceval "Sans faire nul felon samblant" (doing nothing uncourtly seeming) (vs. 4434). Unlike his negative reaction to Sagremor's and Keu's threats, Perceval's reaction to Gauvain's genteel tone and patient understanding is positive. Gauvain alone has risen to the occasion that Perceval has offered to Arthur's knights, understanding that there exists a means other than through the knightly order, represented by armor, to behave toward another. Yet Gauvain's strict and almost blind allegiance to the king thwarts his attempt to participate in it fully, as evidenced by his wearing his armor despite his inclinations to the contrary.[15] This moment most clearly indicates that Perceval will surpass the order of the Arthurian realm. Gauvain does succeed in bringing Perceval to the court, but the two remove their armor before they enter, signifying that they have made human rather than knightly contact. Sagremor and Keu's arming acts in this episode actually create the danger for the knights, whereas Gauvain's arming is functionally empty, since his attitude toward Perceval protects him from the harm that befell the two other knights. Gauvain's functionless arming is similar to the examples from *Jaufre* inasmuch as it reflects and articulates a major theme of *Perceval*, the theme of insufficiency in the Arthurian realm. In the case here as well as in the two cases in *Jaufre*, the arming act has no real purpose but must be understood in the thematic context of the work in order to have meaning. The form of the arming act does not, in these cases, signify protection; rather, the connection between form and meaning must expand to include the interpretation of the act in another—the thematic—context of the romance as a whole.

Another context that often must be considered in order to produce meaning for a clothing act is at the level of the plot. In such instances, clothing acts become both features and motivators of plot. For example, a clothing gift often opens a sequence of actions that requires closure by some form of reciprocation, usually another gift. The first gift is a feature of the plot—it is part of what happens—at the same time that it precipitates further actions, being itself an instigator. The clothing act must then be considered both in terms of its form—a gift that may confer any number of aspects upon the recipient—and of its context as an important feature and motivator of additional acts or actions. In *Cligés*, Guenevere's gift to Alexandre of the *chemise* into which Soredamors has sewn one of her hairs is an honoring gesture that rewards Alexandre's allegiance to Arthur, but it is also an important plot motivator inasmuch as it occasions the free expression of the secret love that exists between Alexandre and Soredamors (vss. 1545–1636). Guenevere's gift is a signifier with two meanings: it conveys the esteem that Arthur's court bears Alexandre, and, considered in its plot context, it gives rise to a second, deeper meaning—the facilitator of the expression of love. In Thomas's account of *Tristan*, there is an even more complex clothing act

---

15. Chrétien uses Gauvain as a counterpoise for his heroes in three of his romances—*Lancelot*, *Yvain*, and *Perceval*. Moreover, as Lacy notes, in *Perceval*, Gauvain "serves as a chivalrous model for Perceval, but he is a model to be surpassed" (*Craft* 100).

that must be interpreted in its plot context. On Tristan's wedding night, as his attendants undress him to prepare him to go to bed with the "false" Yseut, they dislodge the ring that Yseut gave him as a pledge of their love and commitment to each other (vss. 440–59). The main undressing act, in which Tristan refuses to assume the role of agent because of his feelings for the "real" Yseut, precipitates the second undressing act, the dislodging of the ring, and he withdraws into his brooding mind. He later tells her he has a malady that prevents lovemaking, thereby excusing himself from it (vss. 676–97). Once Tristan becomes aware of the ring again, his feelings for the real Yseut are laid bare. His undressing for what would have been a night of carnal love with his new wife ends with the unveiling of his true feelings and the commitment he shares with his true love. The first undressing act's primary meaning is the expression of Tristan's nonengagement in the proceedings: by refusing to undress himself he refuses his own agency. The act, however, precipitates another act—the dislodging of the ring. This second act's primary meaning is the remembrance of the vows taken with the "real" Yseut, and the second act in turn precipitates the lie he tells the "false" Yseut to avoid sleeping with her. Both related acts thus have double meanings, and both precipitate further action. The ability to derive these secondary meanings resides in the interpretation of these acts in their specific plot moments and as plot motivators.

The last of the four categories of context is the broadest—the narrative context. Clothing acts in this category of code manipulation perform specific narrative functions and assist in the elaboration of the narrative. A fascinating example of this category occurs at the end of *Le Bel Inconnu* as Arthur's knights are preparing for the tournament called to lure Guinglain back to court for his marriage to Blonde Esmerée (vss. 5459–97, 5581–5609). In this case, the knights' act of arming themselves takes up a considerable narrative space, and the tournament itself takes up some 637 lines almost at the very end of the romance. The author has his audience witness an elaborate arming scene, followed by a huge two-day tournament, just before escaping his auctorial duties, which is not unlike Guinglain's arming himself to escape three times from the two ladies who love him. The knight first arms himself to escape from Blanches Mains in order to champion Blonde Emerée's cause (vss. 2479–83). Then, after completing his mission, he escapes Blonde Esmerée by arming himself for an imaginary mission so he can find Blanches Mains again (vss. 3875–79). Finally, when he hears about the tournament, he decides to don his armor again over Blanches Mains' objections (vss. 5363–83). Renaut finally imitates his protagonist by suiting up the Arthurian world for a tournament, after which he runs away from his auctorial duties by leaving his protagonist hanging between two women and his audience hanging between two possible endings.[16]

> Mais por un biau sanblant mostrer
> vos feroit Guinglain retrover
> s'amie que il a perdue,
> qu'entre ses bras le tenroit nue.
> Se de çou li faites delai,
> si ert Guinglains en tel esmai
> que ja mais n'avera s'amie.
>
> (vss. 6255–61)

[But if you show a happy countenance, you will make Guinglain find again his lost love and hold her in his arms nude. But if in this you make delay, then Guinglain will have the sorrow of never seeing his love again.]

Renaut provides Guinglain with a vestimentary guise that allows him to accomplish his purpose: his motivation for arming himself is to leave a lady. Guinglain's purposes do not exactly correspond to those of Renaut, however, since Renaut wishes to keep his lady by leaving the ending of the romance open.[17] Renaut's ending is an amplification of Guinglain's repeated escaping, but its purpose is opposite, namely, to assure his lady's continued favor. Therefore, the narrative function of Guinglain's escape through arming himself is to provide Renaut with an escape strategy from the narrative itself. Renaut uses a formally similar device to accomplish one shared purpose, escape, and one set of opposite purposes—leaving a lady versus keeping a lady. The narrative function of this device changes depending on who uses it: Guinglain's use prefigures and facilitates Renaut's, and Renaut's use ends the romance. If we do not consider the sequential arming acts in

---

16. The double ending of the romance has been the subject of several studies. Most notable are those by Peter Haidu ("Realism"), Sara Sturm ("*Bel Inconnu*'s Enchantress"), Alice Colby-Hall ("Frustration and Fulfullment"), and Laurence de Looze ("Generic Clash").

17. Claude Roussel points to *Le Bel Inconnu* as "une oeuvre ouverte" precisely because of its "fin incertaine" (31). He attests, moreover, to the fact that one of the main achievements of the romance is that it conditions readers for such an ending through "la multiplication des fins possibles" throughout the romance and contends that we really cannot ignore "le jeu narratif que représente la juxtaposition en enfilade de ces fins attendues, puis différées, qui contribuent pour une large part au plaisir de la lecture" (31–32).

this narrative context, the full meaning of it eludes us. The armings have a standard meaning of preparation for battle or adventure, but they also have an additional meaning that is only discernible when the narrative strategy of the author is examined. In this narrative context, the armings have the meaning of escape.

Having established the different contexts that have an effect upon the meaning of signifiers, my discussion may turn to a demonstration of the ways in which formally similar clothing acts have different and sometimes multiple meanings based upon these different contexts.[18] The persistence of the gift as a normative clothing act shows that the vestimentary code continues to exist in the corpus of twelfth-century romance and to exert itself as a viable means of expression. Even so, the writers of the period do not seem to hesitate to modify their use of the code, to manipulate or even subvert it to suit their needs. As surely as they manipulate the code, they are transforming it into a signifying system and coming to rely upon the flexibility of the sign in its capacity to represent and convey the arbitrariness and ambiguity that was beginning to be felt in the world. The shift in the representational devices from a symbol-dominated universe toward one imbued with the ambivalence inherent in the sign, that is, from an absolute relationship between form and meaning to contingent meanings, will be best clarified by tracing the use of formally similar clothing acts in light of the transition from highly codified use of clothing to context-dependent uses that require interpretation rather than simply the reading of symbols. The first set of examples involves acts in which one character dresses another, and the second concerns acts in which a character dresses him- or herself. Each of these acts and their different manifestations will be examined in turn.

Dressing another person, according to the standard meaning within the vestimentary code, is an honoring act.[19] This is certainly the case in *Erec et Enide* during the elaborate dressing scenes that punctuate the romance (vss. 1563–1652, 6671–6747). There are many other examples of characters

---

18. If clothing acts are reduced to four basic formal categories, which include dressing oneself, undressing oneself, dressing another, and undressing another, different meanings may be ascribed to acts from the same category, depending upon the context. In the category of dressing oneself, for example, the meaning of the act may be to honor another, to prepare oneself for adventure or battle (if the act involves armor), to prepare oneself to return to action, or to promote oneself. The act of undressing another is equally if not more flexible in its meaning, insofar as it may be an honoring, curative, or even dishonoring act.

19. In the corpus of twelfth-century romance, the act of dressing another person is almost invariably honoring or curative in both intent and effect. However, this fact does not preclude the existence of other effects arising from these acts.

communicating their esteem for another character through dressing acts. In *Lancelot*, the hero's hosts give him, at almost every home that lodges him, a fur mantle; occasionally he receives the mantle directly from the shoulders of another person. This last gesture in particular is a sign of extreme deference. Blancheflor's people honor Perceval by bringing a fur mantle for him to wear (*Perceval* vs. 1779), and Augier's daughter treats Jaufré in a similar fashion (*Jaufre* vss. 4483–84). Lanval is dressed richly by his lady's maidens before they send him back into the world (*Lanval* vs. 173–76). Finally, when Guinglain first arrives in Arthur's court, attendants come to dress him well (*Bel Inconnu* vss. 91–95). In all of these cases, the dressing act communicates the respectful attitude of one character or set of characters toward another.

There are, however, honorific acts of dressing another that have more complex meanings than simply honoring that person and show a clear tendency toward the use of clothing as a signifying system. Philomena, for example, is in the habit of dressing her father every day (*Philomena* vs. 375). Her habit of dressing him not only shows her respect and love for him, but it also provides her father with a reason to cite when he disallows her leaving to accompany Tereus. More important, though, it emphasizes her ability to manipulate cloth, which later serves her well in exacting revenge upon Tereus, as she weaves a tapestry that communicates her plight to her sister and brings about her rescue. Philomena's act of dressing her father must be placed in the context both of plot and character elucidation in order for the full range of its meaning to be discerned. The plot is advanced by her habit of dressing her father because it provides him with his first attempt at justifying his refusal to allow Tereus to take his daughter away from him. Moreover, the character elucidation that her action facilitates is both immediate, in that it honors her father, and delayed, in that it prefigures her competence at using cloth to communicate with her sister and to translate her muted voice into materiality. The signifier of Philomena's habitual dressing act therefore has multiple meanings that are mediated by several different contexts.

Dressing another person may also take a slightly different form in addition to having different meanings. In *Le Bel Inconnu* Guinglain sends Blonde Esmerée to Arthur's court, encouraging her to dress very well (vss. 3630–34). The supposed purpose of her mission is to gain Arthur's blessing for Guinglain's marriage to her. Guinglain, however, is in love with a different woman and thus sends Blonde Esmerée to court in an attempt to delay, if not avert, this marriage. Once she departs, Guinglain goes to seek his love, Blanches Mains. Arthur, for his part, agrees that Guinglain should marry Blonde Esmerée, and when it becomes clear that the knight is in no hurry to return to the court, Arthur decides to host a tournament to lure him (vss. 5196–5300). As a knight, Guinglain cannot resist such a temptation and leaves his lady to participate. Once Guinglain is there, Arthur expresses his wish for him to take Blonde Esmerée as his wife, which he does (vss. 6166–92). Guinglain's plan has failed, but the reason behind this failure is that, although his motivation in sending Blonde Esmerée to court is to avoid marrying her, having her do so in such a way that honors the king is the narrative equivalent of Guinglain's honoring him himself. In sending Blonde Esmerée away in this manner, Guinglain reasserts the power that Arthur has over him, and therefore binds himself to Arthur's decision. In this case, Guinglain's figurative dressing of Blonde Esmerée is a mediated honoring of Arthur that precipitates Guinglain's acquiescence to his will. The meaning of the act is discernible through consideration of the act in terms of its plot context, since it is through this means that we understand the importance of the encouraged act in submitting Guinglain's will to Arthur's. In the same way that Guinglain essentially dresses Blonde Esmerée for the court, Arthur will determine Guinglain's choice of bride. Both are mediated, the first through Blonde Esmerée, the second through the tournament. Moreover, the second is precipitated by and answers the first. Thus, Guinglain's act, though indirect, means both his reluctance to marry Blonde Esmerée and his ultimate acceptance of it. The single act not only has two meanings, but two opposite meanings.

From these examples it is clear how context can mediate meaning for a single form. What is also apparent, however, is that not only did writers take the liberty of placing formally similar clothing acts in different contexts to derive new meanings for them, but they were also perfectly capable of altering the form of the act to incorporate additional nuance and texture from the code. Again, the evidence points to the fact that the writers did not destroy the vestimentary code but incorporated it into their works, finding it useful to employ as it commonly existed in order to exploit its expressiveness, but were equally capable at its manipulation in order to exploit clothing more fully as a sign. I turn my attention now to the second of the two forms of dressing acts that I wish to examine in terms of context mediating meaning—a character's dressing him- or herself.

In the context of the vestimentary code, it is common for characters to dress up to honor a special person or occasion, and often this dressing act occurs as a result of the overcoming of a lack or as part of the effort to overcome a shortcoming of some sort. In *Jaufre*, once Jaufré has defeated

Taulat and freed Melian, he receives a hero's welcome both when he returns to Augier's castle (vss. 6784–97) and when he returns to Brunissen's (vss. 7092–7151). In both places, the inhabitants dress up to celebrate his victorious return, and Brunissen additionally has the streets festooned with fabric to honor him further. Celebratory scenes of this nature abound in the romances, and their examples are too numerous to include here; I discuss this example to demonstrate the normative behavior. Thus, the welcome that Jaufré receives may be considered the normal expression of joyful celebration after the accomplishment of the surmounting of some obstacle.

The deficiency may be personal as well as societal and may take the form of a personal dressing to designate having overcome a lack. Such is the case in *Perceval* when Blancheflor dresses herself after she realizes that Perceval is committed to helping her.

> A l'ajorner s'en retorna
> La pucele en sa chambre arriere;
> Sanz pucele et sanz chamberiere
> Se vesti et appareilla,
> C'onques nului n'i esveilla.
>
> (vss. 2070–74)

> [When day broke, the maiden returned to her chamber again; without (the aid of a) maid or a chambermaid, she dressed and adorned herself, awakening no one at all.]

Brunissen has the same reaction after the night spent with Jaufré (*Jaufre* vss. 7673–75). In both these instances, the lady's unassisted dressing communicates her recent empowerment in an untenable situation. Lancelot also dresses himself after Meleagant's sister cures him following his imprisonment (*Lancelot* vss. 6673–77), and, in *Yvain*, the hero, once cured of his madness, quickly dresses himself in the clothing that the damsels have left for him to find (vss. 3020–35). In both cases, the knights have been restored to their usual vigor and prowess and are thus ready to reassert themselves as knights and heroes. Finally, once the wounds Erec has received during his wanderings are completely healed, Guivret and his people insist on accompanying him, and the text states that Erec, Enide, Guivret, and the others "tuit s'atornent et aparoillent" (all dressed and readied themselves) (*Erec* vs. 5245). Here, the community's dressing itself signals a social healing that both amplifies and underscores the social nature of the marital reconciliation between Erec and Enide, and foreshadows the social healing that Erec's coronation signals at the end of the romance. In all these cases, the purpose of the self-dressing is to reenter the world, and it communicates the character's wholeness following a difficult period, a lack of some sort. A character may preemptively dress well to come before the king to solicit his assistance in overcoming a problem or difficulty. Such acts both honor the king and project hope by prefiguring the vestimentary celebration that will follow a successful resolution.

At the beginning of *Le Bel Inconnu*, Hélie arrives in Arthur's court dressed in samite, a very costly, brilliantly ornate fabric, with a richly dressed dwarf accompanying her in order to plead for assistance in the form of a champion (vss. 137–70). Later, Hélie's dramatic entrance into the court is reflected and amplified when Blonde Esmerée comes into Arthur's court beautifully attired, after having spent a week preparing the fabrics and other necessities before setting out on her journey (vss. 3629–40, 3661–68, 3836–58). She has also taken a great amount of care grooming herself in a luxurious tent directly before coming to see the king (vss. 5142–80). She comes to honor Arthur as king, but also to honor his authority over Jaufré, specifically his authority to choose a wife for him. Like Hélie before her, she asks a favor of the king: to give his blessing to Jaufré's marriage to her. In both of these instances, the supplicant's purpose serves the same narrative function in the text. Hélie and Blonde Esmerée honor the court by dressing well, and the court responds by honoring their requests. This type of clothing act may, like the celebration scenes in *Jaufre*, be considered a normative one: a character's dressing well to go before a person of rank or authority is encompassed in the vestimentary code and represents no divergence from it. Clearly, then, the code persists as a viable means for communicating attitudes in the romances of the period, although this simple and codified relationship between form and meaning is not the only option for the vestimentary signifier.

In *Erec et Enide*, following the episode in which Erec overhears Enide lamenting his abandonment of chivalric exploits, the heroine must find a means to resolve the obstacle in her marriage with the hero. Enide's dressing herself in her best gown on Erec's orders represents Enide's movement toward resolution of the difficulty (vss. 2572–79, 2607–11). It is precisely because Erec has doubts about his wife's opinion of him that Erec submits her to the test of the travels. The lack that Erec attributes to her is but a perceived lack, for she loves and cares deeply for him. What she really lacks is her husband's faith in her devotion to him. Her solitary dressing results from her husband's doubt but also foreshadows the proof that she will eventually provide of her devotion. Enide's motivation in performing this dressing act is to please her husband and ultimately disprove his doubts, and the narrative function of her act is to prefigure her success in proving herself to him and to accentuate her own agency in overcoming the obstacle in her marriage.[20]

In *Perceval*, the hero also must dress himself while in a position of lack, but in his case, the lack is real rather than imagined. When Perceval wakes after the night spent at the Grail Castle, no one answers him and no one comes to assist him in his preparations to leave (vss. 3373–77). This treatment differs greatly from that which he received from the castle inhabitants upon his arrival. Like Enide, he does not wish to dress himself. Yet unlike her, he is unaware of the reason that he must. Whereas Enide has what she needs, but must prove it, Perceval not only does not have what he needs but is completely unaware of his need or lack. He has failed to ask the Grail question, and the absence of the castle's inhabitants for his dressing indicates their tremendous disappointment in him. Perceval's motivation in dressing himself is simply to be on his way, but the narrative function of this scene is to communicate the disappointment of the Fisher King and his attendants. Unfortunately, the message is completely lost upon Perceval.

The same form—a character's dressing well—does not always convey the same meaning. Indeed, there are many cases in which a writer alters the code by changing the context. In *Thèbes*, for example, Jocasta and her two daughters dress richly to go to speak with Polyneices (vss. 4038–4104). Jocasta is going to plead with her son to end the fighting, and to do so, she opens a mutual honoring cycle in which the women's dress communicates their esteem for Polyneices while encouraging him to reciprocate by honoring their request. Thus far, the standard vestimentary code is in operation: the women have dressed well to honor their son and brother. But Polyneices refuses to accept peace on the terms they propose. From a normative standpoint, the purpose of Jocasta's and her daughters' dressing up remains unfulfilled: the act has failed to gain Polyneices's favor. Nonetheless, their attention to dress has not been for nothing. It will serve a different purpose in the text. Upon seeing the beautifully attired Antigone, whose dress

---

20. Enide does not simply submit to Erec's will: she repeatedly disobeys his command that she remain silent whenever she feels that her speaking out can protect him from harm. Each time she does so, however, she pays dearly for her action through her husband's continued consternation, despite the fact that her actions are in his best interest. In the end, Erec realizes that her actions are not acts of defiance but of protection, and his faith in his wife's intentions is renewed.

accentuates her natural beauty and nobility, the Greek Parthenopeus falls in love with her and becomes her suitor.[21] At this point the two sisters each have suitors, one on either side of the dispute (Ismène's suitor, Ates, is Theban), and, although they never categorically take sides, their loyalties effectively split in order for them to support their respective knights. Jocasta's four children, then, are evenly divided, so that in the end, both camps feel the tragedy of loss equally. Both daughters' suitors are killed, as are both sons. Thus, although Jocasta's mission fails, it occasions the establishment of absolute balance within the romance's central tragedy. The *Thèbes* poet has led his audience carefully through a clear and significant manipulation of the vestimentary code. The poet first explains the women's clothing act in the context of the code: their act symbolically communicates their respect as they ask a favor. Yet, in thwarting this attempt, thereby denying the act its normative value, the poet then makes possible and explicit a new meaning for the act. While preserving the form, he requires his audience to interpret the act in light of a particular narrative context—the balance of the tragedy and its effect on the family. The clothing act is stripped of its codified meaning and given a new, contextualized meaning.

Whereas the *Thèbes* example above illustrates the manipulation of the code by shifting a clothing act's context to extract new meaning, Erec's insistence in *Erec et Enide* that Enide not improve her dress for her arrival in Arthur's court (vss. 1353–58) demonstrates an outright subversion of the code. Here, Erec's double purpose in keeping Enide in her ragged dress is identical to the double narrative function that it serves—to honor the authority of the queen by giving her exclusive rights to dressing Enide, and to honor Enide by insisting that only a queen is fit to clothe her. Chrétien has employed an unexpected indicator of the honor Erec wishes to show these two ladies: rather than dress Enide well, the norm in this situation, he will keep her dressed inappropriately. He has subverted the code by keeping Enide dressed in what would be, from a normative standpoint, inappropriate clothing for the occasion. This example clearly demonstrates the movement from an entirely motivated and absolute vestimentary code (in which dressing well unequivocally means honoring another) toward a system of representation that requires the interpretation of signs so that here, because of particular circumstances, dressing poorly actually honors

---

21. Joachim Bumke reminds us that the inclusion of details of dress in the portraits of ladies tend to reveal a great deal about the lady's standing in courtly society and show "the link between the appearance in society and the splendor of a courtly outfit" (144).

another, since Guenevere is the only one worthy of dressing Enide. The form of the clothing act is, in this case, not simply interpreted in context: the context totally determines the form. The subversion of the normative vestimentary code is so complete here that without an understanding of the unique context in which it occurs, the clothing act, or refusal to allow to act, is utterly incomprehensible. In this instance, meaning derives from context rather than from form. Moreover, that context surpasses form in the determination of meaning offers strong evidence of the shift from a monolithic semiotic code to a more fluid signifying system in which contingent rather than absolute meanings predominate. In this example, furthermore, not only are new meanings created, but new forms are as well. The societal implications of such a radical shift in the assignment of meaning remain rooted in the tensions between the nobility, who desired an immutable meaning for themselves in the social hierarchy, and the merchants, who challenged this fixedness by the very fact that their success was determined by ability rather than by birth.

Making and Destroying Clothes

The making of clothing, and the fabric required for it, occupied a special place in medieval society. According to Weiner and Schneider, cloth manufacture itself has traditionally been reserved for

> spinners, weavers, dyers, and finishers [who] harness the imagined blessings of ancestors and divinities to inspire or animate the product, and draw analogies between weaving or dyeing and the life cycle of birth, maturation, death, and decay. The ritual and discourse that surround its manufacture establish cloth as a convincing analog for the regenerative and degenerative processes of life, and as a great connector, binding humans not only to each other but to the ancestors of their past and the progeny who constitute their future. (3)

It is indeed no surprise that we still today refer metaphorically to the "fabric of society." If gifts of cloth and clothing, among other valuables, create binding social ties, the manufacture of cloth does no less. The industries providing the raw materials for cloth production included a great variety of different vocations: farming, raising livestock, manufacturing dyestuffs.

In addition, merchants and traders transported goods to where they were needed. Production also required the work of spinners, weavers, dyers, finishers, and other laborers. The people involved in these commercial relationships were diverse, from different backgrounds and social classes, and of both sexes. Therefore, cloth, in a very real sense, bound society together.

In the Middle Ages, certain types of activities were carried out primarily by men and others primarily by women. Traditionally, spinning, weaving, cutting, and sewing fell into the domain of women's work.[22] Later, as cloth production was steadily becoming an industry of professionals and was increasingly organized and as the technology that supported such production was advancing and becoming more complicated, men began to take over certain formerly female-dominated occupations within the manufacturing process.[23] This shift in the gender assignments of tasks seems to have begun, very predictably, in the larger production centers and to have started as early as the eleventh century, when the horizontal treadle loom began to replace the vertical loom in commercial production (Crowfoot, Pritchard, and Staniland 22).[24] It is important to note, however, that changes of this nature occur over time, and it was certainly the case that at the same time that men were taking over certain occupations in cloth manufacture, women continued to have a significant presence in them for quite a while. In fact, the period during which both men and women were professional producers of cloth stretches over a very long period indeed. Moreover, despite the fact that this shift was occurring in the urban cloth centers, spinning, cutting, and sewing, as well as

---

22. Andrée Lehmann has pointed out that women continued to be the only practitioners of certain trades, such as silk spinning and weaving, hemp and flax dressing, and the production of silk items and garments (436). David Hearlihy treats women's contribution to the cloth trade and their working conditions in *Opera Muliebria*. For a discussion of the attitudes toward the distribution of women's work in the textile trade, see Ruth Mazo Karras's "'This Skill in a Woman is By No Means Despised.'" For a discussion of women's involvement in the guilds, see Maryanne Kowaleski and Judith M. Bennett's "Crafts, Guilds, and Women in the Middle Ages."

23. During the course of the Middle Ages, men began to join with women in such enterprises as commercial embroidery, spinning, and weaving, although women continued to exert a strong presence in these fields. Other trades, however, began to be more and more taken over by men, who were organized into guilds, such as furriers, tailors, tapestry makers, and dyers (Lehmann 436–37).

24. The advantages of the horizontal treadle loom are multiple. Worked by two people, it allows for greater fabric widths and lengths and therefore a more efficient production, as well as making certain weaving techniques, such as texture, possible (Crowfoot, Pritchard, and Staniland et al. 22–23).

private cloth production, continued to be decidedly female tasks until well after the twelfth century.

Nonetheless, twelfth-century romance in France appears to be responding to just this type of gender ambivalence concerning cloth production. These instances are of interest for this study because they once again bear witness to the inscription of ambiguity into the vestimentary code. Further, the ambivalence inscribed by at least two instances pertains to far more than simply gender ambivalence: in depicting the making of cloth in their romances, writers are also providing a deft metaphor for the very process in which they themselves are engaging. The weavers of romance depict weavers of tapestry and makers of fine cloth, all of whom push the meaning of their labor to its very fullest in order to create new meanings. In a sense, the writers depict themselves and their project in the acts of these characters. The process of making cloth and clothing is indeed the most natural place for writers to demonstrate their own process of creating meaning through manipulation of the existing vestimentary code.

My discussion of the making of clothing begins, however, with an examination of the gender ambivalence that appears in two particular textual cases.[25] Both of these examples have in common that, in the end, they problematize the notion that making clothing or cloth is women's work. First, the knight Jaufré refuses to engage in women's work. The Knight of the White Lance promises to let Jaufré pass unharmed if he will renounce knightly pleasures and no longer wear clothes that he has not made himself ("ni vestiment / Non portes si el nol teisia" [*Jaufre* vss. 1448–49]). Although the list of conditions contains items that do not involve Jaufré's making his own clothes, this is the one he seizes on as most absurd. He asks, "E si no sai far vestimens?" (And if I do not know how to make clothes?) (vs. 1455), to which the White Knight responds that he will have him taught: "Eu t'o farai mot ricamens . . . enseinar, / Teiser e cozr e talar" (I will have you expertly taught to weave and sew and cut) (vss. 1456–58). Jaufré insists that he would have too much difficulty learning (vss. 1461–62), but the White Knight believes it would take a strong man like Jaufré only seven years to learn (vss. 1463–64).[26] In the end, Jaufré prefers to fight the knight, thereby reasserting his knighthood. Interestingly, Jaufré does not seem to fear any kind of social demotion from knightly status, but rather worries about his ability

---

25. A modified version of this discussion appears in my "'De fil d'or et de soie.'"
26. Caroline Jewers has noted that the White Knight's estimation of the length of time it would take Jaufré to learn to sew was the same time span necessary for Charlemagne to conquer Spain, and she points to this as the "sly humor" of the romance ("The Name of the Ruse" 192).

to learn women's work. It appears that Jaufré is rather accepting of, or at the very least not outraged by, the gender ambivalence that the knight is proposing, even though he fights him to avoid his proposition. It is seemingly not the reversal of gender roles that so bothers Jaufré but his perceived lack of ability and the prospect of wasting time.

An important counterexample to Jaufré's acceptance of gender ambivalence occurs in *Enéas* with the character of Camille, the queen of Vulcane and a female knight. Camille does not accept gender ambivalence: she simultaneously defies and insists upon it.[27] The text makes clear that Camille is no typical woman of her day, preferring war to traditional women's work:

> el fu toz tens norrie an guerre
> et molt ama chevalerie
> et maintint la tote sa vie.
> Onc d'ovre a feme ne ot cure,
> ne de filer ne de costure.
>
> (vss. 3968–72)

[She was all the time trained in war and loved knighthood well and practiced it all her life. Never did she care for women's work: neither spinning nor sewing.]

Her nonconformist attitude, in addition to her great skill as a warrior, occasionally attracts criticism from male knights.[28] During a battle, Tarcon, a Trojan knight taunts her:

> "Laissiez ester desmesurance,
> metez jus l'escu et la lance
> et le hauberc, qui trop vos blece,
> et ne mostrez votre proëce.
> Ce ne est pas vostre mestier,

---

27. As noted in Chapter 3, Camille's very name is imbued with the gender ambivalence that her character embodies: her name is both masculine and feminine in French.

28. Simon Gaunt has analyzed the gender roles in *Enéas* and has postulated that in the romance—into which an amplification of two thousand lines is inserted in Virgil's original treatment of the scene in which Enéas falls in love with Lavine—feminity, although taking on a larger role, creates a dialogical gender discourse that devalues the female (*Gender* 85). He notes two homophobic diatribes that "reinforce a rigid notion of sexual difference, predicated to a large extent on sexuality" (79). However, he does not treat the character of Camille, who seems to me to be the counterpoint to his argument.

mes filer, coldre et taillier;
en bele chanbre soz cortine
fet bon esbatre o tel meschine."

(vss. 7081–88)

["Calm this excessiveness, put down the shield and the lance and the hauberk that hurts you too much, and do not show your prowess. This is not your profession, but spinning, sewing, and cutting are; a young woman makes a better battle in a nice bedchamber behind the bed curtain."]

Tarcon is making three assertions in his taunt. First, he states that war is not women's work; second, he informs her of what is—spinning, sewing, and cutting; finally, he suggests that if Camille does want to make war, she, as a woman, should be doing it between the sheets. He is thus alternately telling her that she is unfit to be a knight, that her work is inappropriate to her sex, and that she needs to be put in her place. Moreover, he makes reference to clothing or cloth in all three of his assertions, which are emblematic of the relative social positions he is proposing. The hauberk represents the knightly class, from which women are normally excluded. The making of cloth and clothing symbolizes women who manage to become economically autonomous; these women sometimes even escape masculine control. Finally, the bed curtain evokes the traditional role of women as wives and producers of children, a type of production that very rarely assured female autonomy. Tarcon's suggestions, then, slowly demote Camille, progressively removing her autonomy and her equal status with men. Camille, however, refuses Tarcon's "advice," preferring instead to kill him. She wins the battle and fights it on her own terms, as a knight in armor. And, lest there be any lingering doubts, she informs him as he dies: "mialz sai abatre un chevalier / que acoler ne dosnoier; / ne me sai pas combatre anverse" (I know better how to fight a knight than to embrace or love him; I do not know how to do battle on my back) (vss. 7123–25). Here, she is reasserting her status as a knight and, at the same time, refusing the association with the bed curtain image of femininity. She moreover refuses any essentialist reading of her womanhood, stating that what Tarcon suggests comes naturally to women, at least in her own case, does not. She is a knight, like it or not. Whereas Jaufré's refusal to engage in the making of clothing is not a real rejection of women's work, since he worries simply about his own incompetence, Camille's refusal takes on a different tenor as she brandishes her incompetence in female endeavors as though it were another sword. The meaning of the act of refusing to engage in the making of cloth varies according to the contexts. In both cases, the proposition has the meaning of provocation, and, in fact, both episodes end in battle and the death of the party who made the taunt. In Camille's case, however, the act has the additional meaning of reasserting her status as a knight, even a female one.

Despite Camille's reluctance to take on typically female work, women who had skill in working with cloth had the potential for material gains in this society. Clothing and cloth manufacture even provided some women economic autonomy from men. The negative connotations of the word *spinster* derive mainly from this society's fear of powerful women. One such example of a powerful woman is Philomena in Chrétien's Ovidian rewriting.[29] Philomena's ability with textiles, evoked three times in the short narrative poem, is also her saving grace. Her expertise is unmistakable: "Avuec c'iert si bone ovriere / D'ovrer une porpre vermoille / Qu'an tot le mont n'ot sa paroille. / Un diaspre ou un baudequin / Nes la mesniee Hellequin / Seüst ele an un drap portreire" (Also, she was so skilled at working red *porpre* that the whole world contained no equal. She knew how to depict in cloth—in *diaspre* or in *baudequin*—even the followers of Harlequin) (*Philomena* vss. 188–93).[30] This skill is not the only one that Chrétien describes: she, indeed, has many others, so many that Krueger sees in Chrétien's depiction of her a double of the writer himself ("*Philomena*" 94–95).[31] However, this skill is the one that will preserve her from a dismal fate. Her brother-in-law rapes Philomena, after a lengthy discourse between the two, and afterward, he cuts out her tongue to prevent her from telling what has happened to her.[32] Then, he hides her away, entrusting her to a peasant woman who, interestingly,

---

29. For a complete discussion of this work in the context of Chrétien's corpus, see Krueger's "*Philomena*."

30. Colby notes that this design not only would be a very complicated one, probably "conceived of as a band of souls in purgatory, who when driven about in the night, were visible because of the fiery envelope or phosphorescent glow surrounding their bodies," but also would seem to demand the skill of a professional weaver (136).

31. Van Vleck points to the fact that Philomena first "possesses the full power of voice. She can read, write poetry, and play several musical instruments," but that under Tereus's gaze her parole becomes impotent, and she only regains her power of testimony through her weaving abilities, which are ultimately "a medium of indictment and deposition" (35–36).

32. Krueger notes the poignancy of Philomena's loss of speech here, a loss that rivals that of her aggressor ("*Philomena*" 94, 97). Burns, in her "Raping Men," examines the problematic of male rape and its female response in *Philomena*. Hers is a feminist reading that questions the absoluteness of gender-based power structures in these literary works, positing instead that women react through a similar show of force and violence that has the effect of reconfiguring male-female relationships in these episodes.

supports herself through sewing and weaving. She is, according to the text, "une vilainne / Qui vivoit de sa propre painne, / Car filer et tistre savoit" (a commoner who lived by her own labor, for she knew how to spin and weave) (vss. 869–71). This self-sufficient woman unknowingly provides Philomena with the means to escape, reunite with her sister, and regain her own status. Philomena has full access to the woman's sewing and weaving tools and supplies, and one day, she decides to weave a tapestry communicating her plight to her sister (vss. 1083–99). The old woman, who is unaware of Philomena's motivations, procures for her whatever she needs for her task:

> La vieille ne li contredist,
> Mes mout volantiers li eida
> Et trestot quanqu'ele cuida
> Qui a tel uevre covenist
> Porchacier et querre li fist.
> Trestot li quist son aparoil
> Tant que fil inde et fil vermoil
> Et jaune et vert a plante ot,
> Mes el ne conut ne ne sot
> Rien de quanque cele tissoit;
> Mes l'uevre li abelissoit
> Qui mout estoit a feire gries.
>
> (vss. 1108–19)

[The old woman did not impede her but helped her very willingly, and she quickly sought out and found all that she thought necessary for such a task. Soon she (Philomena) asked for the loom and placed threads of indigo, red, yellow, and green on it, but she (the old woman) knew nothing about what she was weaving.]

Meanwhile, Tereus has led Procné to believe that Philomena has died. In response to this news, Procné has mourning clothes brought to her (vs. 1005). This action reflects the peasant woman's action of supplying Procné's sister with materials inasmuch as both actions involve specialized fabric imbued with precise meaning, brought out on Philomena's account. Procné's grief is furthermore so great that she swears never to remove her mourning clothes (vss. 1007–8). When the peasant woman brings her the tapestry, however, her grief ends because she learns that her sister is actually alive. In effect, she trades one cloth for another, one state of being for another: her powerlessness before the death of her sister transforms, through the message of the tapestry, into a position of power. She is now able to save her sister and to exact a gruesome revenge upon her husband for the suffering he has inflicted upon them both.[33] Therefore, in this short narrative poem, three women are empowered through the making of cloth.[34]

This striking example of female empowerment through the manipulation of cloth is interesting in and of itself, but when coupled with the knowledge that we have of the gift economy and the import ascribed to gifts within this society, Philomena's act takes on even more importance and meaning. She manipulates cloth in the same way that writers manipulate the vestimentary code, using cloth and its place in the gift economy insofar as these gifts establish and affirm social ties.[35] Her gift, then, when taken in this context, certainly creates the opportunity for her bonds with her sister to be renewed, but her gift is more than a simple reaffirmation of this relationship. She uses the cloth actually to transmit a crucial message to her sister, which must be seen as the most extensive and interesting manipulation possible of cloth. In the same way that twelfth-century writers use the vestimentary code at "face value," Philomena uses the gift to impart her desire to reestablish bonds with her sister. Yet, just as the writers use clothing signifiers to force the code into a signifying system to create new meanings in their rewriting of old sources, Philomena uses her cloth gift to forge a new meaning from the cloth that she has worked into a message. The meaning of her act of making the cloth is multiple and wide ranging—it exacts revenge, rights wrongs, and restores Philomena to her former place with her sister—but it also has the additional and perhaps more important meaning of providing a metaphor for the new process of signification in which the romance writers engage.

Chrétien provides his audience with another instance in which he represents the innovations in the process of signification, this time in his *Yvain*. In *Philomena* women gain power through the making of cloth; *Yvain* provides a counterexample to this phenomenon. Yvain comes upon a large group of

---

33. This scene has been analyzed in detail by Burns, who interprets Procné's murder of her own son and her cooking and serving of his flesh to his father as an answer to the violence and aggression committed by Tereus against Philomena ("Raping Men" 143–47).

34. The degree of female collaboration in this tale has not gone unremarked by critics; see especially Burns's *Bodytalk* (128–32).

35. For a discussion of the wordplay of Philomena's name, see Nancy A. Jones's "The Daughter's Text" (173).

essentially enslaved noblewomen who toil endlessly sewing clothes.[36] There are three hundred of these *tisseuses*, whose condition is deplorable, yet they produce clothing of great value.

> de fil d'or et de soie ovroient
> chascune au mialz qu'ele savoit;
> mes tel povreté i avoit
> que deslïees et desceintes
> en i ot de povreté meintes;
> et as memeles et as cotes
> estoient lor cotes derotes
> et les chemises as dos sales
>
> (vss. 5190–97)

[They worked with golden thread and silk, each to the best of her ability; but they were of such poverty that many of them were bare headed and ungirdled because of their poverty; and at their breasts and sides their garments were torn and the *chemises* on their backs were dirty.]

The contrast between the quality of the materials they produce and the way they themselves are dressed is striking. One *tisseuse* explains their situation in some detail to Yvain when he shows concern over their treatment: "'toz jorz dras de soie tistrons, / ne ja n'en serons mialz vestues; / toz jorz serons povres et nues, / et toz jorz fain et soif avrons ja tant chevir ne nos savrons / que mialz en aiens a mangier'" ("We will always weave silk cloth, never will this make us better dressed; we will always be poor and naked, and always will we be hungry and thirsty. We will never be able to earn enough to afford better food") (vss. 5292–95). Clearly, these women have been denied the economic fruits of their labor.[37] Whereas sewing, spinning, and weaving

---

36. Krueger points out that Chrétien's hyperrealistic portrayal of the oppression and abjection of the *tisseusses* contrasts directly with the image superimposed upon it at the same castle of the young damsel sitting on the rug, reading with her parents, who will be awarded as a prize to the knight who vanquishes the two *fils de netun*; although the text offers two distinctly different images of women, some enslaved, one courtly and desirable, both images inscribe the female into the patriarchal structure of the society of the twelfth century (*Women Readers* 46–47).

37. Gérard Brault argues against interpreting the *tisseuses* episode as a realistic element of the romance that offers a condemnation of supposed working conditions of the period, as has been argued by some critics, in favor of reading it rather in terms of the conflict between the two sisters over their inheritance that encompasses the episode: "L'épisode . . . oppose le vice de l'aînée à la

normally would provide at least some economic stability and self-sufficiency for women, these *tisseuses* live a life of abject poverty while the males for whom they work reap the benefits.

> Mes bien sachiez vos a estros
> que il n'i a celi de nos
> qui ne gaaint cinc solz ou plus.
> De ce seroit riches uns dus!
> Et nos somes ci an poverte,
> s'est riches de nostre desserte
> cil por cui nos nos traveillons.
>
> (vss. 5307–13)

[But, know this well, there is not one of us who does not do the work to earn five sous or more. With this sum, even a duke would be rich! And we are in poverty, he is rich through our product, the one for whom we work ourselves.]

The situation of these poor ladies is a notable irony in the romance, for their work provides to others what they themselves are denied. Their vocation should, but does not, grant them some hope for an improved economic situation: they have a valued skill. But rather than elevate them in this way, their work simply accentuates their lack. The tattered state of their clothing, moreover, borders on nudity, and this near nudity represents their powerlessness, vulnerability, and lack of social status. Yvain is, in fact, in the process of atoning for his own devaluing of a woman—his failure to keep his promise to Laudine—and he is sensitive to the plight of these women perhaps because of his prior mistake and his fall into nudity and outcast status. The interest that he takes in these women and his ultimate liberation of them helps Yvain along his redemptive path. He understands that despite their truly valuable work, they themselves remain unjustly devalued and economically disadvantaged. Thus, in this episode, Chrétien distorts the earning potential of producing textiles, transforming it instead into a cruel irony. Moreover, Chrétien depicts noblewomen engaged in mercantile activity within the profit economy. This image is shocking for the noble audience, since the nobility of the twelfth century considered such engagements to

---

vertu de la cadette, fait ressortir la force de la coutume, et souligne la justesse de la décision prise par Arthur" (64).

be ignoble. All the characters vilify the forced mercantile activity of these ladies even more than their captivity, and the narrator himself acknowledges the injustice. Fortunately for the young ladies, the situation is rectified by the hero. Ultimately, what originates as a subversion not only of the vestimentary code, for the ladies are dressed in rags, but also of the notion of nobility—the women are engaged in manual and for-profit labor— becomes reinscribed into the signifying system. Their act has meaning if for no other reason than it gives Yvain the opportunity to liberate them, but it has, as does Philomena's act, the additional meaning of providing a model of the code manipulations that become inscribed into the signifying system by the writers of romance. In the same way that the code becomes subsumed in the signifying system, the acts of the *tisseuses* become subsumed.

The converse of making clothing, the act of destroying garments, tends to occur in one of two situations: either a distraught person destroys his or her own clothing to indicate grief, or a person destroys another person's clothing in an act of violence. The first case is a well-documented social behavior and manifests in texts to communicate a character's state of being. There are many examples of this behavior in the literature of the period, but a few will suffice to illustrate my point: Laudine is mourning the death of her fountain-protector when we first see her, ripping and tearing her clothes (*Yvain* vs. 1159); in *Erec et Enide*, Enide has a similar reaction when she believes Erec to be dead (vss. 4576–78). In these cases, grief is made material through the rending of clothing: the inner reality of a character is textually rendered through the depiction of his or her destructive outward actions. The second category appears just as, if not more, frequently than the first type and is an act of aggression. Two examples will suffice to make this point clear. In *Jaufre*, a leper is attempting to rape a maiden, who wails for aid and whom Jaufré subsequently rescues. The leper has ripped her clothing, exposing her breasts in a scene of violence: "E fu sa gonela esquintada / Tro aval desos la tetina" (Her dress was ripped to down below her breasts) (vss. 2304–5). Moreover, the text makes mention of this scene twice more, once around 300 lines later and then around 650 lines after the first evocation of the scene. The author seems to be insisting not only upon the inappropriateness of the act but also upon its violence. In Marie's *Guigemar*, Mériaduc attempts to untie the *ceinture* that the lovers have devised to protect themselves from being loved by anyone else. He is doomed to fail, however, since he is not the lady's love and, more important, because he attempts to release her from the knot, the love token, by force. His effort is characterized by anger and violence, for he prefaces his action with a statement given "par maltalent" (with evil intention) (vs. 726) and then "de sun bliaut trenche le laz" (cuts open the laces of her *bliaut*) (vs. 738). His action is thus done with ill will and aggression and damages her clothing in process. Both these examples fall squarely and unproblematically within the vestimentary code, but just as gifts, dressing and undressing acts, and acts of making clothing at times resist codified meanings, there are acts of destroying clothing that provide evidence of the emerging signifying system. One such case occurs in Chrétien's *Lancelot*, and the vestimentary richness of the scene deserves special note.

In this romance Chrétien constructs a scene in which vestimentary violence is false and actually provokes a great deal more clothing action— the scene of the false rape. In a single scene, characters dress and undress themselves and each other, or refuse to do so; give clothing gifts; and destroy clothing, all to varying degrees and for different purposes. The result is extremely rich vestimentary imagery that develops the character of Lancelot considerably. At the castle of the lady whose lodging is dependent upon his sleeping with her, the lady dresses him, as is customary, in a fur mantle; however, during the false rape scene one of the lady's assailants tears the mantle (vs. 1145). We may initially consider this act of specialized undressing to be one of aggression and dishonoring, yet since the assailant does not destroy the mantle, only tears it a bit, we come to understand that Chrétien is showing us that this act of tearing is quite carefully controlled and that ultimately the violence is only temporary and slight. Indeed, it is false and thus mirrors perfectly the acts of the assailant toward the lady. When Lancelot first enters into the false rape scene, the poet explains that the lady is nude to the navel (vs. 1082). Again, the fact that her nudity is partial signals that the rape is not a real one: all is for show. What is real, however, is Lancelot's prowess and chivalric merit, as he comes to the aid of the maiden. The defense that he mounts on her behalf, as well as the courtly way in which he behaves toward her as she offers her body to him later that evening, lead her to the realization that this knight is indeed exceptional and worthy (vss. 1270–78).

The scene between Lancelot and the maiden is particularly interesting with regard to the use of vestimentary imagery. The bed to which the maiden leads Lancelot for their night together is covered in perfectly white sheets (vss. 1195–99), evoking an impression of purity. This image both defies the lady's amorous attempts and reinforces their ultimate failure, for Lancelot rejects her advances. Lancelot, however, reveals his lack of interest in sleeping with her only after the two have got into bed together. What is remarkable in this passage is the care with which Chrétien points out that neither Lancelot nor the maiden has removed his or her *chemise* (vss. 1201–3; 1213–15). Just as the earlier dishonoring was a false one, so this intimacy is equally false. Upon making this discovery, the lady excuses herself, undresses herself in her own chamber, and remarks that Lancelot is a truly worthy knight. The lady's undressing herself, like the white bedsheets, contrasts and answers both the rape scene, in which the wrong person attempts to undress her, and Lancelot's rejection, in which the right person refuses to undress her. Lancelot implicitly honors her by leaving her clothed, while the rapist, albeit a false one, dishonors her: Lancelot's honoring answers the prior dishonoring. The lady's undressing herself signals her deference toward Lancelot and her esteem for him, even though he is absent from this honoring act. The very next view that both the lady and we, as readers, have of Lancelot is as a fully armed knight, ready to continue his quest of the queen:

> Isnelemant et tost se lieve.
> Et li chevaliers se resvoille,
> si s'atorne et si s'aparoille
> et s'arme, que nelui n'atant.
> La dameisele vient a tant,
> si voit qu'il est ja atornez.
>
> (vss. 1282–87)

[Quickly and early she rose. The knight awoke and dressed; with no help from anyone, he prepared himself and armed himself. At this moment the young lady arrived and saw that he was already attired.]

This image of Lancelot is certainly the only aspect of this episode that unequivocally rings true: the lady has honored him only to provoke his assistance during the staged rape in which both she then he are falsely dishonored, and she has attempted to force him into a false intimacy by insisting that the only way that she will allow him to be lodged in her castle is if he sleeps with her. This attempt at intimacy is foiled, however, by the worthiness of the knight. The image of Lancelot armed and ready to face the only *aventure* that matters to him (recovering the queen from her captor) is, in fact, the only aspect of the episode in which appearance corresponds to reality.

Whereas the acts of making clothing or cloth figuratively represent the process of using the vestimentary code to create a new signifying system, the act of destroying clothes, whether partially or completely, demonstrates a similar but slightly different metaphor. Paradoxically, the very fact of the destroyed or degraded clothing signifier attests to the strength of the system, for in general rent clothing is subsequently reinscribed into the system and continues to generate meanings. In the example from *Lancelot*, once again, the author pushes the code to the limit by presenting false and manipulated vestimentary imagery and then requires his audience to interpret the clothing acts in a different context, with different meanings. He thus forces the code to transcend itself and emerge as a signifying system in which meaning is contingent upon context and the potential for the creation of new meanings is ever present and often realized. As do his characters, Chrétien destroys the absoluteness of the code, destroying order with it, and then allows it to reemerge reconstituted as a more complex system, creating a new order that accounts for ambiguity, ambivalence, and arbitrariness.

The chapter concludes with this last example because it clearly demonstrates to what extent clothing acts may function in a highly developed signifying system. The scene discussed contains many different types of clothing acts, all of which must be interpreted in their specific contexts. These acts, like many of the clothing acts in this literary corpus, signify rather than symbolize. They participate in a system whose rules are starting to show evidence of slippage. Mirroring the larger societal shift in which the nobles were increasingly in commerce with merchants, this reshaping marks the beginning of a new horizontal organization of representation, one in which meaning derives, not from divine or princely ordinance, but rather from relations between words and concepts. The sign, in mentality and in literary practice, is emerging. However, just as the merchants continue to live alongside the nobles, these clothing signs continue to coexist with their symbolic counterparts; in fact, many clothing acts remain whose purposes and functions, narrative and extratextual, continue to align perfectly with one another. Indeed, the vestimentary code is subsumed by the signifying system; however, the possibility of manipulating it is preserved even as it is subsumed, resulting in a remarkably dynamic system in which signifiers have meanings contingent upon context. Accordingly, a great many clothing acts provide striking evidence of the emerging signifying system, insofar as these acts have purposes and meanings that are fully understandable only in relation to their specific contexts. The clothing signifying system is therefore imbued with the ambiguity and ambivalence of the age.

5

CLOTHING AS A STRUCTURING, THEMATIC, AND NARRATIVE DEVICE: THE ART OF WEAVING ROMANCE

THE SYSTEMATIC AND ELABORATE use of clothing in a highly developed signifying system serving the work in a variety of ways and at several levels is characteristic of the courtly literature of the end of the twelfth century. This use of the clothing signifying system is related to the structure of romance and, by extension, of shorter narrative *lais*, in that it is one of the many devices that give romance form.[1] Clothing, as the writers in the twelfth century used it, figures as an element of *conjointure* in that it serves in the process of amplification. The descriptions of clothing are the result of the author's concern for beautifying his or her work through the filling in, or amplification, of certain *topoi* that he or she found to be lacking in the source material.[2] Amplification for the medieval writer was, as Vinaver notes, "an expansion or unrolling of a number of interlocked themes" (*Form* 12). The relationship of theme to structure in twelfth-century romance is very strong indeed. In fact, the structure is determined by, identical to, and indissociable from the elaboration of central themes of the romance.

The structure of medieval narrative has not always been understood or appreciated by modern (that is, postmedieval) critics who were heavily

---

1. I am including narrative *lais* in my discussion of romance because of both the fluidity of medieval genre, which is itself difficult for modern scholarship to define satisfactorily, and the fact that the audience, its reception of the literary work, and the conventions of romance seem to be the same as for the narrative *lais*, such as those by Marie de France that I discuss here. I will, however, continue to refer broadly to the conventions of "romance" while including discussions of these conventions in narrative *lais*. Logan E. Whalen, in his study of Marie's *Lais*, suggests that a *lai* such as *Guigemar* is truly "a romance waiting to happen" (2), because of its development and commonality with the conventions of romance.

2. Kelly has treated the issue of amplification as part of *conjointure* extensively throughout his works on medieval rhetoric and its practice by the romancers of the twelfth century. See particularly his discussions in *The Art of Medieval French Romance*, *The Conspiracy of Allusion*, "Rhetoric in French Literature," and "The Scope of the Treatment of Composition."

influenced by Aristotelian definitions of structure.[3] For centuries, it was believed that the great medieval works were amorphous masses of narrative with no clear organization. Late twentieth-century scholarship, however, became concerned with the reevaluation of medieval literature, paying special attention to rediscovering its particular aesthetics. Such scholarship yielded a much more satisfactory estimation and definition of composition for medieval narrative than had previous, less favorable studies. To illuminate the overall structure of romance, Vinaver describes medieval romance as a tapestry, a work whose complex arrangement is woven in such a way that "a single cut across it, made at any point, would unravel it all" (*Form* 10).[4] Lacy elaborates further, calling the form of romance "a loosely-knit but thoroughly composed structure. All the threads will eventually be tied up, and all the themes taken to their completion, but the links between consecutive episodes are often vague or virtually non-existent" (*Craft* 67). The structure of romance, then, is not linear. Rather, its organization is one in which shape is given to the work as a whole "by patterning of different kinds, mostly through the presentation of parallel situations and often associated with the growth of the hero" (Adams 164). This pattern is, in short, analogy, whereby, in Vinaver's terms, "literary events similar in character but sometimes widely separated in time and space" (*Rise* 99) provide both the content and shape of the text.[5] Moreover, as Lacy asserts, "analogical composition refers not simply to resemblances between episodes, but specifically to the fashioning of episodes so that their resemblances relate them all to the major theme of the work" (*Craft* 68). Much recent scholarship had focused upon the particular devices used to elaborate structure, such as the quest or the portrait.[6] Especially interesting for the present work, since they share parallel concerns, are those studies examining motifs and features that have specific, extratextual

---

3. William W. Ryding's introduction to his *Structure in Medieval Narrative* traces the scholarship on and its conclusions about narrative structure through the centuries and provides an excellent overview of the issues surrounding the evaluation of narrative.

4. Vinaver, however, is far from the first person to draw this parallel. Jean Renart, in his thirteenth-century romance *Le Roman de la rose, ou de Guillaume de Dole*, stresses the similarities between the process of literary creation and cloth production. He describes his own process of embellishing his text through the addition of songs, first, to the process of dyeing fabric with kermes to increase its worth: "car aussi com l'en met la graine / es dras por avoir los et pris, / einsi a il chans et sons mis / en cestui *Romans de la Rose*" (For just as one put the kermes in the cloth to create praise and value, thus he puts songs and chants in this *Romance of the Rose*) (vss. 8–11) and then, to the process of embroidery: "et brodez, par lieus, de biaus vers" (And you embroider, in places, pretty verses) (vs. 14).

5. Vinaver treats analogy thoroughly in *The Rise of Romance*. See particularly his chapter "Analogy as the Dominant Form," from which I am quoting here.

6. See, for example, Lacy's *Craft* and Colby's *Portrait*, respectively.

social reference points, including the conventions of hospitality, customs, and jurisprudence.[7] The conclusions of these studies confirm that romances are highly ordered works of literature that, in part, rely upon the use of such features and motifs to elaborate their themes and develop their plots.

It is my contention that clothing is one of the major devices used by twelfth-century writers of romance to structure and develop their narratives and that these writers use the complex clothing signifying system to inscribe dynamism into their romances at the level of narration. Clothing instances in romance perform a great many different narrative functions and must be interpreted in their unique narrative context. Moreover, each romance tends to use the clothing signifying system in a different way and for different purposes. The meaning and significance of individual clothing acts is therefore contingent rather than absolute. The structure of medieval romance appears to seek this complexity and requires active participation from its readers in order for them to discover it. As Lacy remarks, the poet "adds link to link in a narrative chain," but since he or she does not explicitly connect those links for the reader, "it is the reader who closes them by assembling the related ones" ("Spatial Form" 167–68). Thus the structure of romance necessitates the very act of interpretation that the clothing system does, and if "form is meaning," as Lacy suggests (*Craft* 71), then just as meaning is contingent, so is form. Accordingly, the structure of romance is as dynamic as the clothing signifying system it employs to elaborate its themes, form, and meaning. It is through examining the use of clothing at the structural, thematic, and narrative levels that we are able to appreciate and understand the artistry with which the writers of romance wove together the more static, past material into a new and markedly dynamic literary expression of their changing world.

Clothing and Narrative Threads

One important use of clothing in romance is the opening and closing of narrative threads. This kind of narrative function is perhaps best and most simply exemplified by the clothing gift that opens a cycle and thus necessitates

---

7. Matilda Tomaryn Bruckner discusses the convention of hospitality in her *Narrative Invention in Twelfth-Century Romance*, and Donald Maddox concentrates on customs and their use in the works of Chrétien in his *Arthurian Romances of Chrétien de Troyes*. Peter V. Davies and Angus J. Kennedy have edited a collection of essays titled *Rewards and Punishments in the Arthurian Romances and Lyric Poetry of Mediaeval France*, which treats jurisprudence and other motifs connected with punishment of offenses.

its closing with a countergift, or return in kind, as is the case when a knight gives his protection to the lord who dubbed him and gave him gifts of armor and courtly clothing. Yet many such narrative instances are more complex in nature and use more than clothing gifts to accomplish the articulation of a narrative thread. For example, in Chrétien's *Cligés*, there is a remarkable clothing cycle that opens when Alexandre and his companions come into Arthur's court and that closes with Guenevere's special gift to Alexandre. Upon their arrival in Arthur's court, Alexandre and the Greeks remove their mantles when they first go before Arthur (vss. 306–10), to demonstrate their deference and honor the king and his authority. Several lines later, Chrétien again emphasizes this deference when he describes Alexandre as "Desfublez fu devant le roi" (without his mantle before the king) (vs. 328). Chrétien's insistence here underlines the immense respect that Alexandre bears for this king, and he does so by representing an act of undressing oneself as an honoring gesture. Later, the king will reciprocate this respect when he gives Alexandre his armor (vss. 1121–38). The vestimentary gift is an honoring gesture in which the donor symbolically dresses the recipient. In the same way that Alexandre disrobes to demonstrate deference to the king, Arthur will have Alexandre dressed in armor that is twelve times more valuable than the armor he gives to the other Greeks (vss. 1130–33). The cycle of mutual honoring is completed by the queen's gift of the *chemise* into which Soredamors's hair is sewn (vss. 1144–62). This gesture not only represents the honor that the Arthurian court wishes to bestow upon Alexandre, but also ultimately precipitates the expression and realization of love between Alexandre and Soredamors, thus becoming a plot motivator. The first clothing act, then, opens the narrative thread of the honoring cycle and then requires further articulation of the cycle, in effect requiring the queen's gift, whose value extends far beyond the material, thereby closing the cycle. Alexandre's initial expression of respect is reciprocated by the court's expression of gratitude, through the intermediary of Guenevere's gift. The one act sets the stage for the subsequent acts and thus precipitates the free expression of love, allowing the narrative to continue along the path that the author chooses. Of particular note is the use by Chrétien of several different forms of clothing acts (undressing, gifts, making of clothes) that belong to the same narrative thread and help to articulate its conclusion.

In the same way that the *Cligés* example shows how one honoring clothing act precipitates another in return, the narrative thread in *Erec et Enide* that opens with Erec's refusal (vss. 1353–58), prefigured by her father's repeated refusals (vss. 518–32) to allow Enide to be dressed other than in her old, tattered dress before going to court, illustrates the same overall pattern. In this instance, however, the refusal of the clothing act, combined with Enide's arrival in court dressed in her rags, occasions and even necessitates that Guenevere dress her. Were Enide to be dressed in "acceptable" attire for court by anyone else, the text implies, the queen's action would be unnecessary and therefore superfluous, and clearly superfluity of this kind defies the conventions and aesthetics of this romance. Enide must simply arrive at court in her "natural" state so that the court may recognize her inherent and natural nobility and beauty and so that none other than the queen, the highest lady in the narrative universe, may herself transform Enide's appearance and being from a poor vavasor's daughter to the wife of a wealthy prince, destined to be king. Only Guenevere has such power, and any other attempts to alter Enide's appearance by anyone else could only result in inferior results and, more important, render unlikely if not impossible the queen's personal transformation of Enide into a being like herself. Guenevere herself insists upon the rectitude of Erec's reasoning when she assures him: "'Mout avez bien fait'" ("You have done very well") (vs. 1563). In short, only a queen can make a queen. The narrative, then, depends upon the one clothing instance—the refusal of the dressing acts proposed to improve Enide's appearance before her arrival at court—in order for the second clothing transformational instance to occur. This second clothing instance is crucial not simply to the development of Enide's character but also to the continuation of the narrative: Enide must be dressed as (and by) a queen to merit becoming one. Moreover, the narrative thread opens with the description of Enide's ragged clothing and closes with the evocation of the elaborate dressing scene in which Enide's new clothes are described in detail. The two descriptions thus punctuate the narrative thread, and the clothing acts that accompany them reinforce their impact and indicate attitudes and consequences about the two different states in which Enide finds herself. The entire narrative thread elaborates the major theme of the romance: the theme of growing into one's social role, both reflected in and occasioned by the growing into one's clothes.[8]

In *Bisclavret*, Marie uses clothing to perform a more fundamental transformation—the changing of a human character into a werewolf, which, as a greater transformation, also takes up a greater portion of the

---

8. Sara Sturm-Maddox and Donald Maddox, in their article "Description in Medieval Narrative," examine Chrétien's reliance upon clothing signifiers as emblems of Erec and Enide's progression through life stages.

narrative.⁹ The narrative thread that opens with the transformational clothing act is, in fact, the entire narrative. In this case, as is common in werewolf lore, the werewolf's clothes solidify his rehumanization, just as the removal of them signals his transformation into a beast, the removal of his humanity.¹⁰ Not only is this clothing instrumental, precipitating action in the plot, but, like Guenevere's dressing of Enide, the werewolf's clothing also actually performs the transformation.¹¹ The power of these clothes is revealed by the husband when he refuses to tell his wife where he hides his clothes:

> "Dame, ceo ne dirai jeo pas,
> kar, si jeo les eüsse perduz
> e de ceo feusse aparceüz,
> Bisclavret sereie a tuz jors.
> Ja nen n'avreie mes sucurs
> de si k'il me fussent rendu.
> Pur ceo ne voil k'il seit seü."
>
> (vss. 72–78)

> ["Lady, that I will not tell you, for if I were to lose them and thus be discovered, I would be a werewolf forever. Never would I have help until they were given back to me. For this reason, I do not wish for it to be known."]

Eventually, the wife wrestles the truth from her husband and, as he fears, steals his clothes from the hiding place, rendering impossible his transformation back into a human. It is not until those very clothes are returned to him, at the end of the *lai*, that he is able to regain his humanity. In the

---

9. Gloria Thomas Gilmore points to the tension created in the story through the opposition of two different functions of clothing: one that seeks "to confine in a social role or identity imposed from without," another that wishes "to express a self-definition, chosen or generated from within" (67). The resulting tension is what occasions the action of the narrative, bringing the darker desires of the werewolf, that is, a being that is half human and half beast, into the light of day and society.

10. Edith Joyce Benkov has examined Marie's use of the werewolf lore in detail and has explored how the poet uses "undressing and dressing metaphors for the multiple layers of *her* text" (29). The layers she describes comprise shifts in the narration and narrators that complicate the reception of the *lai* and make room for the surprisingly sympathetic characterization of the werewolf.

11. Benkov asserts that the werewolf's "unwilling transformation is cyclical and is framed by undressing—removing the outward covering or humanness, and redressing—covering savagery that has been exposed" (28–29).

corpus of the *Lais*, Marie imbues no other clothing with more power. The transformational potential of the werewolf's clothing occasions the entire plot, for without this power, the wife's hiding of the clothing would have no meaning in terms of the story. The eventual recovery of the clothing directly answers the theft and restores the balance necessary to complete the narrative. The narrative development of this *lai* depends specifically on the particular power of these clothes to transform, to remove and restore, not just identity, but also humanity.[12] In this *lai*, the entire narrative is a single thread that opens with what Benkov has called an undressing of the truth by which the wife manages to learn about her husband's strange disappearances (29–30).[13] The thread continues through the denouement, which itself is the recovery of the werewolf's clothes and his re-dressing, and rehumanizing, act. Once the hiding, or theft, is answered by the re-dressing, the narrative thread closes and the *lai* ends.

In *Eliduc*, two significant clothing acts create and then resolve tension in the plot and elaborate interpersonal relations in a remarkable way.[14] Marie uses clothing as a synecdochic representation of the young lady to occasion the expression of love between her and Eliduc. After she sends him her ring and belt, she tells him that her gift is in fact the gift of her person to him: "Pur ceo li enveiat l'anel / E la ceinturë autresi / Que de sun cors l'aveit seisi" (She gave him her ring and her belt as well because she had ceded her body to him) (vss. 510–12). In turn, this love affair eventually provokes Eliduc's wife into becoming a nun. She decides to "take the veil" to free

---

12. Gilmore argues that the transformation from human into beast, although made manifest through his removal of clothing, is ultimately a voluntary one: "Reasoning backwards, we may assume that it is the clothing that keeps him from transforming into a werewolf. Hence, it must be a conscious decision on the human hero's part to remove the clothing in the first place, in order to become the 'savage beast'" (72). This suggestion seems to deny the popularly held notion that the transformation is involuntary for the human aspect of the werewolf. It remains unclear in Marie's *lai* in what order the transformation occurs, that is, whether the werewolf removes his clothes before the transformation begins or at some point after it has begun. It therefore appears futile to speculate, as Gilmore does, on the intentions of the werewolf with regard to the transformation.

13. Benkov also argues that Marie interjects herself into the wife's discourse through indirect discourse and usurps the narrative voice in order to further coerce information from the werewolf (30).

14. Bruckner, in *Shaping Romance*, has argued that *Eliduc* is a kind of counterpoint to the process opened at the beginning of the *Lais* with *Guigemar*. She notes that they are the two longest *lais* and follow a similar episodic structure involving a pattern of departures and returns, as well as a pattern of duplication, in the form of two different worlds. In contrast to the multiplicity of men in *Guigemar*, there is a multiplicity of women in *Eliduc*. But perhaps most important, the goal of both *lais* is the selection of the appropriate mate through the process of substitution, and not simply the substitution of one for another, as in other *lais* (163–77).

her husband so that he can marry his new love (vss. 1093–1102). In this case, her decision to perform a special dressing act indicates the resolution of a difficult situation. The veil here is a powerful image because it evokes the notion of hiding. This wife is going to hide herself and her existence behind a veil, an act that will allow her husband and his new lady to come out of hiding and legitimize their own love. This action is, in every sense, an exchange. The motivation for the wife's dressing act is the same as its narrative function: her taking the veil allows her husband to replace her with a new wife. The wife's hiding herself allows Eliduc to replace her with the young lady he now loves. These two female characters actually commodify themselves in identifying themselves utterly with and through the clothing objects. To give herself to Eliduc, the maiden gives him a clothing representation of herself. Only in doing so is she capable of perceiving his love for her. For their love to become open, however, the wife must conceal herself, and she does so through the metaphor of the veil. The clothing gift, then, precipitates the love that necessitates the later clothing act, the taking of the veil. These two acts therefore punctuate the central tension in the plot, one creating it, the other resolving it.

Marie's *Fresne* dramatizes a more complicated integration of narrative threads that resolves tension in the plot. In this *lai*, a progression of three undressing scenes surrounds the climax of the *lai*, the recognition of Fresne as both the lost twin daughter and the rightful spouse for her lord. Twice Fresne removes her mantle in an honoring gesture: first, to honor the marriage bond between her lover and his new wife (her unrecognized twin sister), then, to show deference toward the new mother-in-law of her lover after she has called for Fresne to come before her (vss. 389–405, 429).[15] Another undressing act, this time by the new wife, whose mother encourages her to disrobe for the wedding night, textually divides and reflects the other two (vss. 411–12). Here, the honor Fresne shows, despite her feelings over losing her lover to another, identifies her character as noble and loving. Once her actual identity becomes clear, her qualities will be rewarded by the annulment of her sister's marriage so that she may wed her lover.[16]

---

15. Van Vleck points out that the scene in which the mother begins to suspect Fresne's true identity proceeds like a series of summonses followed by interrogations, and that, in this way, the textile becomes testimony, accompanying and confirming the verbal depositions given (40–42).

16. According to Bruckner: "The substitution of one sister for another is immediately corrected in *Fresne*, when the mother recognizes the blanket and ring she sent along with her baby daughter: the match that appeared wrong for the barons' point of view turns out to be right for

Fresne, in honoring the first marriage by twice removing her mantle, gains the ability to replicate the other undressing act previously performed by her twin: Fresne, too, will be able to undress, for her own wedding night. Although her motivation in her initial undressing acts is to honor, their narrative function is to precipitate her replacement of her sister as wife by proving her nobility and rightful identity. Conversely, the motivation for the sister's undressing act is to prepare to consummate her marriage, but its function ultimately becomes the honoring of her rediscovered twin sister's status. As these sisters dress and undress at different times and for different reasons that entail both surface and hidden functions, clothing structures and facilitates the larger meaning of the episode—the discovery of Fresne's true identity and birthright—and materializes the significance of the scene.

Plot Structuring Through Analogy

Medieval verse romances are highly structured literary expressions that rely on a variety of devices to accomplish their organization. Formally analogical episodes or features provide the framework within which the details of the plot unfold. Moreover, they may be thematically as well as structurally analogical, and each author uses such episodes and features to construct a sophisticated narrative structure with thematic cohesion. Lacy defines thematic analogy as "a technique of structural elaboration which consists of the reflection of the central theme or intrigue of the work in numerous other episodes" ("Structure" 13). Clothing often interacts with a narrative as just such a structuring device. Clothing is thus linked to the overall structure of narrative works both as formal analogy and as thematic analogy.

In *Lanval*, for example, Marie uses two formally analogical descriptions of one lady and the absence of another lady's portrait to initiate and then resolve the central tension of the plot, as well as to reflect a major theme of the work—Lanval's love for his lady and the efforts each will make to preserve it in the face of adversity. Lanval, rejected and forgotten by Arthur's court, is taken by a magical and beautiful lady as her lover. His change in fortune draws the queen's attention to him at court, but he rejects her, claiming to love a lady whose lowest handmaid is more beautiful than the queen. The queen demands that Lanval prove his claim by producing the

---

both the lovers and society" (*Shaping* 171). The barons are those who pushed the knight to marry the sister and thus represent social will, as opposed to personal will.

lady, which he believes to be impossible, since he has vowed never to reveal their love to anyone lest she never visit him again. In the end, however, she comes to court, where she is deemed the most beautiful lady ever seen, thereby saving her lover from doom. Lanval's lady is nothing less than a marvelous creature, with the ability to appear and disappear at will. Marie accentuates the lady's magical aspect by depicting her with her entourage of beautiful maidens wearing unusual clothing. The two episodes in which Marie gives us a portrait of the lady function as analogies of each other. The first instance informs the reader that the lady's beauty is beyond compare and allies the reader with Lanval's position relative to the queen's challenge. When Lanval first sees the lady's attendants, they are described thus: "Vestues furent richement, / Laciees mut estreitement / En deus bliauz de purpre bis" (Richly dressed were they, with laces tightly pulled in two *bliauts* of dark *porpre*) (vss. 57–59). Then he sees the lady herself:

> Ele jut sur un lit mut bel—
> Li drap valeient un chastel—
> En sa chemise senglement;
> Mut ot le cors bien fait e gent.
> Un chier mantel de blanc hermine,
> Covert de purpre alexandrine,
> Ot pur le chaut sur li geté.
> Tut ot descovert le costé,
> Le vis, le col e la peitrine."
>
> (vss. 97–105)

[She lay on a beautiful bed in only her *chemise*; the bedclothes were worth more than a castle. Her body was well formed and handsome. Because of the heat, she had thrown aside an expensive mantle of white ermine covered with Alexandrian *porpre*. Her side, face, neck, and breast were exposed.]

The second instance, in which her surpassing beauty is confirmed by the Arthurian court, does not derive its tension from the reader's uncertainty about the relative beauty of the lady and the queen. The tension arises, rather, from the reader's knowledge that, in light of Lanval's broken promise to the lady, she is unlikely to make her appearance. We question not that she is more beautiful than the queen, but only that she will come to defend Lanval's claim.

His lady does come, however, and Marie describes her arrival:

> Ele iert vestue en itel guise
> De chainse blanc e de chemise,
> Que tuit li costé li pareient,
> Ki de deus parz lacié esteient
> . . . .
> Sis manteus fu de purpre bis,
> Les pans en ot entur li mis
>
> (vss. 559–62, 571–72)

[She was dressed in this manner: in a white *chainse* and *chemise* whose two sides were laced so that her sides were completely revealed. . . . Her mantle was of dark *porpre*; the sides lay around her.]

This second description of the lady, her beauty, and her marvelous clothes is an amplification of the first and derives its narrative power from the circumstances surrounding it. Moreover, the absolute lack of any description of the queen's clothing, or even of her personal appearance, indicates that she offers no competition to the fairy lady either in terms of her beauty or in terms of Lanval's preference.[17] The two descriptions of the lady's clothing thus punctuate the central tension of the plot: the surpassing beauty of the lady, confirmed by the first description is, after all, what offends the queen.[18] The second description of her clothing and her beauty resolves this tension while the conspicuous absence of any analogical description of the queen undermines the notion of threat that the queen proposes, and reinforces the effects of the second portrait of the lady—Lanval's victory over the queen. These three clothing instances provide examples of both formal and thematic analogy within the *lai* and serve both to structure the narrative and to develop and deepen one of the central thematic issues of the work.

In *Le Roman de Thèbes*, there are two dressing scenes that articulate and elaborate the theme of lack in the form of personal loss and offer not only

---

17. I have argued elsewhere that in Arthurian romance, the clothes of Arthur and those of Guenevere, when she is properly performing her function as queen (and not as Lancelot's lover), are rarely accorded descriptions, because as monarchs they are not in competition with the members of the high nobility that serve them. My contention is that this represents a normalizing tendency with regard to the consolidation of the Capetian monarchy. See my "What Was Arthur Wearing?"

18. Van Vleck suggests that the undressing, the "unwrapping," of the fairy-lady's body in this *lai* constitutes a wordless testimony in a judicial process about beauty (47–49).

structural but also rich thematic analogies to each other. When Polyneices and Tydeus first meet in the night outside Adrastus's palace, they begin to fight each other, and the noise of their activity wakes Adrastus (vss. 773–815). The king dresses himself hastily, and thus improperly, in his hurry to investigate the source of the noise (vss. 815–18). A later scene in which Lycurgus's wife comes to investigate a great noise in the middle of the night and hastily dresses herself (vss. 2519–24) reflects the former scene in its structure. The two scenes are thematically linked insofar as they both involve parental figures learning about their children. Adrastus quickly realizes that the knights who are fighting are destined to become his sons-in-law, while Lycurgus's wife learns that her infant son has been killed. What makes the interplay between these two scenes more compelling, however, is that the latter episode serves as a mise en abyme of the larger narrative concerning Adrastus's relationship with Polyneices and Tydeus. Adrastus indeed marries his daughters to these two knights, thereby becoming their surrogate father. But he does not enjoy this relationship for very long before he loses his two new sons in the war between the Greeks and the Thebans. In the same way that Lycurgus's wife grieves the untimely loss of her son, Adrastus will grieve for Polyneices and Tydeus far too soon. The shorter scene involving Lycurgus's wife structurally reflects the first scene in which Adrastus discovers his future sons-in-law, but it also foreshadows Adrastus's grief because of their deaths through a complex thematic analogy. Moreover, these two formally analogical episodes further reinforce the tragic theme of the work as a whole, underlining the tremendous personal cost of the violent war through the depiction of parental mourning.

In Chrétien's *Cligés*, the poet uses clothing to accentuate and elaborate his division of the narrative into two parts—the story of the father and that of the son. These tales inversely mirror each other: the father openly paying respect to the king and secretly longing for his love, the son covertly entering the Arthurian world and ultimately exposing his illicit love, caught in a shameful display of nudity. Chrétien uses clothing to indicate the attitudes of both father and son. Alexandre arrives in Arthur's court and opens an honoring-through-clothing cycle that communicates mutual respect and ends with the queen's gift to him. This gift is, of course, the *chemise* into which Soredamors has sewn her hair, and its giving motivates the plot by precipitating the expression of love between Alexandre and Soredamors. This gift serves a dual function in the text: it is both a sign of appreciation that conforms to other gifts of clothing made in similar situations, and it is a emblematic representation of Soredamors herself, establishing a symbolic closeness between the two characters that prefigures and finally precipitates their love (once she sees the hair in the shirt and recognizes it). The *chemise*, then, has a double function: it is at once the expression of a sentiment and an emblem whose discovery allows two characters to engage in a relationship. If Alexandre arrives at Arthur's court in a position of deference, Cligés arrives with the intention of confusing the court by neither revealing his identity nor allowing the court to recognize immediately that he is the same knight from day to day. Arthur bestowed the gift of armor upon Cligés's father; now Cligés uses his several suits of armor to confuse Arthur and his knights about his identity. This difference alone reveals the chasm that divides the son from the father.[19] Throughout the rest of the romance Cligés will repeat to a large extent the actions of his father, but he will invert them at many turns. The fact that the father and the son approach life and love so differently is made material through the way the two characters use clothing so differently.

In *Jaufre*, clothing helps to structure the romance with a great deal of irony and generally has an important presence in the different narrative sections of the work as a whole. Each of the textual divisions contains references to clothing that may be considered emblematic of that section and also have structural or thematic similarities with other sections of the text. The poet structures his romance through this interweaving. In the opening episode at King Arthur's court, for example, Arthur and the knights don their armor and set out to seek adventure because none has come to seek them (vss. 165–90). Then, when a large horned beast captures Arthur, the knights can do nothing more than tear and rend their clothing as they express their fear and worry for their king (vss. 350–68). Finally, they remove their clothing to build a pile to cushion the king's landing when the beast lets him fall from a peak (vss. 377–410). These three references to clothing all serve the text in a particular way. First, the donning of armor is a supposedly chivalrous act, but in this case, it is devoid of meaning, for the knights cannot save Arthur by using it. Already, the text has revealed to

---

19. Peter Haidu discusses at length the parallel between the father and son in *Cligés* in his *Aesthetic Distance in Chrétien de Troyes* (63–70), in which he explains Alexandre's actions in terms of his belonging to a protocourtly generation, whereas Cligés's generation may be viewed as fully courtly. Haidu argues that in many ways the son surpasses the father, particularly with regard to self-confidence within the courtly milieu. I do not disagree with Haidu's analysis; rather, I find his positing of a generational gap that divides the chivalric realm an extremely satisfactory explanation of the reasons for differences between father and son. However, I would characterize the resulting contrast in temperament in another way: whereas I think Alexandre embodies meekness and deference (with the exception of his very early behavior at his father's court), Cligés is, in my estimation, almost brazen in his deeds.

the reader that appearances are not entirely trustworthy in this romance, for the armed knights of the Round Table should be able to save their king through their prowess at arms and not have to embarrass themselves by removing their clothing to help him. Moreover, armor and the misuse or misappropriation of it will prove to be an important device throughout the rest of the romance. This arming scene, then, announces future scenes involving the unusual use of armor. Next, the knights' ripping and tearing of their clothes, as I will discuss in more detail below, is essentially a leitmotif in this romance. Violent lamentation, accompanied by the rending of clothing, structures the romance through a series of scenes in which similar actions function as thematic analogues of one another. Finally, the use of a pile of clothing to cushion a fall again announces the unorthodox way in which the text uses clothing in general. Additionally, in this scene, when the knights remove their clothing they are erasing their individual identities, to save their king. In this first section of the romance, the author gives us an important taste of what is to come. There are a number of scenes involving unusual uses of armor, including the one in which Jaufré sleeps in his armor one night, despite his being in Brunissen's court at the time. Inappropriate responses to situations seem to be the norm: Jaufré refuses to help a damsel in distress, and Jaufré and Mélian arm themselves in response to Fada's coming to thank them with marvelous gifts. The text is replete with scenes of lamentations and violence in which clothing is destroyed, particularly the ones at Monbrun, and generally deceptive or confusing appearances abound. While clothing is certainly not the only device used to create the ironic tone of this romance, it plays a crucial and consistent role in its elaboration.

The destroying of clothing holds a special place, moreover, in the romance of *Jaufre*. The central episode of the romance concerns itself with an entire region whose inhabitants communally lament and grieve at a seemingly excessive number of precise moments of each day (vss. 3151–70). Brunissen's brother Mélian is the captive of an evil, proud knight named Taulat de Rogimon, who also happens to be the knight whom Jaufré seeks to punish for insulting the Arthurian court. Brunissen's people engage in their communal lamenting because of their intense grief at the capture of their lord. In seeking Taulat, Jaufré comes into Brunissen's lands and disturbs the lady's attempts to sleep. Ironically, it is his need to sleep that occasions his stop in Brunissen's garden in the first place. Yet he is terrified by the lamenting, and furthermore, everyone whom he asks about it refuses to explain the situation to him. Ultimately, he goes on his way to seek Taulat, unwittingly becoming the champion of Mélian as well. His liberating Mélian ends the communal lamenting, establishes him as a hero, and wins Brunissen for him as his wife.

This scene of intense grieving is a central, structuring element of the romance, and many other textual moments reflect it by incorporating scenes of lamentation, often accompanied by the ripping and tearing of clothes. In the very first episode of the romance, Arthur's knights worry about him as he is carried off by a beast. Three times, the text relates how first Gauvain, then all the other knights, rip their clothes in reaction to the peril in which they believe their king to be (vss. 320–68). Later in the text, Jaufré encounters a squire who is tearing his clothes and who warns Jaufré to turn back because of the treachery the squire has endured at the hands of a leperous giant (vss. 2204–50). These instances of intense grief occur before Jaufré arrives at Montbrun, Brunissen's land, but once he leaves, in a state of distress because of the communal lamenting that he cannot understand, he continues to encounter similar scenes. Once away from Montbrun, he comes upon a sympathetic herdsman, who shares food with him, but when he inquires about the reason for the lamenting at Montbrun, the herdsman begins violent lamentations himself and threatens to kill Jaufré (vss. 4307–43). Then, when Jaufré parts ways with Augier to seek Taulat, he asks the knight who hosted him the night before about the strange lamentations. Again, he witnesses a violent grief in reaction to his question, but once Augier calms down, he tells Jaufré where to find Taulat and whom to ask about the lamenting (vss. 4693–4874). The next set of lamenting scenes occurs after Jaufré has defeated Taulat: first, Jaufré encounters a young woman grieving, ripping out her hair and shredding her clothes, claiming that a lady is drowning there, and in this way, she lures him to the fountain to push him in (vss. 8387–8453). Once in, Jaufré is transported to a marvelous land in which he recognizes the lady who had asked him to champion her cause and whom he had refused because of his desire to get married quickly. The young woman's lamenting facilitates Jaufré's disappearance, which, in turn, precipitates lamenting among Jaufré's company, which is described in some detail (vss. 8465–8696). All these instances serve to reflect the larger, central lamenting act and therefore are a structuring device of the romance in general through both formal and thematic analogy.

Thematic Structure Articulated Through Clothing

Very often, and almost always in Arthurian romance, the hero's quest is the major organizing principle of the romance (Lacy, *Craft* 1; Hanning 3). It is the quest that provides the greatest thematic coherence to the work, and therefore, theme becomes a structural feature of the romance. The form and development of the quest, as Lacy argues, provide "the major structural tension of the work: that is the contrast between the conventional, predictable, patterned arrangement of events which points toward a definite conclusion and the open, discursive, indefinitely expandable series of episodes which constitute the typical randomness of the quest" (*Craft* 7). The quest, then, like the clothing signifying system, is used by the writers of romance not merely as a structuring device but also as a means to imbue the work with tension between the opposing poles of stasis and dynamism. Additionally, clothing instances are inextricably linked to the development and articulation of the individual's quest in these works. Clothing helps to elaborate the quest and the themes surrounding and informing it in multiple ways, both in terms of form—description of clothing as well as clothing acts—and with regard to narrative functions. These clothing instances are multivalent, as we have seen. The result is thematic elaboration that is remarkably complex and infused with the same dynamism visible in the clothing signifying system. Moreover, clothing often figures as a major component of the elaboration and articulation of theme.

Chrétien explores the theme of a lack that must be overcome in *Yvain* through the articulation of character nudity, the lack of clothing, as a shameful state to be surmounted. The theme is thus articulated in part through clothing. The hero's passage from husband and knight to mad and naked social outcast, and back again to husband and knight is precisely mirrored in his state of dress. His evolution is equally reflected throughout the poem as other characters endure similar passages. In this romance, Chrétien elaborates on nudity, or the lack of proper clothing, by assigning it a place of predominance both as a direct reflection of the major theme of the romance—Yvain's moral and social devolution and evolution—and as a major plot motivator. Unlike in the *Cligés* example examined earlier, where a single clothing object functions as a plot motivator, in *Yvain* a multivalent clothing act motivates the plot. Yet even before Yvain's madness and nudity, there are some important clothing instances that are thematically analogical to later episodes in the narrative and thus provide structure as well as thematic elaboration.

When we see Laudine for the first time, she is grieving the death of her husband and is ripping and tearing her clothes: "ses mains detuert et ront ses dras" (she was twisting her hands and rending her garments) (vs. 1159).[20] A brief time later, when King Arthur comes to her land and finds Yvain married to this lady, the poet gives us a description of her clothing, stating that she is "plus bele que nule contesse" (more beautiful than any [other] countess) (vs. 2369). These two passages punctuate the period of time during which Laudine progresses from a loss of social status with no one to defend her fountain to an elevated state in which she has the most valiant knight of the Arthurian court at her side. This passage is an inverted foreshadowing of the progression that Yvain will make from sanity and high social status to madness and outcast status. Yvain's plight is also represented through vestimentary imagery. Even as the maiden messenger arrives to deliver her message to Yvain, the clothing image is operative. When she approaches the encampment of Arthur's knights, she removes her mantle. Her undressing can be seen not only as an honoring gesture toward the king, whom she cordially and respectfully greets, but also as a dishonoring gesture toward Yvain, whom she shames publicly with the admonitions that her lady has sent (vss. 2704–72). Immediately upon hearing the news that his lady has reclaimed the ring, the symbol of her love for him, Yvain destroys his clothes, slipping into madness (vs. 2806), his nudity becoming a sign of his insanity and his retreat from society. The three undressing acts—the lady's removal of her mantle, Yvain's removal of the ring, and his removal of his clothing—form a short but highly charged series. The same vestimentary act occurs three times in quick succession, each time inching Yvain ever closer to outcast status. The maiden's appearance in court, accompanied by the removal of her mantle, reminds him of his broken promise and formally prefigures his undressing act; the reclamation of the ring (itself an unclothing act) physically manifests his separation from her; and the removal of his own clothes signals his leaving society. Without his sanity, Yvain has lost his ability to function in society, and without his clothes, he has lost his social identity. The hermit with whom he has his first social contact during his madness recognizes him as mad from the fact that he is nude (vs. 2832), while the ladies who once knew him have a very difficult time recognizing him undressed (vss. 2892–2912). Furthermore, Yvain himself, once he comes back to his senses and recognizes his nudity, is ashamed and quickly dresses himself in the clothing that the damsels have

20. Kelly has identified this description of Laudine as a dynamic one, since, as he explains: "While Laudine quite literally is in the process of tearing apart and corrupting her beauty, Yvain is reconstructing her in his mind, in effect restoring in his imagination the harm Laudine does herself" ("Art" 200).

left for him (vss. 3020–22). Thus, his passage from society to outcast status, from husband to rejected lover, is both reflected and occasioned by a series of undressing acts that progressively confer shame and madness upon him, whereas his rehabilitation is completed and externally signaled by his later self-dressing act.

Yvain is not the only character in the poem for whom shame is linked to the absence of clothing. The giant who menaces Gauvain's relatives threatens that he will take the gentleman's daughter and will reduce her to state of lice-ridden nudity (vs. 4116). The giant himself is described primarily with regard to his poor accoutrements, emphasizing the shameful state of his life (vss. 4086–95). Lunete's fall from grace is characterized by her reduction to near nudity. She is taken to be burned at the stake "trestote nue en sa chemise" (completely naked in her *chemise*) (vs. 4316). However, as the other ladies realize that Lunete has been too harshly judged, they lament the fact that she can no longer provide them with beautiful clothes to wear (vss. 4360–61). In the end, they decide to send a mantle to her to cover herself, thus reducing her shame (vss. 4368–73). Finally, the situation of the three hundred *tisseuses*, as I discussed in Chapter 3, represents a notable irony within the text: these wretched women are forced to toil to make fine clothing but are themselves dressed completely in rags (vss. 5294–96). Their near nudity materially represents and articulates their powerlessness, vulnerability, and lack of social status, while their work provides to others what is denied to them. In all these cases, Yvain provides deliverance from shame and nudity. Yvain has thus come full circle: he first saves Laudine from her grief (after having provoked it, however); then he himself endures madness and nudity but manages with some help to return to sanity and society; and finally he must save others from their shame and nudity, which ultimately wins back the love of Laudine. Yvain's clothing and nudity provide a direct parallel to his changing identity. The development of his identity as a hero and as an individual is his quest, and therefore his clothing both confirms and renders material the achievement of his quest, articulating the major theme of the romance.

In *Lancelot*, Chrétien explores clothing as a marker of an identity that is alternately constant and shifting, calling appearances and motivations into question throughout the romance and reflecting the major theme of the work—Lancelot's quest to be the queen's worthy lover. Almost everyone honors Lancelot, and his seeming ability to suit his task so well as the liberator of the people, through dressing acts, most often in the form of a mantle placed upon his shoulders. The text is replete with references to his special aptitude for the task. Several episodes accentuate the fact that he fits the requirements of his task so precisely, including the one in which Lancelot borrows armor from one of his hosts to fight the proud knight. The text emphasizes that these arms fit Lancelot extremely well, so well indeed that one would believe he had been born wearing them: "qu'il fu ensi nez et creüz / de ce voldroie estre creüz" (that he had been born and raised [wearing them], on this, I would like to be believed) (vss. 2675–76). Chrétien insists that his readers believe him, and his emphasis serves to identify Lancelot both with the armor and as the obvious savior of the captives. Lancelot fits his armor and his destiny perfectly, unlike Gauvain, who has failed at his mission and is finally found at the Water Bridge, bobbing up and down in the water with his armor spread about on the shore (vss. 5105–28). Obviously, Lancelot has the appropriate tools for the job, whereas Gauvain is decidedly lacking. Yet herein lies an artful subtlety in Chrétien's text: although all of the poem's characters conclude that the earlier episodes are signs of Lancelot's particular aptitude for the task, they do not understand that Lancelot, although well suited for the liberation of the people of Logres, is undertaking the task for very different reasons. Since the people of Logres will be freed from Meleagant along with the queen, Lancelot is only incidentally their liberator. He is the knight worthy of the task of liberation, as is indicated by the repeated gifts of mantles, yet he pursues this task only to fulfill his own desires, thereby subverting the meaning of the clothing acts despite their accumulation.

Lancelot's single-mindeness with regard to finding the queen is an integral part of his identity. His dedication to his task is never more apparent than when he climbs into the cart to reach her more quickly. In the same way that the cart was only superficially shameful and that the rape scene, discussed in detail in Chapter 3, was staged, his identity as the worthy liberator is only superficial. The queen is indeed the only character in the poem who is consistently capable of determining Lancelot's identity. She is the one to name him, just as she is the one who can recognize him in any clothes or armor. First and foremost he wishes to save his lady, the queen, and his ability to remain focused on her never wavers—except, of course, for the "two steps" of hesitation for which he must atone throughout the rest of the romance. For Guenevere, Lancelot's identity, like his attention to the queen, remains constant, regardless of his clothing. Chrétien creates an identity for Lancelot that only one other character is capable of perceiving. For everyone else, Lancelot remains an enigma, and his constantly changing clothes reflect this confusion.

From a structural point of view, the accumulation of dressing acts confers on the protagonist the identity of a hero who is perfectly suited to liberate the people of Logres and the queen, while he is, in fact, truly seeking only the queen, driven by his love to find her. In the same way that his focus remains uniquely on her, she is the only one capable of unconditionally recognizing his true identity, despite shifts in his appearance. The honorific dressing scenes of Lancelot provide contrast to the two notorious disarming scenes of Gauvain, both of which demonstrate Gauvain's inability to complete his task and punctuate the two main divisions of the plot. Once the search for the queen has ended with Lancelot's defeat of Meleagant, the hero finds Gauvain disarmed by the Water Bridge, and after Lancelot returns from imprisonment and self-imposed exile to fight Meleagant at the appointed date, his arrival necessitates the disarming of Gauvain so that the hero may do his work. The repetition of scenes in which other people dress or arm Lancelot establishes their expectation of his heroic act, functioning as a repeated anticipation of the final arming scene. Gauvain's double disarming inversely reflects these scenes and structurally contrasts with them. Yet Chrétien subverts Lancelot's heroic identity that the repetition of the dressing and arming scenes serves to establish, bringing his audience to understand instead that Lancelot's identity is anything but clear. He does this by associating clothing with concealment at a crucial moment in the story. As Lancelot prepares to set out to join the queen for their tryst, the poet evokes the covering quality of the night by using a clothing metaphor:

> Tant a au jor vaintre luitié
> que la nuiz molt noire et oscure
> l'ot mis desoz sa coverture
> et desoz sa chape afublé.
>
> (vss. 4543–45)

[In its battle against the day, dark and somber night finally prevailed and covered its light beneath its covering and hid it beneath its cloak.]

In the same way that the *chape* of night cloaks the adultery of Lancelot and Guenevere, the mantles that Lancelot receives along the way and the armor that fits him so perfectly conceal his true motivations and his identity as an adulterer.

In *Perceval*, the hero's evolution as a knight is marked by his clothing, as is his final atonement, with regard both to the Lady of the Tent and to his family. As has been noted by Lacy, Perceval's main problem is that he fails to interpret properly the appearance of objects to arrive at an understanding of them and their place in the world (*Craft* 16–20). This is never more obvious than when he mistakes the knights he sees in his mother's forest first for devils, then for angels (vss. 100–154). Interestingly, when he hears the sound of the noisy armor, he believes the knights to be devils, but when he catches sight of them in their shining armor, he thinks they are angels. Furthermore, it is precisely because of this erroneous perception of them that he sets out to find King Arthur so that he too can be a knight: he is simply attracted to their appearance rather than to their social function. As Lacy points out, "To the naïve youth, armor constitutes identity ("On Armor" 366).[21] It is also significant that he begins his quest dressed inappropriately for his new calling: he wears the Welsh clothes that his mother has made for him: "A la meniere et a la guise / De Gales fu appareilliez: / Uns revelins ot en ses piez" (In the Welsh fashion he was dressed, with buckskin shoes on his feet) (vss. 602–4), repeatedly refusing to abandon them in favor of a more courtly costume. With Ivonet, he gives reasons for his refusal, citing the inferiority of the clothing that the squire Yonez proposes. Perceval not only refuses these clothes but insults them as well, insisting that the ones that his mother made for him are far superior. However, we know, as the medieval audience would have known, that the clothes he describes as inferior are of the finest materials, and we understand that the notion of dressing the part of a knight is lost upon Perceval. Yet despite his refusal to wear the clothes of a knight, he does manage to acquire a suit of armor, although he has no idea how to use his arms.[22]

---

21. Lacy argues for a distinction between identity, or who a character is, and identification, who one is perceived to be. Perceval is confused by this distinction, failing to make it early in the romance (*Craft* 26–27).

22. In fact, Perceval's very procurement of the set of armor evokes and reinforces his complete misunderstanding of its use and purpose, for once he has killed the Red Knight to take his armor, Perceval believes he must resort to chopping up the knight to bits to remove his armor: "Mais ains avrai par charbonees / Trestot esbrahoné le mort / Que nule des armes en port, / Qu'eles se tienent si au cors / Que ce dedens et che defors / Est trestot un, si com moi samble, / Qu'eles se teinent si ensamble" (But I will have have to cut up this dead man in tiny pieces before being able to wear a single piece of his armor, so well they are held fast to his body that there is no inside or outside but all of a single piece, and it's all holding tightly together) (vss. 1136–42). It is only with the arrival of Yonez that Perceval is instructed in the appropriate removal of armor, although he remains unaware of its use.

At the next stop on Perceval's journey, he encounters Gornemant, who, we learn, is not only a valiant knight but also a perfectly courtly gentleman. It is finally Gornemant who is able, if not entirely to convince Perceval of the superiority of the courtly clothes, at least to persuade him to wear them to please his new mentor and who takes it upon himself to teach Perceval how to use his armor. When he asks Perceval if he knows how to use his arms, the youth replies that the only knowledge he has of his arms and armor is how to put them on and take them off:

> "Jes sai bien vestir et retraire,
> Si com li vallé m'en arma
> Qui devant moi en desarma
> Le chevalier qu'avoie mort;
> Et si legierement les port
> Qu'eles ne me grievent de rien" (vss. 1392-97)

> ["I know how to put them on and take them off, as the valet (showed me) who armed me and, in front of me, disarmed the knight I had killed, and they are so light to wear that they do not bother me at all."]

Not only is his knowledge extremely superficial on a practical level, but his understanding that there could be social or relational implications to the acts of arming and disarming is completely absent. Perceval thus both fails to know and fails to understand. These two shortcomings are eloquently brought to our attention in this one short clothing passage.

By the time Perceval reaches Blancheflor's castle, he has almost entirely overcome his shortcomings within the chivalric world. Upon his arrival, he is disarmed by Blancheflor's servants (vss. 1776–80); that is, he is perceived for the first time as a true knight. They further honor him by bringing a fur mantle for him to wear (vss. 1779–80). Perceval is now fully educated in his use of arms and fully courtly, and others treat him as such: he is accepted and respected by everyone he encounters. The two notable exceptions to this general attitude toward the new knight are the lack of attention accorded him as he exits the Grail Castle and the admonition he receives from the pilgrims on Good Friday. These rejections are encoded in vestimentary imagery as well. Although the inhabitants of the Grail Castle receive Perceval with much honoring, bringing him mantles and allowing him to sleep in the bed of the Fisher King, they completely ignore him the following morning;

no one arms him, no one answers his calls, and no one bids him farewell (vss. 3356–91). He has failed the Fisher King and the inhabitants of the Grail Castle in not asking the question he should have asked. They extended great hospitality to Perceval, only to find that his chivalric training had undermined the very reason he had been sent into their midst. Their overwhelming disappointment in him is demonstrated textually by their refusal to dress him, arm him, or answer him, and this rejection is made all the more poignant by the contrast with their warm welcoming of him the night before.

This episode contrasts greatly with Perceval's previous sojourn in Blancheflor's castle. Although he is received in the same fashion—with great hospitality—his subsequent treatment by Blancheflor and her people is vastly different. This difference can only be explained by the fact that in this case, Perceval does not fail to save Blancheflor: he succeeds grandly. In fact, after the night of apparent love between Perceval and the lady, she willfully dresses herself to demonstrate her newfound ability to defend herself against her foe, while Perceval at the Grail Castle is forced to fend for himself as the inhabitants abandon him. In one case, dressing oneself is a positive act of self-sufficiency; in the other, it is a condition imposed upon an individual by those he has disappointed.

The second rejection that Perceval endures is from the pilgrims on Good Friday, when he is admonished for wearing armor on this sacred occasion (vss. 6264–6330). Again, it is Perceval's ignorance—for he does not even know what day it is—combined with his complete subservience to the ideals of the Arthurian universe that has led him astray. Thus it is specifically for becoming too involved in the chivalric world that Perceval suffers this affront, and his armor becomes a sign of shame. At this point in the text, Perceval has forgotten the church, his courtly clothing, and the clothing that his mother made for him. He is presented to us as a chivalric shell. Yet it is at this moment that Perceval remembers these objects, and when he arrives at the home of the hermit, the text indicates that he "si descent et si se desarme" (descends and disarms himself) (vs. 6339), an undressing act that removes shame.[23] Since this is the last reference to the clothing of Perceval and in light of the fact that so much of the early part of the poem was devoted to describing his accoutrements in detail, we

---

23. Interestingly, in the thirteenth-century *Queste del Saint Graal*, various churchmen admonish knights to don the "armes de Sainte Eglise" (62, line 27) which is not actually armor but ecclesiastical clothing. Perceval seems, at least nominally, to be performing just this sort of disarming (from chain mail) and rearming (in a habit).

may assume that he has lain his arms aside forever, rejecting the Arthurian chivalric world for the religious one that he now seeks with his uncle the hermit.[24] Perceval has gone from a youth dressed in the Welsh fashion who confuses the appearance of knights with that of devils, then angels, to a brave and chivalrous knight who sports courtly clothing when not in battle, then to a tired and disillusioned knight who wears nothing but his armor. The confusion with which the romance opens concerning whether the knights are devils or angels seems to announce the estimation Perceval now makes of himself as his part of the romance closes: he is uncertain if, in becoming one of Arthur's knights, he has allied himself with good or evil. He has doubts about whether he has become more of an angel than a devil. Finally he abandons his armor for what we can assume to be the clothes of a religious hermit. In the end, he is not far from where he started, having returned to his religious and familial "roots" and to his natural simplicity after discovering firsthand the shortcomings of Arthurian chivalry. Through the description of Perceval's clothing and clothing acts, Chrétien demonstrates clearly every step he takes on his journey. Perceval's quest and evolution as a hero are thus articulated and materialized by vestimentary references that in turn develop and elaborate the thematic structure of the romance.

Reading a Narrative Through Clothes

Romance writers in the twelfth century used clothing not only to provide shape and contours to their narratives but also to give meaning to a work as a whole. The author "Crestïens," in his *Guillaume d'Angleterre*, and Marie, in her *Guigemar*, for example, employ clothing both to structure the plot and reflect its themes and to provide a parallel, vestimentary narrative. In these two works, it is possible to read the narrative through clothing. In other words, references to it consistently occur at plot junctures, although, as we have seen, each clothing instance may contribute to the elaboration of several different levels of the work. In the following discussion, I provide a detailed analysis of clothing in regard to character, plot, and thematic and

---

24. Of course, since Chrétien left the romance unfinished, it is unclear what his intentions may have been. It may have been his plan, for example, to form some sort of synthesis between the Arthurian, terrestrial world and the celestial one of religious brotherhood. In the absence of an ending, though, this interpretation remains speculative. My reading of this episode is based on what does appear in the text, and as such, this episode is the last one in which Perceval appears, and this undressing act is his last action in the romance.

narrative development for both works to demonstrate to what extent the audience can read the romance through clothes. My detailed reading of these two particularly illuminating works, lengthier than any other discussion of a single text thus far, functions as a conclusion to my entire study insofar as they illustrate all the principles adduced throughout my study and demonstrate clearly the narrative richness achievable through the use of clothing as a complex signifying system. Without attention to the use of clothing at the narrative level, it is impossible to appreciate fully the interplay between form and meaning in the clothing signifying system and the larger implications of this interplay upon the meaning of the narrative as a whole. I do not mean to suggest that these are the only two twelfth-century works that may be read in this way—indeed many may—but *Guigemar* and *Guillaume d'Angleterre* are exemplary in this capacity.[25]

Guigemar

Marie's *Guigemar* is the story of a young knight whom, we are told at the beginning of the *lai*, Nature has deprived of the ability to love.[26] After an encounter with a speaking, prophesying hind and a ride in the cabin of a magical ship, Guigemar falls in love with a young lady who is married to an old, jealous man. The two manage to live together in her luxurious prison for a time until the old man catches them together and sends Guigemar on his way in his ship. Finally, the lovers are reunited through a recognition rite that only the two of them can perform. What makes this *lai* interesting for a study of the narrative use of clothing is that the audience is able to read the narrative through the clothing references in the text.[27]

When we first meet the protagonist of our *lai*, he is leaving to serve a king who will dub him a knight. Once he is in the service of the king, the dubbing is represented in the text by the following two lines: "Le reis l'adube richement / Armes li dune a sun talent" (The king dubbed him richly and gave him arms to his liking) (vss. 47–48). The description of the king's

---

25. Several scholars have, in fact, advanced remarkably similar arguments for two works in particular: *Erec et Enide* and Béroul's *Tristan*. See, for example, Sara Sturm-Maddox and Donald Maddox's "Description in Medieval Narrative," Jacques Le Goff's chapter on *Erec et Enide* in *The Medieval Imagination*, and François Rigolot's "Valeur figurative du vêtement dans le *Tristan* de Béroul."

26. A slightly modified version of this discussion appears in my "*Chemise* and *Ceinture*."

27. Bruckner analyzes the attraction, separation, and assorting of opposites through the two separate plots of the *lai*, which are "tied together, again separated, and finally reunited through a series of events designed to reduce the difference between Guigemar and the lady. . . . Bipartition and tripartition are not surprisingly coordinated in this effort" (*Shaping* 165).

dressing Guigemar in armor, the clothes of a knight, is what informs us of his new vocation. Therefore, the very first narrative event that engages the protagonist is represented through the clothing that he receives and wears. His identity as a knight is dependent upon his taking on the appearance of a knight, that is, wearing the accouterments of one. Once Guigemar's new social status is established in the text, Marie turns our attention away from the identificatory power of clothing and will henceforth present clothing through its various performative functions.

The first of these functions is dependent upon clothing's material quality. After Guigemar injures the hind and hears her prophesy (that only a woman with whom Guigemar is desperately in love and who suffers as much as he does may heal his wound), he dismisses the prophesy as absurd: "Il set assez e bien le dit / K'unke femme nule ne vit / A ki aturnast s'amur / Ne kil guaresist de dolor" (He knew and said to himself that to no woman he had ever seen had he wanted to offer his love, nor one who could heal his wound) (vss. 129–32). This prophecy is true and, through its veracity, functions here as a prolepsis. Guigemar has his servant take leave of him to seek assistance, but not before the servant attends to his master's wound by dressing it with his shirt. "De sa chemise estreitement / Sa plaie bende fermement" (He firmly and tightly bound his wound with his *chemise*) (vss. 139–40). Clothing here performs the function of a bandage, an entirely natural use for something made of cloth. The first attempt at healing Guigemar's wound is made possible through a normal yet nonvestimentary use of clothing. Nonetheless, the bandage, while not being used as clothing, still envelops a part of Guigemar's body; he is, after all, *wearing* the bandage. This clothing element is therefore both ordinary and exceptional. Marie's use of an article of clothing here has in no way challenged our expectations, for it is not unusual that one would bandage a wound with what is at hand—one's clothes. She has brought to our attention the fact that clothing can perform many functions, an important fact to bear in mind as the hero continues on his journey.

We are, however, forewarned by the hind that this attempt to heal Guigemar's wound cannot be successful. Indeed, bewildered, alone, and in pain, Guigemar wanders about and comes upon a marvelous ship in a harbor. The poet describes the ship as very beautiful, and in fact, the knight cannot resist boarding it. Once aboard, Guigemar is surprised to find no one there. He does, however, find a magnificent bed that is beautifully arrayed. The fact that Marie devotes twelve lines to the description of the bed and its bedclothes signals its importance.

En mi la nef trovat un lit
Dunt li pecul e li limun
Furent a l'ovre Salemun
Taillié a or, tut a triffoire,
De ciprés e de blanc ivoire.
D'un drap de seie a or teissu
Ert la coilte ki desus fu.
Les altres dras ne sai presier,
Mes tant vos di de l'oreillier:
Ki sus eüst sun chief tenu
Jamais le peil n'avreit chanu.
Li coverturs de sabelin
Vols fu de purpre alexandrin.

(vss. 170–82)

[In the middle of the ship he found a bed whose posts and frame were made in the style of Solomon, worked in gold, all inlaid, of cypress and white ivory. The quilt upon it was made from silk woven with gold. For the other bedclothes, I cannot give a value, but I can tell you this about the pillow: whoever rested his head upon it would never have white hair. The sable bedspread was lined with Alexandrian *porpre*.]

It provides a place of rest for Guigemar in his second attempt to heal his wound. The text tells us: "Il s'est sur le lit apuiez; / Repose sei, sa plaie doelt" (He lay down on the bed; he rested, but his wound hurt him) (vss. 188–89). Once again, Guigemar envelops his wound (and the rest of his body) in cloth; this time, however, the clothes are those of the magnificent bed. During his slumber, the ship sails itself out to sea, and Guigemar finds that his rest has not been effective in healing his wound: "Kar grant dolur out en sa plaie" (For great pain he had in his wound) (vs. 198). The cloth used to envelop Guigemar while he sleeps in this episode performs a strikingly similar function to the one the bandage performed in the episode before: both represent attempts to heal the wound, and both fail because the woman whom Guigemar must love is missing. Without this element, we know that he cannot be healed, and that any attempt is bound to end in failure. Guigemar's rest between the beautiful sheets has, however, placed him in an advantageous position: the boat has sailed him to the port where he will meet the lady who can heal him. So, while the *chemise* used as a bandage is an entirely vain attempt to heal the wound, sleeping enveloped in the sheets advances Guigemar's healing. This cloth, along with the magic ship itself, performs the function of physically transporting Guigemar to where he needs to be. Here, the cloth's function is entirely extraordinary while nonetheless seeming ordinary, for nothing is more normal than sheets on a bed. Marie has found a device for transporting her knight to where he must go that in no way shocks the reader but extends and deepens her use of clothing, gradually sustaining the clothing metaphor that she established at the very beginning of the *lai*.

However, whereas the *chemise* used as a bandage and the rest enjoyed between the beautiful sheets have both been ineffective, the ship has brought Guigemar to the port of the lady who will heal his wound. When the ship carrying Guigemar arrives in the harbor beside the lady's prison tower, the lady and her attendant go to meet it. The lady is too fearful to go aboard, so her attendant, her niece, must do so. The young lady removes her mantle when she boards the ship where Guigemar is resting (vss. 277–80). This action indicates the young maiden's peaceful, good intentions as she goes to meet whoever is waiting aboard. She removes a layer of protection from around her body to demonstrate her openness, her fearlessness, and her trust in the good intentions of whoever is on board. Not only does her action represent her attitude in boarding, it also announces the intimacy that Guigemar will enjoy in the company of this maiden and her mistress. The two women will make good on this implicit promise to Guigemar through the maiden's simple act of removing her mantle: they will take him into their private realm. Thus this undressing act illustrates her attitude of friendliness and deference while at the same time foreshadowing the intimacy between Guigemar and the lady. The undressing act also inversely mirrors the two prior wound dressings and therefore formally reverses Guigemar's inability to heal his wound, for the maiden brings him into contact with her lady, his healer. The young maiden will even lend him her bed while her lady nurses him back to health:

> En bacins d'or ewe aporterent,
> Sa plaie e sa quisse laverent;
> A un bel drap de cheisil blanc
> Li osterent entur le sanc;
> Puis l'unt estreitement bendé
> Mut le tienent en grant chierté
>
> (vss. 369–74)

> [In a golden basin they brought water, his wound and his thigh they washed; with a beautiful piece of white linen, they removed the blood then they bound it tightly, treating him with very great care.]

Guigemar has at last found the woman who can earn his love, thereby healing his wound; she becomes his lover. Jacques Ribard has remarked that the choice of dressing for the wound, "cheisil blanc," makes reference to the clothes worn at a baptism, which would mean that Guigemar is undergoing a similar rite of passage (138). He is being "baptized" into the realm of love. At this point in the text, cloth has become instrumental, finally healing Guigemar's wound.[28]

Unlike prior attempts to dress his wound, this dressing act involves the woman he loves, and therefore it has the curative powers necessary for healing. The hind made it clear that only one person would be capable of successfully dressing his wound, and this exclusivity will immediately appear a second time, doubled. One day the lady has a premonition that they will soon be caught, so she asks Guigemar for an oath.

> "Amis, de ceo m'aseürez!
> Vostre chemise me livrez;
> El pan desuz ferai un plait:
> Cungié vus doins, u ke ceo seit,
> D'amer cele kil defferat
> E ki despleier le savrat."
>
> (vss. 557–62)

> ["Lover, of this assure me! Give me your *chemise*; I'll make a knot in the side: I'll give you leave to love the woman, whoever she is, who can untie this knot."]

She forms a knot in Guigemar's *chemise* that only she can untie, and he places a *ceinture* around her waist that only he can unfasten.

---

28. Pickens has noted a similar progression in the text but focuses instead solely upon the wound and its centrality to the hero's passage through "stages representing his growing consciousness of his identity as a man. The stages of his coming to consciousness are indicated by ever more expansive reiterations of symbolic themes" ("Thematic Structure" 330). The stages to which Pickens refers are identical to the clothing stages that I outline.

> Le plet i fet en teu mesure,
> Nule femme nel deffereit,
> Si force u cutel n'i meteit.
> La chemise li dune e rent.
> Il la receit par tel covent
> Qu'el le face seür de li;
> Par une ceinture autresi,
> Dunt a sa char nue le ceint,
> Par mi le flanc aukes l'estreint:
> Ki la bucle purrat ovrir
> Sanz depescier e sanz partir,
> Il li prie que celui aint.
>
> (vss. 564–75)

[She made the knot in such a way that no woman could untie it without using scissors or a knife. She gave him back the *chemise*. He received it on the condition that she make a similar pledge to him; by means of a *ceinture* upon her naked flesh he cinched her, tightened it also around her sides: whoever could open the buckle without breaking or severing it, he would ask her to love that man.]

The mutual oaths manifest as representational undressing acts. Before either of the lovers may open him- or herself up to accepting love from another, a clothing obstacle must be overcome. In this way, their clothing is a metonymical representation of the two lovers, who render themselves unattainable to the outside world, at least with regard to love. These complementary undressing acts are just as exclusive as the wound dressing had been, and it is also reciprocal, as is their love.

Later that very day, the husband's chamberlain does indeed see the two together through the window. The husband comes to his wife's chamber with three of his men and, finding the knight with his wife, orders him killed. A scene ensues in which Guigemar defends himself by warding off his would-be attackers with "Une grosse perche de sap / U suleient pendre li drap" (a thick rod of fir where they hung clothes [to dry]) (vss. 595–96). His use of an instrument for drying clothes, that is, an instrument to make them wearable again, to ward off his attackers is what saves his life. Marie's specification here of the device used by Guigemar has a dual function: it divides the text into two parts and reflects the actions immediately before and after this division. In the same way that the rod restores clothing to its normal function, the lady's care has restored Guigemar to his normal level of functioning—it has healed him. Also, the husband's discovery of the two sends Guigemar away, returning the lady to the solitude, her normal situation, that the husband desires.

After this episode, Guigemar's ship carries him to his home, where he is restored to power over his lands. His people begin to press him again to take a wife, but this time, Guigemar has a foolproof way to refuse—the knot in his *chemise*. The text informs us that every woman in the land tried to untie the knot (vss. 652–54). Meanwhile, the ship has returned for the lady and has brought her into the domain of Mériaduc. He is surprised to find the lady aboard this mysterious ship in his harbor, but when he removes her from the boat, his rudeness in handling her is apparent: "Il la saisit par le mantel, / Od lui l'en meine en sun chastel" (He seized her by the mantle and led her with him into his castle) (vss. 705–6). Although the situation of this disembarkation scene bears a resemblance to the one in which Guigemar arrived as an unknown passenger aboard the mysterious ship, this scene of almost violent force contrasts greatly with the gracious welcome that Guigemar received from the lady and her attendant. The attendant removed her mantle before boarding to show her respect and good intentions to whoever was aboard; Mériaduc, by contrast, tries to force her into loving him, later even attempting to unfasten her *ceinture* after cutting open the laces of her *bliaut*: "Il la receit entre ses braz, / De sun bliaut trenche les laz: / La ceinture voleit ovrir, / Mes n'en poeit a chief venir" (He took her into his arms, and cut the laces of her *bliaut*: he wanted to untie the *ceinture*, but he was not able to do so) (vss. 737–40). Once he realizes his failure, he has all his knights attempt to unfasten the girdle as well.[29] Both lovers thus endure many unwanted attempts by others to gain their favor by force, but their clothing oath provides the means to resist the violence and protects their bodies and their love from violation at the hands of others.

Finally, the two lovers reunite and perform the recognition rite, thereby closing the narrative thread commenced as a result of the lady's premonition.

---

29. Bruckner underlines the importance of repetition in this episode: Meriaduc attempting to untie the *ceinture*, hearing the lady explain what the knot means, and remembering hearing of a knight nearby with a similar story. This repetition is "the key element that allows Meriaduc to discover the link already connecting the lovers. By marking the boundaries that set the couple apart from those who pursue them, repetition and variation each have a role to play in the sorting-out process, each are identified in turn with selection and substitution" (*Shaping* 166).

> Quant ele ot le comandement,
> Le pan de la chemise prent,
> Legierement le despleiat.
> Li chevaliers s'esmerveillat;
> Bien la conut, mes nequedent
> Nel poeit creire fermement.
> A li parlat en teu mesure:
> "Amie, duce creature,
> Estes vus ceo? Dites mei veir!
> Lessiez mei vostre cors veeir,
> La ceinture dunt jeo vus ceins."
> A ses costez li met ses meins,
> Si ad trovee la ceinture.
> "Bele, fet il, queil aventure
> Que jo vus ai issi trovee!"
>
> (vss. 809–23)

[When she heard his command, she took the tail of his *chemise* and easily untied it. The knight was astonished; he recognized her well, but nonetheless he could could not quite believe it. He spoke to her in this way: "Love, sweet creature, is that you? Tell me the truth! Let me see your body, and the *ceinture* I tied around you." He put his hands on her sides and found the *ceinture*. "Beautiful one, he said, what a (happy) adventure that I have found you here!"]

The two parallel references to exclusive clothing acts punctuate the main action of the *lai* and divide it into two corresponding parts. The hind's prophesy, functionally a prolepsis, opens a textual situation that must later be closed by Guigemar's encounter with the lady. In the meantime, Guigemar attempts, unsuccessfully, to heal his wounds twice. The lady's premonition, itself a sort of prophesy that also functions as a prolepsis, produces the need for the oath, a restrictive undressing act. This act, like Guigemar's two attempts to heal his wound without the necessary conditions having been met, textually appears twice before its successful completion (although both textual references represent many attempts by many people). Marie has, in this *lai*, used clothing at three distinct levels. She uses clothing to develop the character of Guigemar with his donning armor to become a knight; she uses it to motivate the plot by twice necessitating clothing acts by prophesy;

and she uses it to structure the narrative with two parallel threads mirroring each other. Moreover, the plot of this *lai* may be read through the clothing references: the clothing becomes a parallel. The *lai* itself may, in fact, be seen as a weaving together of textile references, and indeed, the narrative depends upon these references for its form and meaning. Guigemar and his lady find each other through the healing powers of cloth, then separate, only to rediscover each other later through their special vestimentary device. Their love, like the structure of the *lai*, takes on a woven form.

Guillaume d'Angleterre

In the hagiographic romance *Guillaume d'Angleterre* the clothing motif reflects and supplements the central themes of the text.[30] In the story, the king of England is ordered by God to abandon his worldly success and live poorly. When Guillaume follows this order, he loses his wife and his newborn twin sons, but through multiple trials and much time, the four are reunited and restored to their rightful place in society. Their success is made possible because they first humbled themselves to receive higher honor and then lived according to their inherent nobility, making them worthy of the honor. The author of the *Guillaume* uses clothing as part of a complex signifying system in which signs carry more than one meaning and infuse the work with a supple and dynamic quality that the reader must interpret. Although the use of clothing to represent metonymically (and uniformly) characters' states of being and attitudes is a common convention in medieval literature, the author of the *Guillaume* calls upon his readers to

---

30. The authorship of *Guillaume d'Angleterre* has been the topic of much debate for some time now. The author of this work signed it simply "Crestïens," leading some critics to believe that the writer is indeed Chrétien de Troyes. During the earlier stages of the debate, there were, at least in print, roughly equal numbers of scholars rejecting and supporting the *Guillaume* as the work of the Champenois poet. Those against attributing the work to Chrétien de Troyes, such as Jean Frappier, have largely deemed the composition to be literarily beneath such a refined poet and raconteur, while those in favor, including Paul R. Lonigan, have shown that the differences are not so large and derive mostly from the nature of the Guillaume legend itself and the tradition from which it sprang, namely, that of the saint's life. In recent years, however, somewhat fewer scholars find reasons to doubt that the author of such romances as *Le Chevalier de la charrete* and *Le Conte del Graal* wrote the *Guillaume*, and studies have begun appearing on the *Guillaume* that explore it as a literary work in and of itself rather than concentrating on various aspects of its construction in the hopes of determining its authorship. Interestingly, it is precisely this type of direct inquiry that has produced some of the most convincing arguments for attributing the *Guillaume* to Chrétien de Troyes. See, for example, Harry F. Williams's article "The Authorship of *Guillaume d'Angleterre*." Throughout my discussion, I refer to the author of this romance as Chrétien, since this name is the one used by the author to sign his work. By my use of this name, I do not mean in any way to argue for or against the identification of this author with Chrétien de Troyes.

interpret textual (and here, textile) signs in their unique context, that is, their meaning is contingent upon the context in which they occur. Yet the poet also inverts the signifying system that he has developed throughout the course of the romance, whereby meaning is context based, since the main character remains constant despite the varied contexts in which he finds himself and despite his continually changing appearance. Guillaume's tendency to create his contexts (as opposed to re-creating himself) is textually rendered by the fact that he becomes a seller of dyes. Lacy has convincingly proposed an interpretation of the poem in terms of instruction about "how to get ahead in the world" (*Craft* 121). He notes that, although the prologue of the poem conditions the reader for a text with a primarily religious message (like that of a saint's life), the tone immediately changes once the divine commandment has been heeded and Guillaume and his wife are reduced to a state of absolute poverty with nothing but the clothes on their backs (121). The rest of the work, he remarks, describes how the three separate groups of characters (consisting of Guillaume himself; then his wife, Gratienne; and finally their two sons) descend into poverty and subsequently ascend anew to material success (122). They accomplish this by exemplifying two guiding principles set forth in the text. As Lacy states: "First we are told that the person who humbles himself will be exalted (vs. 1024) and that one gives in order to receive (vss. 147–65). . . . The second of the work's principles or theses, a common one in medieval literature, is that *nature passe nourriture*; this . . . is applicable to all the characters, but especially the two sons" (122).

An obvious example of clothing reflecting the first of these principles (humility and generosity) at work is the motif of Guillaume's coat, which he destroys by cutting large strips out of the sides to provide cloth to swaddle his two infant sons. The scene is described tenderly and can leave no doubt that this act is one of generosity and love. When the first son is born,

> Li rois, qui l'enfant ot mont chier,
> Se panse ou lou pourra couchier,
> Lors a traite s'espee nue;
> D'une cote qu'il ot vestue
> A jus lou destre pan copé,
> S'i a l'anfant anvelopé
> Et jus a la terre l'a mis.
>
> (vss. 477–83)

[the king, who cherished the child greatly, wondered where he could lay him to sleep, so taking his naked sword, he cut the right side out of his *cote* and enveloped the child within it and lay him on the earth.]

And, when the second is born, the king reacts in the same way, providing for his sons:

> Et li rois de tant I escote
> Que l'autre pan ra de sa cote
> Tout jus a la terre trainchié,
> S'i l'anfant mis et couchié.
>
> (vss. 501–4)

[And the king did the same with the other side of his *cote*, cutting it to the ground, and lay it on the earth and put the child upon it.]

In this episode, the king has simultaneously shown humility and generosity. He has sacrificed his own clothing, his own appearance (he will soon be taken for a beggar by merchants—an event that precipitates the separation of the family), but in doing so, has provided for his sons but in a way that (without his knowledge, of course) goes well beyond their immediate needs. For it is through the pieces of cloth cut from the king's own coat that the reunion of the family will be sealed at the conclusion of the poem. The gift of this cloth, which must be seen as a great one, since we know that he left his castle with only the clothes on his back, exceeds any intentions of the king. This gift is so generous, in fact, that when his wife calls upon him to give more (to feed her), he can only offer his own flesh—he offers this willingly, but fortunately his wife rejects it. In addition, though the future significance of the pieces of cloth in no way negates his generosity, the cloth itself becomes a physical emblem, a sign of the rightful lineage of the two sons. The pieces of cloth are their birthrights, in both a literal and a figurative sense. They are the only physical manifestations of their relationship with the king and also represent the mechanism by which reunion, as well as restoration to their rightful place in society, is made possible.

Between the time of the sons' birth and the reunion that will follow, the pieces of cloth become painful reminders for the sons that they are not who they had previously believed themselves to be. After the king loses his two sons, they are taken in by two merchants, who raise them and later try to persuade them to enter the merchants' trades. When the two reject trade, the merchants reveal to them (separately) the truth of the sons' childhood: that they were found abandoned, wrapped in the pieces of cloth, Marin aboard a ship and Lovel being carried by a wolf.

This revelation is carried out in a hateful and angry way by the merchants, first by Fauchiers, the adoptive father of Marin:

> Tant s'est danz Fourchiers eschaufez
> Seur Marin, qui vers lui s'orgueillie
> Ne ne viaut rien feire qu'il vueillie,
> Si l'apela garçon frarin,
> Et dist qu'an l'apela Marin
> Pour ce que une garce remeise
> Ou viez pan d'une cote esrese
> L'ot mis sor mer droit a l'issue
> D'une forest de Giernemue,
> Si fu an un batel trovez.
> Eur s'est li vileins esprovez,
> Eur a sa nature provee,
> Eur avez la sausse trovee
> Qui est feite d'escamonie.
> Laingue de vilein soit honie!
> Houniz soit ses cuers et sa boiche!
> Quant Marins oÿ le reproiche,
> Grant honte en ot et grant angoisee,
> Et li vileins le bat et roisse,
> Come fel et de put asfeire,
> Et par esnui et par contreire
> Court a sa huiche, si a pris
> Lou pan que il i avoit mis,
> Si l'aporte, puis si li rant.
> Marins mont volantiers lou prant,
> Si l'a souz sa chape bouté,
> Estroitement anvelopé
>
> (vss. 1466–92)

[Fauchiers became so angry with Marin, who stood up to him and would not do his will, that he called the boy a loser. He told him he called him Marin because a young servant girl had wrapped an old piece of a *cote* around him and placed him on the sea outside the forest of Yarmouth, and he had found him in a boat. Thus the lowborn has shown himself, proven his nature. Now you see the sauce made from scammony. May the lowborn's tongue be shamed! Shamed be his heart and his mouth! When Marin heard the reproach, he was greatly ashamed and in anguish, and the lowborn beat and battered him, like a scoundrel would do. He ran to his chest and pulled out the piece of cloth he had put there, and he brought it and gave it back to him. Marin took it voluntarily and hid it under his cloak, tightly wrapped.]

This passage serves as a contrast between the way in which the sons (in this case Marin) received the pieces of cloth from their true father and the way in which it was returned to them by their adoptive fathers. Unlike Guillaume, who demonstrated compassion when he bestowed his gift on his sons, the merchant uses his knowledge about the discovery of the boy in such conditions to injure him. He also maligns the piece of cloth by referring to it as threadbare (*esrie*), assuming that it could have been only a servant girl (someone dramatically lower on the social scale than the merchant himself) who left the boy there. When he throws the cloth at Marin, he is literally throwing the latter's past up at him, and doing so in the most injurious way he can find. The young man leaves his adoptive father's house shocked and ashamed at what he has just learned, believing himself to be of low station and knowing nothing about his heritage.

While the picture that Fourchiers paints of the young man's past is clearly derogatory, the account does not conceal the position taken by the narrator. The latter is unequivocally condemning the merchant for his very nature: he is drawing a contrast between the nature of Marin, whom the reader knows to be noble, and the nature of the merchant, who shows himself to be base and shameful (in case the reader had any doubt). Through the act of returning the piece of cloth to Marin, itself the physical manifestation of the revelation he makes, Fourchiers shows his true nature and drives the youth away from his adoptive home. The surrendering of the cloth reflects the revealing of the past and therefore becomes a motivating and necessary element which occasions the youth's return to his noble station (in the interim, his becoming a knight in the service of the king of Quatenasse) and places him firmly on the path finally leading to the recovery of his place among royalty (his return to England with his family).

In the meantime, Lovel has had an equally rude awakening at the hands of his adoptive father, Goncelins; Lovel, "Que batu ot come un gaignon / Dans Goncelins et traïné" (who had been beaten like a mongrel by Goncelins, then dragged) (vss. 1500–1501), was told the truth about his origins:

> Et mont vilmant ot ramponé
> Dou pis que dire li savoit:
> Si com au lou tolu l'avoit,
> Et si com il estoit lïez
> Ou viez pan d'une cote viez.
> Li vileins tost li reproicha,
> Come cil que male boiche a,
> Et dit e feit au plus qu'il peut,
> Si com de nature li meut.
> Toutevoie tant de bien fist,
> Sanz ce que garde ne s'an prist
> N'a bien feire n'i antandi,
> Qu'il a l'anfant lou pan randi
> Ou anvelopé lou trova.
>
> (vss. 1502–15)

[and very vilely insulted in the worst way he knew how: and he had taken him from a wolf, wrapped up in an old piece of an old *cote*. The lowborn reproached him for all of this in as foul a way as possible, and he said and did all he could as his nature dictated. Nevertheless, he did a good thing, without understanding it, without realizing or meaning to, when he returned to the child the cloth in which he had been enveloped.]

For a second time, the reader sees the merchants throw insults at the sons and abuse them physically. However, Goncelins will later consider his actions (at the prompting of his charge's tears and gracious acknowledgment of the merchant's generosity in raising him) and will insist on equipping Lovel with what he needs to go out into the world. Here again, a father figure gives him the gift of clothing (among other things): "Cil li done une chape buire / Et heuses et esperons viez" (He gave him a sackcloth cloak and boots and old spurs) (vss. 1618–19). This gift certainly provides Lovel with what he needs as he departs and makes his way in the world, but when compared with the one made by his real father so long ago, it appears far less generous and ultimately less valuable. In the first place, the merchant does not truly give of his own accord: he realizes that Lovel needs specific things, but he is quick to point out how his providing them is not entirely to his liking: "Te donrai je, mais mont m'esnuie" (I will give them to you, but it bothers me greatly) (vs. 1611). This image of fatherly love truly pales in comparison with the one we have of Guillaume cutting apart his own coat for the well-being of his newborn sons and to his own detriment. Lovel's needs are met by the merchant only after he is shamed into it by the boy's acknowledgment, and even then the gift is accompanied by the merchant's statement of how much it will cost him. In contrast, the king immediately recognized the needs of his sons and quickly took of himself whatever was necessary, without a thought for the personal cost.

The reason for this difference, as the poet tells us in his discussion of nature versus nurture, is that the king has an inherently noble and gracious nature that will always surpass that of the merchant. This fact becomes clear when the poet reveals that the sons have maintained their nobility, their nature, despite being raised by the merchants. The youths do not wish to follow in the footsteps of the men who raised them as sons, for no other reason than that they are adhering to what is in their nature. Once they leave their former homes, the youths are taken in by the king of Quatenasse and are, by his orders, trained in the arts that are appropriate for men of noble condition: hunting and hawking. Furthermore, when they meet their true father again, they are dressed as knights. In the fictional universe developed by our poet, if these youths who were raised by merchants and of unknown birth had been anything less than noble, they would not have been capable of promoting themselves so well. The text states that the king of Quatenasse provided them all the accouterments appropriate for men of noble rank (vss. 2712–16). The sons have thus gone from being swaddled in the threadbare remnants of a coat to wearing armor and sumptuous clothes fit for a knight. This evolution in vestimentary condition signifies in every sense a progression in social condition. They have transcended the condition of poverty at their birth, the poet tells us, first and foremost because their nature has won out over their upbringing: they are noble in nature and this fact is rewarded in the world. *Nature passe nourriture*.

Finally, the time arrives when Guillaume reaps the benefit of what he has sown: he begins to receive after having given so much, begins to be exalted after having humbled himself to such an extent. First, he is reunited with his wife, who is now the lady of a large domain. When the two are in each other's presence for the first time in twenty-four years, he does not at first recognize her, because she is wearing a veil. It is through the recognition of a ring that she had given to her husband that the queen realizes the identity of this man standing before her. This episode is the first of two times when recognition occurs because of a vestimentary gift given years earlier. Later, while Guillaume is hunting in the woods outside Gratienne's castle, he trespasses on the land of the king of Quatenasse and comes face to face with his own sons. At this moment, all is recounted and recognition is possible, but Guillaume asks his sons to prove their true identities by producing the pieces of cloth. When they do so, their joy is immediate:

> De rien ne vostrent samblant feire
> Jusqu'il orent les pans veuz;
> Li rois les a bien queneüz
> Et dist por voir que ce sont il,
> Lors li font joie andui si fil.
> Li rois, que molt s'an esjot,
> Les rebaise et si les conjot,
> Si font tuit troi tel joie ansamble
> Que li ostes dist qu'il resamble
> Que li aient borse trovee.
>
> (vss. 2858–67)

[They had the desire to do nothing besides see the pieces of cloth; the king recognized them easily and said that truly they were his sons, and the sons rejoiced. The king, who rejoiced greatly, kissed and hugged them, and joy was so strong among them that one would say they had found a purse.]

The comparison that the poet makes at the end of this passage is an important one because it demonstrates the fact that the discovery, or recovery, of the king's sons is indeed a treasure for the king. It represents the fulfilling of the "give in order to receive" principle. The king gave all he had to give to his two newborn sons: he gave them pieces of his coat, and he endowed them with a noble nature. The pieces of cloth have served the sons well: at the very beginning of their lives, the cloth provided clothing; later, it precipitated their flight from the merchant's way of life; and, in the end, it reunites them with their family and proves once and for all that their nobility of nature indeed results from nobility of birth.

The character of the sons, then, illustrates the principle that nature is stronger than nurture, their return to their rightful place indicated by their position relative to a piece of cloth in which their father wrapped them at birth. The plight of the father, however, illustrates the principle of being well rewarded for giving and for humbling oneself, although it must also be noted that Guillaume's success as a merchant is surely attributable to his personal worth, thus his nature. As for the merchants, they too are ultimately rewarded for what they have given. They did, after all, raise the two young princes. Upon being reunited with her husband and sons, Gratienne wishes to bestow upon the two merchants gifts of clothing. The clothes are very valuable, and the merchants delight in contemplating how much money they will receive in selling them. Gratienne insists that the merchants wear the clothes she has given them, and to ensure that they do so, she buys the clothes back from them. She immediately returns the clothes to the two merchants and they wear them. The poet comments on the appearance of the two merchants sporting their new clothes:

> Lors se vestent des robes chieres;
> Lor contenances et lor chieres
> Furent si folles et si nices
> Que des mantiaus et des pelices
> Samble qu'an lor ahust presté.
>
> (vss. 3205–9)

[When they donned their new expensive outfits, their appearances and expressions were so silly and so foolish that the mantles and the fur-lined garments seemed that they had been loaned to them.]

In short, they look ridiculous. Their clothes are not in accordance with their station, not because they are not wealthy—Gratienne has promised them that they will want for nothing—but because they are not noble. Their nature, which is in no way comparable with that of Guillaume and his family, cannot be altered even with the nurturing that Gratienne promises them. This is never clearer than when they want to exploit the clothes for their commercial value: these men are merchants, and they will never be anything else. In the same way that humble surroundings could not prevent the manifestation of the inherent nobility of Marin and Lovel, Fourchiers and Goncelins will never be capable of transcending their materialistic and bourgeois nature to assimilate to the aristocratic surroundings that they now occupy. The characters of the merchants, reflected here in their attitude toward the clothes, therefore also illustrate the principle that *nature passe nourriture*.

In addition to the poet's use of clothing to reflect the central themes of the work as these themes are developing, there are also instances in which the poet uses clothing or an item closely related to clothing (a ring, for example) to accentuate more localized thematic features within the poem. One example of this occurs when Gratienne first comes aboard Guillaume's ship to collect the port tax by laying claim to the object of her choosing. She is wearing a veil that prevents Guillaume from recognizing her even as she asks about objects whose personal value to him only his wife could understand. Here, the clothing object alters the appearance of the person wearing it, delaying recognition on the part of the other character, and permitting this part of the story to proceed at a slower pace.

Guillaume himself has had some experience with appearance-changing substances. When he arrives upon Gratienne's shore, he is returning from a merchant trip to England, his former kingdom. During his sojourn there, his former subjects recognize in him a strong resemblance with their long-lost king Guillaume. The reigning king, Guillaume's nephew, comes to speak with this man and is so impressed with him that he offers him a job as his seneschal. Guillaume refuses, preferring to continue his trade, but he does inform himself about the reception he would receive if he returned as king. When Guillaume's nephew asks the king his name, the latter responds:

> "Sire, j'ai nom Gui de Galvaide,
> Ou j'ai assez garance et gaide
> Et alun et bresil et gregne,
> Dom je tieng mes dras et ma legne."
>
> (vss. 2225–28)

["Sire, my name is Will of Galway, where I have plenty of madder and woad and alum and brazil nut and kermes with which I dye my silk and my wool."]

Guillaume sells dyes! He sells a substance that changes the color of clothing, a substance that alters appearances.[31] Here is the king, essentially recognized by

---

31. Eamon asserts that the process of dyeing is, for the medieval mind, inherently linked to transformation, especially to alchemical transmutations. He explains that ancient alchemists, whose works were highly influential in the Middle Ages and who were "impressed by the observation that

the people, but claiming to be something that he is not—a merchant—and claiming not to be something that he is, the king. However, what he claims to sell is a substance whose only function is to alter appearances, even deceive the eye. Given the circumstances, it is hardly possible that he should be anything but a person peddling the power to change. He began as a king, an aristocratic man born into a position of wealth, power, and prestige. He became a pauper by giving away all his possessions, his crown, and his throne. He became a father, and soon after, a beggar, but lost the three people who were dearest to him. He became the servant to a merchant to whom he was remarkably loyal and who saw in him the potential to become something greater. He became a merchant, and a very rich one at that. Finally, in quick succession, he once again became a husband, a father, and a king. Through all of his incarnations, however, Guillaume retains the one thing that he could never lose—his noble nature.

Chrétien's use of clothing in this poem conforms to the notion of "multivalent symbols" (Williams 22). In such a system, certain signs carry more than one meaning and infuse the work with a supple and dynamic quality that the reader must interpret. This is the case with Guillaume's coat: the coat of a king, it becomes torn and ragged, but the reader cannot forget that the reason for this wear is that Guillaume is following divine prescriptions. When the coat is cut to shreds, it is for distinctly noble, generous reasons—the newborn infants need clothing. Thus, Guillaume's coat comes to signify different things in different contexts. The pieces of cloth that remain of the coat also undergo transformations: first, they are protection and the only material thing their father can offer his sons; then, at the hands of the overly materialistic merchants, they become signs of shame; finally, they signify restored identity by presenting proof. Acts may also be classified in this system of multivalent signs: when Guillaume gives his sons the pieces of cloth, he does so selflessly, nobly; yet the same act carried out by the merchant is seen by the merchant only in terms of his own loss. The third father figure to give Marin and Lovel gifts of clothing is the king of Quatenasse, and he does so specifically because he recognizes their inherent nobility. The act of giving clothing, then, assumes different significance when carried

---

certain dyestuffs could completely transform the outward appearance of fabrics, believed they had discovered the secret of the transmutation of all matter" (31). This belief has wide-ranging implications for the present study because it underlines the importance of dyestuffs in their capacity for transformation of appearance, especially considering the extent to which, for the medieval mind, the changing of outward appearance equated with a more fundamental change. Guillaume, in peddling dyes, peddles transformation.

out in different contexts, by different characters. However, the interpretation of this act seems to fall along class lines: noble characters imbue the act with their nobility, as a way to express it or recognize it, while the merchants see it as a purely material exchange in which they either lose or gain (as when they wish to sell the clothes given them by Gratienne). Finally, we cannot ignore Guillaume's ability to remain constant despite changes: the king takes on a multitude of appearances and roles, but he is always noble. In this case, the poet inverts the system in which a sign must be interpreted through its context: here, the contexts must be interpreted based on its sign. The man does not re-create himself, he creates his contexts: he is the seller of dyes.

If, as I have argued throughout this study, the clothing signifying system used by the writers of twelfth-century romance is an open, generative one, then it follows that all the features of romance that it touches are also infused with this same quality, whether those features are structural, thematic, or narrative. The dynamism is thus inscribed into the meaning of the romance as a whole. The expansive and discursive quality of the literary expression of romance is crucial to that expression because it reflects the movement and changes of the society of the period and in which the audience found itself. The writers of romance were clearly speaking to their times as they wrote and were moreover doing so in remarkably effective ways. Their use of the clothing signifying system both to structure their works and to elaborate their major themes, also a structuring process, attests to their capability of producing an expression of rich, often contingent meaning, imbued with all the ambivalence, arbitrariness, and ambiguity that were becoming increasingly present in their world. The ability among the most talented writers of the day to exploit clothing to its fullest representational potential, namely, as a parallel narrative, provides overwhelming evidence of the consciousness of their art and their attention to narrative detail. The use of the clothing signifying system to create new meanings from existing material is part and parcel of a major tenet of the prevailing literary aesthetic; that is, it is a component of the *conjointure* to which Chrétien refers. This art of composition is thus inherently dynamic, and it is the clothing system, among other features, that guarantees and expresses its dynamism. Furthermore, just as *conjointure* contributes to and has effects at all levels of the narrative, so does the clothing signifying system as it serves many different narrative purposes and has multiple expressions with varied, contingent meanings.

CONCLUSION

THAT THE TEXTUAL FEATURES OF ROMANCE include a great many textile elements is clear. The medieval art of composition, or *conjointure*, is primarily a technique of weaving a narrative, both from a methodological perspective and from an aesthetic perspective, since writers sought to choose among many possible elements those that would please and regale their audience. The clothing signifying system, as part of *conjointure*, is likewise a major component of romance at many different narrative levels, and the principal reason for its use must be traced to the importance placed on the vestimentary code and appearance by its noble audience. The shifting concerns of this class are indicative of and cause for changing perspectives, changing mentalities. Representation is in the process of moving from a fixed, static state, a symbolic state, toward a freer, more dynamic expressive system exemplified by the sign. One of the mechanisms that writers use to portray this changing world is the complex clothing signifying system that they fashion from the vestimentary code and exploit to its fullest representational potential.

The shift in representation perhaps begins with a change in the art of description and involves a movement away from the established, codified, and static "types" of character description, which consistently includes clothing description, toward more complicated, even problematic descriptions that inscribe ambivalence into both the characterization and the text. Such ambivalence takes different forms: sexual, gender, class, and economic or material ambivalence. The resulting descriptions are dynamic and help elaborate character identity, whether social or personal. This dynamism extends into the very material nature of clothing: its capacity to conceal as much as it reveals. Disguise is a kind of normalized subversion of the vestimentary code that, in fact, undermines it both because it occurs frequently and almost always successfully in courtly literature, and because it represents a dramatic subversion of the identity that clothing helps elaborate. This potential for subversion within the code actually provides a point of entry for more widespread manipulation of it. The writers exploit this feature of the code whenever it suits their narrative needs to do so.

Moreover, they also manipulate the vestimentary code in much more fundamental ways, with great impact on it as well as on the process of signification. The variety of different types of manipulation may be seen along a continuum, progressing from the least invasive to the most dramatic. First, writers may choose to duplicate the code but give it different conventions, a process that incurs changes only at the level of the signifier. Such changes involve the use of a parallel semiotic system in which different meanings are arbitrarily assigned to a signifier, as in the case of Tristan's ring, which unequivocally identifies him to Yseut but only to her, the ring having no special meaning for any other character.

Second, writers may decide to alter the process of signification through changes either in the linguistic community or in the context in which clothing references appear. Community-based meanings for signifiers involve those instances in which only certain members of a linguistic community are capable of deciphering the meaning of a signifier, as in the case in *Guillaume d'Angleterre* when the pieces of cloth cut from the king's coat identify the two youths as Guillaume's sons but only to Guillaume himself. Guillaume is the only member of that linguistic community for whom the pieces of cloth have their real and true meaning. Changes to context, by contrast, may occur at several interrelated levels: character, theme, plot, or narrative. All these levels provide contexts that may effect the meaning of a single clothing signifier. In other words, a clothing act may have a different meaning when viewed in light of character motivation than the meaning it has when viewed in light of plot motivation or in narrative context. For example, when Jocasta and her daughters dress themselves well and beautifully to go before Polyneices to entreat him to end the war with his brother, their attempt fails, but their action instead enhances Antigone's beauty and precipitates Parthenopeus's falling in love with her, resulting in a symmetry in the narrative. In this case, the apparent failure of the act in the context of character motivation is countered by its significance with regard to the action it provokes and the ensuing narrative symmetry in the work. Thus the act's deeper meaning may be determined only in light of these additional contexts.

Finally, there exists the possibility of code absence. These are situations in which clothing signifiers are otherwise completely indecipherable or confused, as when Lancelot wears different armor to the tournament, but continue to have meaning for another character who reads beyond the signifier, as does Guenevere when she recognizes her lover despite his unknown armor. Although this last position on the continuum of manipulation is certainly the most extreme and most dramatic, all manipulations of the vestimentary code actually help transform it. Taken together, their effect on it is, in fact, so significant that it transcends its own conventions of a strict and single connection between form and meaning. The code thus becomes a true signifying system with the potential, most often realized in these courtly works, to create rather than simply reiterate predetermined, fixed meanings.

Whereas, with the emergence of the clothing signifying system, clothing descriptions become increasingly dynamic, clothing acts, by their very nature as alterations of appearance, provide perhaps the most compelling examples of this dynamism. Even the most normative acts, the giving of clothing in the context of a gift economy, potentially change characters' identities, social and sometimes personal, and attest to an increasing fluidity within the code. Moreover, there are instances in which gifts possess a surplus of meaning that derives from their occurrence in several different layers of context at once and that often defy the conventions of gift-giving as they are inscribed in the gift economy. The changing relationship of form to meaning, reflected in the transition from symbol to sign occurring in the larger representational system, as discussed earlier, is perhaps the most salient characteristic of the developing clothing signifying system. In this system, not only must descriptions and acts be interpreted rather than simply read as unproblematic symbols, but they may also have multiple and varying meanings depending upon the context or narrative level in which they are considered. In other words, a single clothing act may have several different but complementary meanings when viewed from different perspectives. The writer of romance, then, pushes the codified connection between signifier and signified to its limits and often beyond them to create new meanings for established clothing referents and even to create, through the total inversion of convention, new forms for preexisting ideas.

The depiction of making cloth or clothing gives writers the occasion to represent the very process in which they are engaged: a fashioning of materials into meanings, a fashioning of a code into a signifying system. These processes involve the transference of meaning through established clothing norms but are not limited to the narrowness of the codified, symbolic relationship between form and meaning. Rather, in both the process of cloth(es)-making and that of making a signifying system, signifiers may be imbued with additional, unconventional, and often very specific and peculiar meanings, and the interplay between signifier and signified itself may take on provocative new meanings as well. The increased capacity for signification and flexibility that accompanies the metaphoric inscription of the writer's process onto the represented universe allows further opportunities for the integration of additional ambivalence into the text. Certainly Chrétien's depiction of the noble yet degraded *tisseuses* both distorts the normative practices of clothes-making and subsequently resolves the tension and even shock that such an image provokes, while nonetheless inscribing a degree of economic and class ambiguity despite the restoration at the end of the episode. Chrétien portrays the subversion of the ladies' nobility through their forced economic activity and their lamentable state and then repairs it through Yvain's liberation of them, but the damage has been done to the code's conventions, forcing it to accommodate increased flexibility and less static expression. The vestimentary code at its most creative, that is, the codified behavior and meaning of making clothes, thus becomes, in romance, a self-reflexive and highly interpretive vehicle to depict the craft of the writers.

Significantly, the representation of the destruction of clothing does not evoke or equate with the destruction of the code but instead the destruction of its absoluteness. An extraordinary illustration of this phenomenon occurs in Chrétien's *Lancelot* during the complex scene of the false rape in which the partial destruction of the lady's clothing cannot fundamentally mean what it might in other circumstances—dishonoring her—but instead has the opposing and misplaced effect of further honoring Lancelot, all the while powerfully reasserting the theme that honoring and dishonoring are inverted in this romance. But just as the *tisseuses* scene in *Yvain* inscribes ambivalence into the code, so this inverted dishonorable destruction imbues both ambiguity and arbitrariness into it. Moreover, just as the destruction of the lady's garment was partial and ultimately not dishonoring, so too this transgression of convention does not, in fact, destroy the code but instead assists in its expansion. Indeed, just as destroyed or compromised clothing is also reinscribed into the system, the vestimentary code itself is subsumed by the signifying system. Destruction of clothing, then, may in essence be as creative a process as the making of clothing.

The dynamism of the clothing signifying system does not occur merely at the level of the signifier, the image, or the act but touches all levels of the narrative, sometimes even producing a parallel vestimentary narrative to be read through the clothing references of a text. The structure of a work, along with all the thematic and narrative elements that produce it, is therefore imbued with this dynamism. Clothing instances often form cycles or narrative threads that sometimes elaborate and reinforce the major themes of a work, sometimes motivate the plot through the precipitation of further actions. Such instances are important structuring devices for the romance, frequently providing structure through analogical composition, whether formal or thematic analogy. Thematic elaboration, intricately related to structure in the courtly literature of the twelfth century, is also well served by the use of the clothing signifying system. In much the same way that writers of romance use clothing to elucidate character, they often have recourse to vestimentary imagery and the depiction of clothing acts to develop thematic content across large expanses of text in order to link various and otherwise unconnected episodes to one another. This type of textual coherence derives not from formal unity but from thematic relatedness and is emblematic of the romance genre of this period. It is precisely this kind of structure that gives form and meaning to complex textile works such as tapestry, as Vinaver noted (*Form* 10).

In romance, text and textile are, in fact, indissociable. Indeed, the relationship between the two is not simply metaphorical but rather actually describes the relationship between the thematic and the formal, between the actions of the characters within the text and the process of composition in which the writers engage to create the text. The vestimentary signifying system, with its contingent meanings that are dependent upon context and its signifier whose relationship to adjacent signifiers is fluid, could easily be compared to the fibers of cloth, bound and twisted together, woven into new forms, dyed with the color of specific meanings, and made into the fabric of fiction. The manipulation of this fabric, both a manual and a material act, produces ever changing, ever dynamic surfaces. These surfaces form an impression that, like the very weave of cloth, both reveals and conceals its own threads, its own wearer, and its own constituents at different points and in different ways. Romance, with its propensity for detailed descriptions of and many acts involving clothing, is a more dynamic genre as a whole for having dressed itself in the changing fabric of the society in which it was generated, revealing itself, concealing itself, and playing with the system until that system becomes material in the text, material in the world. The art of romance, Chrétien's *molt bele conjointure*, is an art of weaving, and the clothing signifying system that the practitioners of this art created is a crucial and beautiful feature of that weave.

BIBLIOGRAPHY

PRIMARY SOURCES

Amadas et Ydoine. Ed. John R. Reinhard. Paris: Champion, 1974.
Bernard of Clairvaux. *The Letters of St. Bernard of Clairvaux*. Trans. Bruno Scott James. London: Burns and Oates, 1953.
Béroul. *Le Roman de Tristran*. Ed. and trans. Norris J. Lacy. New York: Garland, 1989.
———. *Le Roman de Tristan: Poème du XIIe siècle*. Ed. Ernest Muret. Paris: Champion, 1982.
La Chanson de Roland. Ed. Joseph J. Duggan et al. Turnhout: Brepols, 2005.
Chrétien. *Guillaume d'Angleterre*. Ed. A. J. Holden. Geneva: Droz, 1988.
Chrétien de Troyes. *Le Chevalier au lion (Yvain)*. Ed. Mario Roques. Paris: Champion, 1982.
———. *Le Chevalier de la charrette (Lancelot)*. Ed. Jean Frappier. Paris: Champion, 1962.
———. *Cligés*. Ed. Alexandre Micha. Paris: Champion, 1982.
———. *Erec et Enide*. Ed. Mario Roques. Paris: Champion, 1966.
———. *Erec et Enide*. Ed. and trans. Carleton W. Carroll. New York: Garland, 1987.
———. *Lancelot, or The Knight of the Cart*. Ed. and trans. William W. Kibler. New York: Garland, 1981.
———. *Perceval (Le Conte du Graal)*. Ed. Keith Busby. Tübingen: M. Niemeyer, 1993.
———. *Philomena: Conte raconté d'après Ovide*. Ed. C. de Boer. Paris: Librairie Paul Geuthner, 1909.
———. *The Story of the Grail (Li Contes del Graal), or Perceval*. Ed. and trans. Rupert T. Pickens and William W. Kibler. New York: Garland, 1990.
Enéas: Roman du XIIe siècle. Ed. J.-J. Salverda de Grave. Paris: Champion, 1925.
Floire et Blancheflor. Ed. Margaret M. Pelan. Paris: Société d'Edition, 1956.
Gautier d'Arras. *Eracle*. Ed. Guy Raynaud de Lage. Paris: Champion, 1976.
———. *Ille et Galeron*. Ed. Yves Lefèvre. Paris: Champion, 1988.
Geoffrey of Vinsauf. *Poetria Nova of Geoffrey of Vinsauf*. Trans. Margaret F. Nims. Toronto: Pontifical Institute of Mediaeval Studies, 1967.
Guillaume de Lorris and Jean de Meun. *Le Roman de la rose*. Ed. Daniel Poirion. Paris: Garnier-Flammarion, 1974.
Heldris de Cournuälle. *Le Roman de Silence*. Ed. Lewis Thorpe. Cambridge: Heffer, 1972.
———. *Le Roman de Silence*. Ed. and trans. Sarah Roche-Mahdi. East Lansing: Colleagues Press, 1992.
Jaufre. Ed. Clovis Brunel. Paris: Société des Anciens Textes Français, 1943.

Macrobius. *The Saturnalia.* Trans. Percival Vaughan Davies. New York: Columbia University Press, 1969.
Marie de France. *Les Lais de Marie de France.* Ed. Jean Rychner. Paris: Champion, 1983.
Matthew of Vendôme. *The Art of Versification.* Trans. Aubrey E. Galyon. Ames: Iowa State University Press, 1980.
Narcisus: Poème du XIIe siècle. Ed. M. M. Pelan and N. C. W. Spence. Paris: Les Belles Lettres, 1964.
Piramus et Tisbé: Poème du XIIe siècle. Ed. C. de Boer. Paris: Champion, 1921.
La Queste del Saint Graal. Ed. Albert Pauphilet. Paris: Champion, 1984.
Renart, Jean. *Le Roman de la rose, ou de Guillaume de Dole.* Ed. Félix Lecoy. Paris: Champion, 1966.
Renaut de Bâgé. *Le Bel Inconnu: Roman d'aventures.* Ed. G. Perrie Williams. Paris: Champion, 1929.
———. *Le Bel Inconnu.* Ed. Karen Fresco. Trans. Colleen P. Donagher. New York: Garland, 1992.
Le Roman de Thèbes. Ed. Guy Raynaud de Lage. Paris: Champion, 1966.
Thomas. *The Romance of Horn.* 2 vols. Ed. Mildred K. Pope. Oxford: Anglo-Norman Text Society, 1955–1964.
Thomas of England. *Le Roman de Tristan: Poème du XIIe siècle.* Ed. Joseph Bédier, 1902.
———. *Tristran.* Ed. and trans. Stewart Gregory. New York: Garland, 1991.

SECONDARY SOURCES

Abbott, Reginald. "What Becomes a Legend Most? Fur in the Medieval Romance." *Dress* 21 (1994): 4–16.
Adams, Alison. "The Shape of Arthurian Verse Romance (to 1300)." *The Legacy of Chrétien de Troyes.* Vol. 1. Ed. Norris J. Lacy, Douglas Kelly, and Keith Busby. Amsterdam: Rodopi, 1987. 141–65.
Anquetil, Jacques. *Silk.* Paris: Flammarion, 1995.
Arthur, Ross G. Introduction. *Jaufre: An Occitan Arthurian Romance.* Trans. Ross G. Arthur. New York: Garland, 1992. ix–liii.
Auerbach, Erich. *Mimesis: The Representation of Reality in Western Literature.* Trans. Willard R. Trask. Princeton: Princeton University Press, 1953.
Badel, Pierre-Yves. *Introduction à la vie littéraire du Moyen Age.* Paris: Bordas, 1969.
Baldwin, John W. "The Capetian Court at Work Under Philip Augustus." *The Medieval Court in Europe.* Ed. Edward R. Haymes. Munich: Willem Fink, 1986. 71–91.
Baker, J. N. L. *Medieval Trade Routes.* London: Historical Association, 1938.
Barnard, Malcolm. *Fashion as Communication.* London: Routledge, 1996.
Barthes, Roland. *L'Aventure sémiotique.* Paris: Seuil, 1985.
———. *Système de la mode.* Paris: Seuil, 1967.
Baudrillard, Jean. *L'Échange symbolique et la mort.* Paris: Gallimard, 1976.
———. *Le Système des objets.* Paris: Gallimard, 1968.
Baumgartner, Emmanuèle. "Le Défi du 'chevalier rouge' dans *Perceval* et dans *Jaufré*." *Le Moyen Age* 83 (1977): 239–54.

Beazley, C. Raymond. "Medieval Trade and Trade Routes." *Geographical Teacher* 2 (1903–4): 114–21.
Bell, Quentin. *On Human Finery*. London: Hogarth, 1967.
Benkov, Edith Joyce. "The Naked Beast: Clothing and Humanity in *Bisclavret*." *Chimères* 19.2 (1988): 27–43.
Berger, Arthur Asa. *Reading Matter: Multidisciplinary Perspectives on Material Culture*. New Brunswick: Transaction, 1992.
Berlow, Rosalind Kent. "The Development of Business Techniques Used at the Fairs of Champagne from the End of the Twelfth Century to the Middle of the Thirteenth Century." *Studies in Medieval and Renaissance History* 8 (1971): 3–31.
Blanc, Odile. "Historiographie du vêtement: Un Bilan." *Le Vêtement: Histoire, archéologie et symbolique vestimentaires au Moyen-Age*. Ed. Michel Pastoureau. Paris: Cahiers du Léopard d'Or, 1989. 7–33.
Bloch, Marc. *La Société féodale*. 2 vols. Paris: Albin Michel, 1939–40.
Boucher, François. *20,000 Years of Fashion: The History of Costume and Personal Adornment*. New York: Harry Abrams, 1987.
Bourdieu, Pierre. *La Distinction: Critique social du jugement*. Paris: Minuit, 1979.
Bourgain, L'Abbé L. *La Chaire française au XIIe siècle d'après les manuscrits*. Paris: Société Générale de Librairie Catholique, 1879.
Bourquelot, Félix. *Etudes sur les foires de Champagne, sur la nature, l'étendue et les règles du commerce qui s'y faisait aux XIIe, XIIIe et XIVe siècles*. Paris: Imprimerie Impériale, 1865.
Braudel, Fernand. *Civilisation matérielle et capitalisme (XVe–XVIIIe siècle)*. Tome 1. Paris: Armand Colin, 1967.
Brault, Gérard J. "Fonction et sens dans l'épisode du Château de Pesme Aventure dans l'*Yvain* de Chrétien de Troyes." *Mélanges de langue et littérature françaises du Moyen Age et de la Renaissance offerts à Monsieur Charles Foulon*. Tome 1. Rennes: Institut Français de l'Université de Haute-Bretagne, 1980. 59–64.
Breward, Christopher. *The Culture of Fashion: A New History of Fashionable Dress*. Manchester: Manchester University Press, 1995.
Bruckner, Matilda Tomaryn. "*Le Chevalier de la charrette*: That Obscure Object of Desire, Lancelot." *A Companion to Chrétien de Troyes*. Ed. Norris J. Lacy and Joan Tasker Grimbert. Cambridge: D. S. Brewer, 2005. 137–55.
———. *Narrative Invention in Twelfth-Century Romance: The Convention of Hospitality (1160–1200)*. Lexington: French Forum, 1980.
———. "Of Beasts and Men in *Bisclavret*." *Romanic Review* 82.2 (1991): 251–69.
———. "Repetition and Variation in Twelfth-Century French Romance." *The Expansion and Transformations of Courtly Literature*. Ed. Nathaniel B. Smith and Joseph T. Snow. Athens: University of Georgia Press, 1980. 95–114.
———. "The Shape of Romance in Medieval France." *The Cambridge Companion to Medieval Romance*. Ed. Roberta A. Krueger. Cambridge: Cambridge University Press, 2000. 13–28.
———. *Shaping Romance: Interpretation, Truth, and Closure in Twelfth-Century French Fictions*. Philadelphia: University of Pennsylvania Press, 1993.
Brundage, James A. *Law, Sex, and Christian Society in Medieval Europe*. Chicago: University of Chicago Press, 1987.
Bumke, Joachim. *Courtly Culture: Literature and Society in the High Middle Ages*. Trans. Thomas Dunlap. Berkeley and Los Angeles: University of California Press, 1990.

Burgess, Glyn S. *The Lais of Marie de France: Text and Context*. Athens: University of Georgia Press, 1987.

Burns, E. Jane. *Bodytalk: When Women Speak in Old French Literature*. Philadelphia: University of Pennsylvania Press, 1993.

———. *Courtly Love Undressed: Reading Through Clothes in Medieval French Culture*. Philadelphia: University of Pennsylvania Press, 2002.

———. "Ladies Don't Wear *Braies*: Underwear and Outerwear in the French *Prose Lancelot*." *The Lancelot-Grail Cycle: Texts and Transformations*. Ed. William W. Kibler. Austin: University of Texas Press, 1994. 152–74.

———. *Medieval Fabrications: Dress, Textiles, Clothwork, and Other Cultural Imaginings*. New York: Palgrave Macmillan, 2004.

———. "Raping Men: What's Motherhood Got to Do with It?" *Representing Rape in Medieval and Early Modern Literature*. Ed. Elizabeth Robertson and Christine M. Rose. New York: Palgrave, 2001. 127–60.

Cameron, Rondo. *A Concise Economic History of the World*. New York: Oxford University Press, 1997.

Colby, Alice M. *The Portrait in Twelfth-Century French Literature*. Geneva: Droz, 1965.

Colby-Hall, Alice M. "Frustration and Fulfillment: The Double Ending of the *Bel Inconnu*." *Yale French Studies* 67 (1984): 120–34.

Contamine, Philippe, Marc Bompaire, Stéphane Lebecq, and Jean-Luc Sarrazin. *L'Économie médiévale*. Paris: Armand Colin, 1993.

Contamine, Philippe, Thierry Dutour, and Bertrand Schnerb. *Commerce, finance et société (XIe–XVIe) siècles): Recueil de travaux d'histoire médiévale offert à M. Le Professeur Henri Dubois*. Paris: Presses de l'Université de Paris-Sorbonne, 1993.

Contini, Mila. *Fashion from Ancient Egypt to the Present Day*. New York: Odyssey Press, 1965.

Corbellari, Alain. "Les Jeux de l'anneau: Fonctions et trajets d'un objet emblématique de la littérature médiévale." *De Sens rassis: Essays in Honor of Rupert T. Pickens*. Ed. Keith Busby, Bernard Guidot, and Logan E. Whalen. Amsterdam: Rodopi, 2005. 157–67.

Cordwell, Justine M., and Ronald A. Schwartz, eds. *The Fabrics of Culture: The Anthropology of Clothing and Adornment*. The Hague: Mouton, 1979.

Corrigan, Peter. "Interpreted, Circulating, Interpreting: The Three Dimensions of the Clothing Object." *The Socialness of Things: Essays on the Socio-semiotics of Objects*. Ed. Stephen Harold Riggins. New York: Mouton de Gruyter, 1994. 435–49.

Crowfoot, Elisabeth, Frances Pritchard, and Kay Staniland. *Textiles and Clothing, c.1150–c.1450*. London: HMSO, 1992.

Culler, Jonathan. *Structuralist Poetics: Structuralism, Linguistics, and the Study of Literature*. Ithaca: Cornell University Press, 1975.

Davies, Peter V., and Angus J. Kennedy, eds. *Rewards and Punishments in the Arthurian Romances and Lyric Poetry of Mediaeval France*. Cambridge: D. S. Brewer, 1987.

Davis, Fred. *Fashion, Culture, and Identity*. Chicago: University of Chicago Press, 1992.

de Looze, Laurence. "Generic Clash, Reader Response, and the Poetics of the Non-ending in *Le Bel Inconnu*." *Courtly Literature: Culture and Context*. Ed. Keith Busby and Erik Kooper. Amsterdam: John Benjamins, 1990. 113–23.

Demay, G. *Le Costume au Moyen Age d'après les sceaux*. Paris: Dumoulin, 1880.

Deslandres, Yvonne. *Le Costume, image de l'homme*. Paris: Albin Michel, 1976.

Dicthfield, Philip. *La Culture matérielle médiévale: L'Italie mériodionale byzantine et normande.* Rome: Ecole Française de Rome, 2007.
Diverres, A. H. "Tristan and Iseut's Condemnation to the Stake in Béroul." *Rewards and Punishments in the Arthurian Romances and Lyric Poetry of Mediaeval France.* Ed. Peter V. Davies and Angus J. Kennedy. Cambridge: D. S. Brewer, 1987. 21–29.
Dronke, Peter, ed. *A History of Twelfth-Century Western Philosophy.* Cambridge: Cambridge University Press, 1988.
Dubois, Jean, Mathée Giacomo, Louis Guespin, Christiane Marcellesi, Jean-Baptiste Marcellesi, and Jean-Pierre Mével. *Dictionnaire de linguistique.* Paris: Larousse, 1991.
Duby, Georges. *Art et société du Moyen Age.* Paris: Seuil, 1997.
———, ed. *A History of Private Life: Revelations of the Medieval World.* Trans. Arthur Goldhammer. Cambridge: Harvard University Press, 1988.
———. *Les Trois Ordres ou l'imaginaire du féodalisme.* Paris: Gallimard, 1978.
———. *Guerriers et paysans, VII–XIIe siècle: Premier essor de l'économie européenne.* Paris: Gallimard, 1973.
Eamon, William. *Science and the Secrets of Nature: Books of Secrets in Medieval and Early Modern Culture.* Princeton: Princeton University Press, 1994.
Eco, Umberto. *Art and Beauty in the Middle Ages.* Trans. Hugh Bredin. New Haven: Yale University Press, 1986.
———. *The Open Work.* Trans. Anna Cancogni. Cambridge: Harvard University Press, 1989.
———. *A Theory of Semiotics.* Bloomington: Indiana University Press, 1976.
Elliott, Dyan. "Dress as Mediator Between Inner and Outer Self: The Pious Maiden of the High and Later Middle Ages." *Mediaeval Studies* 53 (1991): 270–308.
Enlart, Camille. *Manuel d'archéologie française depuis les temps mérovingiens jusqu'à la Renaissance.* Tome 3: *Le Costume.* Paris: Picard, 1916.
Evans, Joan. *Dress in Mediaeval France.* Oxford: Clarendon Press, 1952.
Ewing, Elizabeth. *Dress and Undress: A History of Women's Underwear.* London: Batsford, 1978.
Faral, Edmond. *Les Arts poétiques du XIIe et du XIIIe siècle.* Genève: Slatkine, 1982.
Fleishman, Suzanne. "*Jaufre* or Chivalry Askew: Social Overtones of Parody in Arthurian Romance." *Viator* 12 (1981): 101–29.
Frappier, Jean. *Chrétien de Troyes: L'homme et l'œuvre.* Paris: Hatier, 1957.
Fraser, Veronica. "Humour and Satire in the Romance of *Jaufre*." *Forum for Modern Language Studies* 31 (1995): 223–33.
Gaunt, Simon. *Gender and Genre in Medieval French Literature.* Cambridge: Cambridge University Press, 1995.
———. *Love and Death in Medieval French and Occitan Courtly Literature: Martyrs to Love.* Oxford: Oxford University Press, 2006.
———. "Romance and Other Genres." *The Cambridge Companion to Medieval Romance.* Ed. Roberta A Krueger. Cambridge: Cambridge University Press, 2000. 45–59.
Geary, Patrick. "Sacred Commodities: The Circulation of Medieval Relics." *The Social Life of Things: Commodities in Cultural Perspective.* Ed. Arjun Appadurai. Cambridge: Cambridge University Press, 1986. 168–91.
Gellrich, Jesse M. *The Idea of the Book in the Middle Ages: Language Theory, Mythology, and Fiction.* Ithaca: Cornell University Press, 1985.

Genette, Gérard. *Figures II*. Paris: Editions du Seuil, 1969.
———. *Figures III*. Paris: Editions du Seuil, 1972.
Gies, Frances, and Joseph Gies. *Daily Life in Medieval Times*. New York: Black Dog and Leventhal, 1999.
Gilmore, Gloria Thomas. "Marie de France's *Bisclavret*: What the Werewolf Will and Will Not Wear." *Encountering Medieval Textile and Dress: Objects, Texts, Images*. Ed. Désirée G. Koslin and Janet E. Snyder. New York: Palgrave Macmillan, 2002. 67–84.
Giraudias, Etienne. *Étude historique sur les lois somptuaires*. Poitiers: Société Française d'Imprimerie et de Libraire, 1910.
Goddard, Eunice Rathbone. *Women's Costume in French Texts of the Eleventh and Twelfth Centuries*. Baltimore: Johns Hopkins University Press, 1927.
Grimbert, Joan Tasker. "*Cligés* and the Chansons: A Slave to Love." *A Companion to Chrétien de Troyes*. Ed. Norris J. Lacy and Joan Tasker Grimbert. Cambridge: D. S. Brewer, 2005. 120–36.
Gurevich, Aron J. "The Merchant." *The Medieval World*. Ed. Jacques Le Goff. Trans. Lydia G. Cochrane. London: Collins and Brown, 1990. 243–83.
Haidu, Peter. *Aesthetic Distance in Chrétien de Troyes: Irony and Comedy in* Cligés *and* Perceval. Geneva: Droz, 1968.
———. "Narrativity and Language in Some XIIth Century Romances." *Yale French Studies* 51 (1974): 133–46.
———. "Realism, Convention, Fictionality, and the Theory of Genres in *Bel Inconnu*." *L'Esprit Créateur* 12 (1972): 37–60.
Hanning, Robert W. *The Individual in Twelfth-Century Romance*. New Haven: Yale University Press, 1977.
Hansen, Henry Harold. *Costumes and Styles*. New York: E. P. Dutton, 1956.
Harris, Jennifer. "'Estroit vestu et menu cosu': Evidence for the Construction of Twelfth-Century Dresses." *Medieval Art: Recent Perspectives*. Ed. Gale R. Owen-Crocker and Timothy Graham. Manchester: Manchester University Press, 1998. 89–103.
———, ed. *5000 Years of Textiles*. London: British Museum Press, 2004.
———. "'Thieves, Harlots, and Stinking Goats': Fashionable Dress and the Aesthetic Attitudes in Romanesque Art." *Costume* 21 (1987): 4–15.
Harte, N. B., and K. G. Ponting, eds. *Cloth and Clothing in Medieval Europe: Essays in Memory of Professor E. M. Carus-Wilson*. London: Heinemann, 1983.
Heller, Sarah-Grace. "Fashion in French Crusade Literature: Desiring Infidel Textiles." *Encountering Medieval Textiles and Dress: Objects, Texts, Images*. Ed. Désirée G. Koslin and Janet Snyder. New York: Palgrave Macmillan, 2002. 103–19.
———. *Fashion in Medieval France*. Cambridge: D. S. Brewer, 2007.
———. "Light as Glamour: The Luminescent Ideal of Beauty in the *Roman de la Rose*." *Speculum* 76 (October 2001): 934–59.
Herlihy, David. *Opera Muliebria: Women and Work in Medieval Europe*. Philadelphia: Temple University Press, 1990.
Hindman, Sandra. *Sealed in Parchment: Rereadings of Knighthood in the Illuminated Manuscripts of Chrétien de Troyes*. Chicago: University of Chicago Press, 1994.
Hollander, Anne. *Seeing Through Clothes*. New York: Viking, 1978.
Hotchkiss, Valerie R. *Clothes Make the Man: Female Cross Dressing in Medieval Europe*. New York, Garland, 1996.

Howell, Martha C. "Women, the Family Economy, and the Structures of Market Production in Cities of Northern Europe During the Late Middle Ages." *Women and Work in Preindustrial Europe.* Ed. Barbara A. Hanawalt. Bloomington: Indiana University Press, 1986. 198–222.
Huizinga, Johan. *The Waning of the Middle Ages.* New York: St. Martin's Press, 1924.
Huchet, Jean-Charles. "*Jaufre* et le Graal." *Vox Romanica* 53 (1994): 156–74.
———. "Le Roman à nu: *Jaufre.*" *Littérature* 74 (1989): 91–99.
Hunt, Alan. *Governance of the Consuming Passions: A History of Sumptuary Laws.* New York: St. Martin's Press, 1996.
Hunt, Tony. "*Le Chevalier au lion*: Yvain Lionheart." *A Companion to Chrétien de Troyes.* Ed. Norris J. Lacy and Joan Tasker Grimbert. Cambridge: D. S. Brewer, 2005. 156–68.
———. "*Texte* and *Prétexte: Jaufre* and *Yvain.*" *The Legacy of Chrétien de Troyes.* Vol. 2. Ed. Norris J. Lacy, Douglas Kelly, and Keith Busby. Amsterdam: Rodopi, 1988. 125–41.
Hutson, Lorna. *The Usurer's Daughter: Male Friendship and Fictions of Women in Sixteenth-Century England.* London: Routledge, 1994.
Irwin, Robert. *Le Monde islamique.* Paris: Flammarion, 1997.
Jewers, Caroline. "Fabric and Fabrication: Lyric and Narrative in Jean Renart's *Roman de la Rose.*" *Speculum* 71.2 (1996): 907–24.
———. "The Name of the Ruse and the Round Table: Occitan Romance and the Case for Cultural Resistance." *Neophilologus* 81.2 (1997): 187–200.
Jones, Nancy A. "The Daughter's Text and the Thread of Lineage in the Old French *Philomena.*" *Representing Rape in Medieval and Early Modern Literature.* Ed. Elizabeth Robertson and Christine M. Rose. New York: Palgrave, 2001. 161–88.
Karras, Ruth Mazo. "'This Skill in a Woman Is By No Means to Be Despised': Weaving and the Gender Division of Labor in the Middle Ages." *Medieval Fabrications: Dress, Textiles, Cloth Work, and Other Cultural Imaginings.* Ed. E. Jane Burns. New York: Palgrave Macmillan, 2004. 89–104.
Kellogg, Judith L. "Economic and Social Tensions Reflected in the Romances of Chrétien de Troyes." *Romance Philology* 39.1 (1985): 1–21.
———. *Medieval Artistry and Exchange: Economic Institutions, Society, and Literary Form in Old French Narrative.* New York: Peter Lang, 1989.
Kelly, Douglas. "The Art of Description." *The Legacy of Chrétien de Troyes.* Vol. 1. Ed. Norris J. Lacy, Douglas Kelly, and Keith Busby. Amsterdam: Rodopi, 1987. 191–221.
———. *The Art of Medieval French Romance.* Madison: University of Wisconsin Press, 1992.
———. *The Arts of Poetry and Prose.* Turnhout: Brepols, 1991.
———. *The Conspiracy of Allusion: Description, Rewriting, and Authorship from Macrobius to Medieval Romance.* Leiden: Brill, 1999.
———. *Medieval French Romance.* New York: Twayne, 1993.
———. *Medieval Imagination: Rhetoric and the Poetry of Courtly Love.* Madison: University of Wisconsin Press, 1978.
———. "Narrative Poetics: Rhetoric, Orality, and Performance." *A Companion to Chrétien de Troyes.* Ed. Norris J. Lacy and Joan Tasker Grimbert. Cambridge: D. S. Brewer, 2005. 52–63.

———. "Rhetoric in French Literature: Topical Invention in Medieval French Romance." *Medieval Eloquence: Studies in the Theory and Practice of Medieval Rhetoric.* Ed. James J. Murphy. Berkeley: University of California Press, 1978. 231–51.

———, ed. *The Romances of Chrétien de Troyes: A Symposium.* Lexington: French Forum, 1985.

———. "The Scope of the Treatment of Composition in the Twelfth- and Thirteenth-Century Arts of Poetry." *Speculum* 41.2 (1966): 261–78.

———. "'Senpres est ci et senpres la': Motif Repetition and Narrative Bifurcation in Béroul's *Tristan*." *Voices of Conscience: Essays on Medieval and Modern French Literature in Memory of James D. Powell and Rosemary Hodgins.* Ed. Raymond J. Cormier. Philadelphia: Temple University Press, 1977. 131–42.

———. *Sens and Conjointure in the* Chevalier de la Charrette. The Hague: Mouton, 1966.

Kowaleski, Maryanne, and Judith M. Bennett. "Crafts, Guilds, and Women in the Middle Ages: Fifty Years After Marian K. Dale." *Sisters and Workers in the Middle Ages.* Ed. Judith M. Bennett et al. Chicago: University of Chicago Press, 1989. 11–38.

Kraemer-Raine, Pierre. *Le Luxe et les lois somptuaires au Moyen-Age.* Paris: Ernest Sagot, 1920.

Kristeva, Julia. "Du symbole au signe." *Le Texte du roman: Approache sémiologique d'une structure discursive transformationnelle.* The Hague: Mouton, 1970. 25–35.

Krueger, Roberta A., ed. *The Cambridge Companion to Medieval Romance.* Cambridge: Cambridge University Press, 2000.

———. "*Philomena*: Brutal Transformations and Courtly Transformations in Chrétien's Old French Translation." *A Companion to Chrétien de Troyes.* Ed. Norris J. Lacy and Joan Tasker Grimbert. Cambridge: D. S. Brewer, 2005. 87–102.

———. "Questions of Gender in Old French Courtly Romance." *The Cambridge Companion to Medieval Romance.* Ed. Roberta A. Krueger. Cambridge: Cambridge University Press, 2000. 132–49.

———. *Women Readers and the Ideology of Gender in Old French Verse Romance.* Cambridge: Cambridge University Press, 1993.

Lacy, Norris J. *The Craft of Chrétien de Troyes: An Essay on Narrative Art.* Leiden: Brill, 1980.

———. "Deception and Distance in Béroul's *Tristan*: A Reconsideration." *Journal of the Rocky Mountain Medieval and Renaissance Association* 6 (1985): 33–39.

———. "On Armor and Identity: Chrétien and Beyond." *De Sens rassis: Essays in Honor of Rupert T. Pickens.* Ed. Keith Busby, Berdard Guidot, and Logan E. Whalen. Amsterdam: Rodopi, 2005. 365–74.

———. "Spatial Form in Medieval Romance." *Yale French Studies* 51 (1974). 160–69.

———. "Thematic Structure in the *Charrette*." *L'Esprit Créateur* 12.1 (1972): 13–18.

Lacy, Norris J., Douglas Kelly, and Keith Busby, eds. *The Legacy of Chrétien de Troyes.* 2 vols. Amsterdam: Rodopi, 1987.

Laver, James. *The Concise History of Costume and Fashion.* New York: Harry N. Abrams, 1969.

———. *Costume.* London: Cassell, n.d.

Lazard, Madeleine. "Le Costume dans 'Jehan de Saintré': Valeur sociale et symbolique." *Studi Francesi* 78.3 (1982): 457–64.

Le Goff, Jacques. *The Medieval Imagination.* Trans. Arthur Goldhammer. Chicago: University of Chicago Press, 1992.

Lehmann, Andrée. *Le Rôle de la femme dans l'histoire de la France au Moyen Age.* Paris: Berger-Levrault, 1952.
Leix, Alfred. "Medieval Dye Markets in Europe." *Ciba Review* 10 (1938): 324–29.
———. "Oriental Dye Markets of the Middle Ages." *Ciba Review* 10 (1938): 330–36.
———. "Trade Routes of the Middle Ages." *Ciba Review* 10 (1938): 314–23.
Lejeune, Rita. "A propos de la datation de *Jaufre*: Le Roman de *Jaufre*, source de Chrétien de Troyes?" *Revue Belge de Philologie et d'Histoire* (1953): 717–47.
———. "La Date du roman de *Jaufre*." *Le Moyen Age* (1948): 257–95.
Lénat, M. R. "L'Adoubement dans quelques textes littéraires de la fin du XIIe siècle: Clergie et chevalerie." *Mélanges de langue et littérature françaises du Moyen Age et de la Renaissance offerts à Monsieur Charles Foulon.* Tome 1. Rennes: Institut Français de l'Université de Haute-Bretagne, 1980. 195–203.
Lériget, Marthe. *Des lois et impôts somptuaires.* Montpellier: L'Abeille, 1919.
Little, Lester K. *Religious Poverty and the Profit Economy in Medieval Europe.* Ithaca: Cornell University Press, 1978.
Lonigan, Paul R. "The Authorship of the *Guillaume d'Angleterre*: A New Approach." *Studi Francesi* 47–48 (1972): 308–14.
Lubell, Cecil. *Textile Collections of the World.* Vol. 3: *France.* New York: Van Nostrand Reinhold, 1977.
Luchaire, Achille. "Louis VII—Philippe Auguste—Louis VIII (1137–1226)." *Histoire de France depuis les origines jusqu'à la Révolution.* Ed. Ernest Lavisse. Vol. 3. Paris: Hachette, 1901.
Lurie, Alison. *The Language of Clothes.* New York: Random House, 1981.
Mackay, Angus, and David Ditchburn, eds. *Atlas of Medieval Europe.* London: Routledge, 1997.
Maddox, Donald. *The Arthurian Romances of Chrétien de Troyes: Once and Future Fictions.* Cambridge: Cambridge University Press, 1991.
Maddox, Donald, and Sara Sturm-Maddox. "*Erec et Enide*: The First Arthurian Romance." *A Companion to Chrétien de Troyes.* Ed. Norris J. Lacy and Joan Tasker Grimbert. Cambridge: D. S. Brewer, 2005. 103–19.
Martin, Janet. *Treasure in the Land of Darkness: The Fur Trade and Its Significance for Medieval Russia.* Cambridge: Cambridge University Press, 1986.
Mauss, Marcel. "Essai sur le don: Forme et raison de l'échange dans les sociétés archaïques." *Sociologie et anthropologie.* Paris: PUF, 1973. 143–279.
Munro, John H. "The Medieval Scarlet and the Economics of Sartorial Splendour." *Cloth and Clothing in Medieval Europe: Essays in Memory of Professor E. M. Carus-Wilson.* Ed. N. B. Harte and K. G. Ponting. London: Heinemann, 1983. 13–70.
Muthesius, Anna. "Byzantine Silks." *5000 Years of Textiles.* Ed. Jennifer Harris. London: British Museum Press, 2004. 75–79.
———. "Sicilian Silks." *5000 Years of Textiles.* Ed. Jennifer Harris. London: British Museum Press, 2004. 165–66.
———. "Silk in the Medieval World." *The Cambridge History of Western Textiles.* Vol. 1. Ed. David Jenkins. Cambridge: Cambridge University Press, 2003. 325–54.
———. *Studies in Byzantine and Islamic Silk Weaving.* London: Pindar Press, 1995.
Neuburger, M. C. "Medieval Dyeing Techniques." *Ciba Review* 10 (1938): 337–40.
Netherton, Robin. "When Cut Drives Fashion: The Norman Woman's Sleeve Shape." *Costume Research Journal* 12.4 (2001): 4–11.

Pastoureau, Michel. *Armorial des chevaliers de la Table Ronde*. Paris: Léopard d'Or, 1983.

———. *Figures et couleurs: Étude sur la symbolique et la sensibilité médiévales*. Paris: Léopard d'or, 1986.

Pastoureau, Michel, and Dominique Simonnet. *Le Petit Livre de couleurs*. Paris: Editions du Panama, 2005.

Peirce, Charles Sanders. *Peirce on Signs: Writings on Semiotic by Charles Sanders Peirce*. Ed. James Hoopes. Chapel Hill: University of North Carolina Press, 1991.

Pickens, Rupert T. "*Le Conte du Graal*: Chrétien's Unfinished Last Romance." *A Companion to Chrétien de Troyes*. Ed. Norris J. Lacy and Joan Tasker Grimbert. Cambridge: D. S. Brewer, 2005. 169–87.

———, ed. *The Sower and His Seed: Essays on Chrétien de Troyes*. Lexington: French Forum, 1983.

———. "Thematic Structure in Marie de France's *Guigemar*." *Romania* 95 (1974): 328–41.

Pigeonneau, H. *Histoire du commerce de la France*. Paris: Léopold Cerf, 1885.

Pinasa, Delphine. *Costumes: Modes et manières d'être*. Paris: Rempart, Desclée de Brouwer, 1995.

Piponnier, Françoise. *Costume et vie sociale: La Cour d'Anjou XIVe–XVe siècle*. Paris: Mouton, 1970.

Piponnier, Françoise, and Perrine Mane. *Se vêtir au Moyen Age*. Paris: Adam Biro, 1995.

Pirenne, Henri. *Economic and Social History of Medieval Europe*. New York: Harvest, 1936.

Postan, M. M., and Edward Miller. *The Cambridge Economic History of Europe*. Vol. 2: *Trade and Industry in the Middle Ages*. Cambridge: Cambridge University Press, 1987.

Quicherat, Jules. *Histoire du costume français depuis les temps les plus reculés jusqu'à la fin du XVIIIe siècle*. Paris: Hachette, 1877.

Rémy, Paul. "A propos de la datation du roman de *Jaufre*." *Revue Belge de Philologie et d'Histoire* 28 (1950): 1349–77.

Reyerson, Kathryn L. "The Merchants of the Mediterranean: Merchants as Strangers." *The Stranger in Medieval Society*. Ed. F. R. P. Akehurst and Stephanie Cain Van D'Elden. Minneapolis: University Press of Minnesota, 1997. 1–13.

Ribard, Jacques. "Le *Lai de Guigemar*: Conjointure et senefiance." *Amour et merveille: Les Lais de Marie de France*. Ed. Jean Dufournet. Paris: Champion, 1995. 133–45.

Riggins, Stephen Harold, ed. *The Socialness of Things: Essays on the Socio-semiotics of Objects*. New York: Mouton de Gruyter, 1994.

Rigolot, François. "Valeur figurative du vêtement dans le *Tristan* de Béroul." *Cahiers de Civilisation Médiévale* 10 (1967): 447–53.

Roach, Mary Ellen, and Joanne Bubolz Eicher, eds. *Dress, Adornment, and the Social Order*. New York: John Wiley and Sons, 1965.

Roche, Daniel. *The Culture of Clothing: Dress and Fashion in the "Ancien Regime."* Trans. Jean Birrell. Cambridge: Cambridge University Press, 1994.

Roussel, Claude. "Point final et points de suspension: La Fin incertaine du *Bel Inconnu*." *Le Point Final: Actes du colloque international de Clermont-Ferrand*. Ed. Alain Montandon. Clermond-Ferrant: Faculté des Lettres et Sciences Humaines de l'Université de Clermont-Ferrand II, 1984. 19–34.

Ruck, E. H. *An Index of Themes and Motifs in Twelfth-Century French Arthurian Poetry.* Cambridge: D. S. Brewer, 1991.
Ryding, William W. *Structure in Medieval Narrative.* The Hague: Mouton, 1971.
Saussure, Ferdinand de. *Cours de linguistique générale.* Paris: Payot, 1960.
Southern, R. W. *The Making of the Middle Ages.* New Haven: Yale University Press, 1953.
Sponsler, Claire. "Narrating the Social Order: Medieval Clothing Laws." CLIO 21.3 (1992): 265–83.
Spufford, Peter. *Handbook of Medieval Exchange.* London: Offices of the Royal Historical Society, 1986.
Staines, David. Introduction. *The Complete Romances of Chrétien de Troyes.* Ed. and trans. David Staines. Bloomington: Indiana University Press, 1990. vii–xxix.
Sturm, Sara. "The *Bel Inconnu*'s Enchantress and the Intent of Renaut de Beaujeu." *French Review* 44.5 (1971): 862–69.
———. "The Love Interest in *Le Bel Inconnu*: Innovation in the *Roman Courtois*." *Forum for Modern Language Studies* 7.3 (1971): 241–48.
———. "Magic in *Le Bel Inconnu*." *L'Esprit Créateur* 12 (1972): 19–25.
Sturm-Maddox, Sara, and Donald Maddox. "Description in Medieval Narrative: Vestimentary Coherence in Chrétien's *Erec et Enide*." *Medioevo Romanzo* 9 (1984): 51–64.
Van Vleck, Amelia E. "Textiles and Testimony in Marie de France and *Philomena*." *Medievalia et Humanistica* 22 (1995): 31–60.
Vance, Eugene. *Mervelous Signals: Poetics and Sign Theory in the Middle Ages.* Lincoln: University of Nebraska Press, 1986.
Veale, Elizabeth M. *The English Fur Trade in the Later Middle Ages.* Oxford: Oxford University Press, 1966.
Vinaver, Eugène. *A la recherche d'une poétique médiévale.* Paris: Nizet, 1970.
———. *Form and Meaning in Medieval Romance.* Cambridge: Modern Humanities Research Association, 1966.
———. *The Rise of Romance.* Oxford: Clarendon, 1971.
Weiner, Annette B., and Jane Schneider, eds. *Cloth and Human Experience.* Washington, D.C.: Smithsonian Institution Press, 1989.
Whalen, Logan E. *Marie de France and the Poetics of Memory.* Washington, D.C.: Catholic University Press, 2008.
Wilcox, R. Turner. *The Mode in Costume.* New York: Charles Scribner's Sons, n.d.
Williams, Harry F. "The Authorship of *Guillaume d'Angleterre*." *South Atlantic Review* 52.1 (1987): 17–24.
Wingate, Isabel B. *Fairchild's Dictionary of Textiles.* New York: Fairchild, 1979.
Wolf-Bonvin, Romaine. *Textus: De la tradition latine à l'esthétique du roman medieval*, Le Bel Inconnu, Amadas et Ydoine. Paris: Honoré Champion, 1998.
———. "Un Vêtement sans l'être: La Chemise." *Le Nu et le vêtu au Moyen Age (XII–XIIIe siècles): Actes du 25e colloque du* CUER MA. Aix-en-Provence: Publications de l'Université de Provence, 2001. 383–94.
Wright, Monica L. "'De fil d'or et de soie': Making Textiles in Twelfth-Century French Romance." *Medieval Clothing and Textiles* 2. Ed. Robin Netherton and Gale R. Owen-Crocker. Woodbridge: Boydell, 2006. 61–72.

———. "*Chemise* and *Ceinture*: Marie de France's *Guigemar* and the Use of Textiles." *Courtly Arts and the Art of Courtliness: Selected Papers from the Eleventh Triennial Congress of the International Courtly Literature Society.* Ed. Keith Busby and Christopher Kleinhenz. Cambridge: D. S. Brewer, 2006. 771–77.

———. "Dress for Success: Béroul's *Tristan* and the Restoration of Status Through Clothes." *Arthuriana* 18.2 (2008): 3–16.

———. "Superlative Silk: Samite and the Grail." Forthcoming in *Medieval Clothing and Textiles.*

———. "Their Clothing Becomes Them: The Narrative Function of Clothing in Chrétien de Troyes." *Arthurian Literature* 20 (2003): 31–42.

———. "What Was Arthur Wearing? Discrepancies in Dress Descriptions in Twelfth-Century French Romance." *Philological Quarterly* 81.3 (2002): 275–88.

Zumthor, Paul. *Essai de poétique médiévale.* Paris: Seuil, 1972.

———. *Langue et techniques poétiques à l'époque romane (XIe–XIIIe siècles).* Paris: Klincksieck, 1963.

INDEX

Abbott, Reginald, 31, 50, 59, 60
accessories. *See* adornment
Adams, Alison, 164
adornment, 7, 20–21, 23, 31 n. 18, 43, 70 n. 27
Adrastus, 134
agriculture, 28
Alexandre, 62, 67, 81, 88–89, 98, 126, 134–35
alum, 32, 164
Amadas et Ydoine, 63–64, 81, 86, 88
ambiguity, 41, 44, 77, 79, 121, 166
   class, 56, 170
   identity, 75–77
   instability of meaning, 15, 18, 36, 93, 101, 110
   material, 9
   multiplicity of meaning, 73
   refusal of, 39
ambivalence, 2, 77, 79, 121
   class, 40–41, 56
   gender, 53–56
   identity, 74–75
   material, 9, 36
   semantic, 36
   sexual, 50–53, 56
   symbolic, 101
   vestimentary, 57
amplification, 12–13, 100, 104–5, 111 n. 28, 123, 133
analogical structure, 5, 124, 131, 133–34, 138, 171
analogy, 7, 44, 137
Angrés, Count, 67
anneau. *See* rings
Anquetil, Jacques, 28 n. 14, 31–32
anxiety. *See* class anxiety
apparel. *See* clothing
arbitrariness, 40, 41, 77, 79
   linguistic, 15–19
   in signifiers, 95, 168, 170
   signifying system, part of, 101, 121, 166
arming, 95–101, 136, 142, 144
armor
   abandonment of, 95, 145–46
   ambiguity, 75–76, 112, 141
   deception, 67–68, 73, 75
   description of, 7 n. 1
   fine, 14, 85
   gift of, 34, 36, 81–82, 85, 88, 126, 135
   and identity, 73–76, 82
   innovations in, 74
   lack of, 57 n. 11, 85
   misread sign, 75–76, 142, 144, 168
   narrative device, 86–87
   necessity of heraldry, 75
   protection, 97–98
   social identity of wearer, 62, 73, 82
   symbol of knighthood, 16, 36, 143, 161
   synecdoche, 61–62
Arthur, King, 2, 4, 47, 49, 57, 62, 72–73, 81–84, 88, 92, 96–99, 102–3, 105, 107, 126, 131, 134–35, 137, 139, 143, 146
Asia, 32
Ates, 85, 107
attire. *See* clothing
aune (measurement of fabric), 39 n. 28
aventure, 39, 120, 154

Baldwin, John W., 8 n. 3
Barnard, Malcolm, 17, 19–20, 38
Barthes, Roland, 21, 27 n. 11, 39
battle dress, 36, 101 n. 18
baudequin, 113
Baudrillard, Jean, 18
Baumgartner, Emmanuèle, 40 n. 30
beasts, 49, 49–50 n. 5, 53–54, 96, 135–37. *See also Bisclavret*

beauty, 59–60. *See also* clothing, and beauty
Beazley, C. Raymond, 28, 37 n. 24
bed-curtains. *See* bedclothes
bedclothes, 8, 112, 119–20, 132, 148–50
bedcover. *See* quilt
bedsheets. *See* bedclothes
Bel Inconnu (Renaut), *Le*, 45–53, 56, 57, 87, 99, 100 n. 16, 102–3, 105
Bell, Quentin, 64
bellatores, 75
Benkov, Edith Joyce, 128 n. 10, 128 n. 11, 129
Bennett, Judith M., 109 n. 22
Berger, Arthur Asa, 16, 20
Bernard of Clairvaux, 25 n. 8
Béroul, 7, 65–67, 70, 89–94, 147 n. 25
birds, 53–54
Bisclavret (Marie), 127–28
Blancheflor, 58–61, 102, 104, 144–45
Blanches Mains, 47–53, 56, 57, 99, 102–3
bliaut, 7, 24–25, 39 n. 29, 45, 47–48, 53–55, 57–58, 72, 91, 119, 132, 153
Bloch, Marc, 28, 29, 34–35, 64
Blonde Esmerée, 45–53, 99, 102–3, 105
bodice, 26
borders. *See* trim
Boucher, François, 24–25, 28
Bourgain, L'Abbé L., 25 n. 8
bourgeoisie, 17, 109
Bourquelot, Félix, 32, 37
braies, 24
Brault, Gérard J., 116 n. 37
brazilwood, 32, 33
britches, 24
brocade, 32 n. 18, 38 n. 27, 48
Bruckner, Matilda Tomaryn, 73 n. 30, 75–76, 87 n. 7, 125 n. 7, 129 n. 14, 130 n. 16, 147 n. 27, 153 n. 29
Brunissen, 81, 96, 104, 136–37
buire, 160
Bumke, Joachim, 25 n. 8, 38 n. 28, 107 n. 21
Burns, E. Jane, 19 n. 24, 24 n. 4, 25 n. 6, 36, 64, 113 n. 32, 115 n. 33, 115 n. 34

Calogrenant, 62 n. 16
Cameron, Rondo, 27–29
Camille, 2, 53–57, 111–13
Capaneüs, 61
ceinture, 50, 88, 118, 129, 151–54
cendal, 31, 31–32 n. 18, 84
ceremonial garments, 26–27, 31, 33, 36, 51, 59
chain-mail. *See* mail
chainse, 7, 24, 57, 133
Champagne, 29–30, 37

chanson de geste, 7, 11, 11 n. 11, 13, 64 n. 19, 82
chanvre, 24 n. 3
chape, 24, 26, 66, 142, 158, 160
chasuble, 24
chausses, 24
checkered fabric, 48, 53
chemise, 4, 7, 24, 51–52, 56–57, 66, 86, 88–89, 98, 116, 120, 126, 132–35, 140, 148–54
Chevalier au lion (Chrétien). *See Yvain*
Chevalier de la charrette (Chrétien). *See Lancelot*
chivalry, 11, 14, 37, 48, 93, 95, 146
Chrétien de Troyes, 7, 10–12, 14, 24 n. 2, 24 n. 3, 30, 45, 58–61, 64 n. 19, 76, 98 n. 15, 116 n. 36, 121, 125 n. 7, 127 n. 8, 135 n. 19, 155 n. 30, 166, 171. *See also Cligés; Erec et Enide; Lancelot; Perceval; Philomena; Yvain*
Christianity, 84, 91, 95 n. 13
church, 9 n. 6, 10 n. 10, 25, 90–91, 145
class anxiety, 36–41, 58
Cligés (Chrétien), 24 n. 3, 62, 67, 81, 88–89, 98, 126, 134–35, 138
cloak, 24–26, 66, 142, 159–60
cloth, 17 n. 16, 25 n. 6, 27 n. 12
  as class marker, 24–25
  economy of, 27–31
  manufacture of, 28, 30–33, 113–18
  manipulation of, 70–71
  and narrative structure, 3
  provenance of, 4
  trade, 32
cloth shearers, 28
clothing
  and beauty, 25–26, 51–60, 107, 127, 132–33, 168
  and character development, 44–61
  degradation of, 89–90
  destroying, 118–21
  and healing, 104–5, 148–51, 155
  and identity, 17, 41, 43–44, 61–68, 70–72
  instrumental, 60
  making, 108–18
  and narrative threads, 125–31
  plot device, 131–37
  reading narrative through, 146–66
  and seduction, 50–53
  social meaning of, 19–22
  and thematic structure, 137–46
  tight, 25–26, 55, 132, 143 n. 22, 152
  twelfth-century terminology of, 23–27
coats of arms, 62, 74–75
cochineal. *See* kermes
code manipulation, 65–77, 80, 89, 94, 99, 118

code subversion, 58, 61, 68, 107–8
coilte, 149
Colby-Hall, Alice M. (Colby, Alice M.), 45, 100 n. 16, 113 n. 30, 124 n. 6
commerce. *See* trade
commercial practices, 30, 37 n. 24
conjointure, 7, 11–14, 41, 58 n. 12, 123, 166–67, 171
Constantinople, 87
consumption, 18, 25, 38
Contamine, Philippe, 28
Conte du Graal. See *Perceval*
Corbellari, Alain, 93 n. 12
Cordwell, Justine M., 21
coronation, 21, 58 n. 13, 82, 105
Corrigan, Peter, 38 n. 25
cote, 66–67, 116, 156–60
cotton, 27, 69
countergift, 34, 85, 126
court, arrival at, 102, 105, 107, 126–27, 133, 134–35
courtliness, 11, 13–14, 36
courtly love, 10 n. 9, 11
coverlet, 149
credit, 30, 37, 38
crocodile, 49–50 n. 5
Crowfoot, Elisabeth, 33, 109
Crusades, 17 n. 16, 28, 31, 37 n. 23
Culler, Jonathan, 69, 76, 80 n. 2
cut. *See* style

damaging. *See* destruction
Davies, Peter V., 125 n. 7
Davis, Fred, 17–18
de Looze, Laurence, 100 n. 16
debt, 37, 39
decoration. *See* ornamentation
degradation. *See* clothing, degradation of
descriptio, 13–14, 45
description, 13, 21–22, 45–61
  dynamic, 14, 50–61
  static, 14, 45–50, 53
design. *See* style
Deslandres, Yvonne, 23 n. 1, 28, 38
destruction, 83–84, 89–90, 108, 118–21, 136–39, 156, 170
diagonal stripe, 32 n. 18
diaspre, 49, 83, 113
Dinas, 90–91
dirty clothing, 116
disarming, 95–96, 142–45
disguise, 65–68, 70–71, 75, 91–92, 94, 167
display, 29, 37–38, 60, 134

distaff, 28
donations. *See* gifts
dragon, 49–50 n. 5
dressing, 20, 72, 91, 94–108, 119, 127–30, 133
  assisted, 86, 101–2, 148
  complex scenes of, 102–3
  identificatory, 142–43
  to persuade, 105, 106–7
  unassisted, 89, 101 n. 18, 104–6, 140
  wound, 151
dubbing, 21, 33–36, 81–82, 147
Dubois, Jean, 69 n. 24
Duby, Georges, 8–9, 27 n. 12, 28, 34–35
dwarf, 57 n. 11, 105
dyers, 28, 32–33, 108–9
dyestuff, 32–33, 108, 164 n. 31, 165 n. 32. *See also specific dyes*

eagle (*escramor*), 49–50 n. 5
Eamon, William, 164 n. 32
east. *See* Levant
Eco, Umberto, 36
economic expansion, 7, 27, 28, 30, 34, 36–41, 60
edge, 26, 87
edging. *See* trim
Eicher, Joanne Bubolz, 20–21, 38, 43, 61 n. 15
Eliduc (Marie), 88, 129–30
Elliott, Dyan, 10 n. 10
embellishment. *See* ornamentation
embroidered fabric, 27, 32 n. 18, 50, 54–55
embroidery, 26, 32 n. 18, 49, 54, 109 n. 23, 124 n. 4
Enéas, 2, 53–57, 111–13
England, 27, 38 n. 28, 90 n. 10, 155, 159, 164
Enide, 1, 2, 14, 56–58, 72–73, 85, 87, 104–8, 118, 126–28
Enlart, Camille, 26 n. 9
epic. See *chanson de geste*
Erec et Enide (Chrétien), 1, 2, 11–12, 14, 56–58, 72–73, 85, 87, 101, 104–8, 118, 126–28, 147 n. 25
Erec, 1, 57–58, 72–73, 81–82, 85, 87, 104–7, 118, 126–27
ermine, 21, 26, 31, 38 n. 28, 45–51, 53, 58–59, 83, 90, 132
  symbolism of, 31
ethos, 21, 96 n. 14
Evans, Joan, 24–25, 27
Evrain, King, 87
Ewing, Elizabeth, 17 n. 17, 19, 26, 39 n. 29
exchange, 28, 34–35, 66, 83–85, 130, 166

exotic garments, 19, 23–29, 31–32, 50, 53, 49, 163
export, 27–28, 32
exportation of cloth, 27–28

fabric. *See* cloth
fabrication, 108–18. *See also* cloth
Fada, 96–97, 136
Fairs of Champagne, 29–30, 37
fairy, 1, 46, 53–54, 81, 102, 131–33
fairy lady. See *Lanval*
fashion, 17–19, 23, 39 n. 29, 69
Fauchiers, 158
femininity, 53, 55–56, 112
feudal society, 8
feudalism, 34
fish, 53–54
fit. *See* style
Flanders, 11 n. 10, 27, 30, 32
Fleishman, Suzanne, 84 n. 5, 96 n. 14
flying serpent, 49–50 n. 5
Frappier, Jean, 155 n. 30
Fraser, Veronica, 84 n. 5
Fresne (Marie), 87, 130–31
funeral, 21
fur, 26, 26 n. 10, 30, 31, 39, 45–47, 49, 52 n. 6, 58–59, 91, 102, 119, 144, 163. *See also specific types of fur*

Gaunt, Simon, 13 n. 14, 111 n. 28
Gauvain, 73 n. 31, 75 n. 34, 97–98, 137, 140–42
Gawain. *See* Gauvain
Geary, Patrick, 34
gender, 12 n. 12, 53–56, 109–11, 113 n. 32, 167
generosity, 91, 154, 157, 160. *See also* largess
gift economy, 34–36, 37, 80–82, 85, 115, 169
gifts, 14, 43
   church, made to, 90–91
   gratitude, expression of, 136, 163
   identificatory, 87–88, 141, 157, 162, 165
   largess expression of, 81–86, 94
   love, expression of, 88–89, 129–30, 134
   narrative device, 125–26
   plot device, 93
   reconciliatory, 49
   refusal of, 91–94
   restorative, 86–87, 115
   and social function, 57, 10, 81–83, 135
   and social ties, 18 n. 21, 34–36, 80–93, 115, 159–61
Gilmore, Gloria Thomas, 128–29
Giraudias, Etienne, 39 n. 28

Girlet, 67
Goddard, Eunice Rathbone, 24
gold, 26 n. 9, 28, 32 n. 18, 38 n. 27, 47–51, 54–56, 58, 62, 73 n. 29, 75, 88–89, 116, 149, 151
Goncelins, 160, 163
gonelle, 25 n. 7
Gornemant, 144
Gratienne, 156, 162–64, 166
grief, 85, 114–15, 118, 134–37, 140
gris, 31, 86, 90
Griselda. See *Philomena*
Guenevere, 4, 52 n. 6, 72–74, 76, 88, 98, 108, 126–28, 133 n. 17, 141–42, 168
Guigemar (Marie), 5, 81, 87–89, 118, 123 n. 1, 129 n. 14, 146–55
guilds, 109
Guillaume d'Angleterre, 5, 9 n. 6, 72, 124 n. 4, 146–47, 155–68
Guinglain, 47–52, 87–88, 99–100, 102–3
Guivret, 104
Gurevich, Aron J., 29

Haidu, Peter, 100 n. 16, 135 n. 19
Hanning, Robert W., 64 n. 19, 137
harmony, 47, 50
harness, 86
Harte, N. B., 33 n. 19
hauberk, 8, 56, 62, 91, 112
headdress, 28 n. 14. *See also* veil; wimple
Hélie, 105
Heller, Sarah-Grace, 17–19, 23, 31 n. 17, 90 n. 9
helmet, 8, 56
hem, 26, 87
hemline, 25
hemp, 24 n. 3, 32, 109 n. 22
heraldry, 62, 74–75
heterovalence, 18
history of clothing, 3–4, 18–19, 23–27, 30–33
Hollander, Anne, 17, 24–25, 64
honoring, 47, 80–82, 86, 98, 101–7, 120, 126, 130–34, 139–44, 170
horse, 14, 67, 81, 83, 86
hose, 24
Huchet, Jean-Charles, 40 n. 30
Huizinga, Johan, 16
humiliation, 24 n. 3
Hunt, Alan, 38
Hunt, Tony, 40 n. 30

identity. *See* clothing, and identity
impersonation. *See* disguise

impoverishment. *See* poverty
imprisonment, 104, 142
incognito, 75–76
indebtedness, 37, 39
indigo, 32, 33, 114
individual, 43–44, 61, 64, 138, 140, 145
insanity. *See* madness
investiture, 21
Irwin, Robert, 32 n. 18
Iseut. *See* Yseut
Islamic world. *See* Levant
Ismène, 107
Isolde. *See* Yseut
Italy, 27, 28, 30, 31, 32
ivory, 28, 56, 149

Jaufre, 40, 81–84, 96–98, 102–5, 110–12, 118, 135–37
jewelry, 8, 18 n. 19, 69, 70 n. 27
Jewers, Caroline, 84 n. 5, 110 n. 26
Jocasta, 106–7, 168
Jones, Nancy A., 115 n. 35

Kaherdin, 70–71
Karras, Ruth Mazo, 109 n. 22
Kay. *See* Keu
Kellogg, Judith L., 37, 61 n. 14
Kelly, Douglas, 11–14, 45, 57–59, 66, 91 n. 11, 123 n. 2, 139 n. 20
Kennedy, Angus J., 125 n. 7
kermes, 32–33, 124 n. 4, 164
Keu, 97–98
King Arthur. *See* Arthur
knighthood, 16, 36, 93, 95–96, 110–11
knightly clothing, 86, 93, 97, 110, 112
Kowaleski, Maryanne, 109 n. 22
Kraemer-Raine, Pierre, 37 n. 23
Kristeva, Julia, 9, 15–16, 18
Krueger, Roberta A., 10 n. 9, 12 n. 12, 13 n. 14, 74 n. 33, 113, 116

La Chanson de Roland, 7 n. 1
La Queste del Saint Graal, 145 n. 23
laborers, 27–28, 109
lacca, 32
lacing, 10 n. 10, 19, 26, 39 n. 29, 51, 55, 119, 132–33, 153
lack, 60
  of armor, 36, 57
  in Arthurian chivalry, 97
  of *bliaut*, 57
  of description, 133
  in Gauvain's character, 141

overcoming through dressing, 103–6
perceived, 105, 111
real, 106, 144
of resources, 21, 117
in source, 123
structuring device, 133–34
theme, 138–41
Lacy, Norris J., 68 n. 23, 73 n. 31, 89 n. 8, 93 n. 12, 98 n. 15, 124–25, 131, 137–38, 143, 156
Lais. *See* Marie de France
lamentation. *See* grief
Lancelot (Chrétien), 4, 13 n. 14, 52 n. 6, 73–76, 86–87, 98 n. 15, 102, 104, 119–21, 133 n. 17, 140–42, 168, 170
Lanval (Marie), 1, 81, 102, 131–33
Lanval's lady, 1, 81, 102, 131–33
largess, 8–9, 34–36, 43, 80–81, 83–86, 89, 93–94
Laudine, 14, 86, 117–18, 138–40
Laver, James, 25 n. 7
Lavine, 111 n. 28
laws, 38
layering, 23–24
Le Goff, Jacques, 147 n. 25
Lehmann, Andrée, 109 n. 22, 109 n. 23
Leix, Alfred, 32–33
Lejeune, Rita, 40 n. 30
Lénat, M. R., 95 n. 13
length of garment, 25
leopard, 49–50 n. 5
Lériget, Marthe, 38 n. 28
Levant, 23, 25, 27–28, 31–33, 37, 46, 48–49
lichen, 33
linen, 24, 27, 32, 62 n. 16, 88, 90, 151
linguistic community, 4, 65, 68–69, 71–72, 168
linguistics, 15, 69 n. 24
lion, 49–50 n. 5
Little, Lester K., 80, 85
Lonigan, Paul R., 155 n. 30
looms, 28
love token, 88–89, 94, 118, 151–55
Lovel, 158, 106–61, 163, 165
Luchaire, Achille, 8 n. 3
luminosity, 31
Lunete, 85–86, 140
Lurie, Alison, 28 n. 14
luxury, 8–10, 24–27, 29–30, 35, 38, 43, 47
Lycurgus, 134

Mackay, Angus, 29 n. 15
Macrobius, 12

madder, 33, 164
Maddox, Donald, 125 n. 7, 127 n. 8, 147 n. 25
madness, 5, 86, 104, 138–40
magic
  creature, 54
  lady, 131
  objects, 87 n. 7
  ship, 147
  of silk, 31
mail (*maille*), 62, 145 n. 23
manches, 24–26, 88
Mane, Perrine, 25, 28 n. 13, 32 n. 18, 33, 43, 82, 90
mantle, 26–27, 33, 36, 45–55, 58–59, 72, 73 n. 29, 82–83, 86, 102, 119, 126, 130–33, 139–42, 144, 150, 153, 163
manufacture, 108–18. *See also* cloth, manufacture of
marble, 28
Marc, 89–94
Marie de France, 5, 7, 11–12, 71, 88, 118, 127–33, 146–52, 154. *See also Bisclavret; Guigemar; Eliduc; Fresn; Lanval; Milun*
Marin, 158–59, 163, 165
markets, 32
masculinity, 56
matching attire, 62–63
materia, 11–13
Mauss, Marcel, 34 n. 21, 85
meaning, 9, 18, 40, 44
  absolute, 52, 65, 68, 73, 75, 108
  contextual, 94–108
  contingent, 101, 166, 171
Meleagant, 86, 104, 141–42
Melian, 96–97, 104, 136
mercantile economy, 6, 27, 29, 34, 36, 90 n. 9
merchant class, 28, 37, 39, 43, 80
merchant fairs, 29, 32
merchants, 8–9, 15, 19–20, 29–30, 37, 60, 108–9, 121
Mériaduc, 89, 118, 153
merit, 47, 57, 119
metonymy, 152, 155
mill, 28
Miller, Edward, 31, 33
Milun (Marie), 71
miniver, 31, 49
mistaken identity, 72
moiré, 31
monovalence, 17
Munro, John H., 32 n. 18, 33 n. 19

murex, 32 n. 18, 33 n. 20
Muthesius, Anna, 32

nakedness. *See* nudity
narrative coherence, 7, 11
narrative structure, 41, 131
narrative threads, 5, 8, 124–30, 153, 155, 170–71
Netherton, Robin, 19, 26
Neuburger, M. C., 33
non-recognition, 64–65, 74, 88
Normans, 32
nosepiece, 74
nostalgia, 10, 12–13, 23
nudity
  seduction, 52
  shame, 134
  social definition, 4, 24 n. 3
  lack of status, 64–65, 116–19, 138–40
  vulnerability, 85–86, 157
nuptials. *See* wedding

oaths, 36, 66, 89, 92–94, 99, 151–54
occupation, 36, 109, 112, 113 n. 30
offerings. *See* gifts
ofrois (orfrey), 26 n. 9
Ogrin, 89–91
Ordericus Vitalis, 25 n. 8
ornamentation, 13, 25, 26, 31, 46
orseille, 33
ostentation, 6, 18 n. 21
osterin, 31, 31–32 n. 18, 49
outcast, 5, 117, 138–40

paile, 31, 31–32 n. 18, 90
pantine, 49–50 n. 5
Parthenopeus, 107, 168
Pastoureau, Michel, 12 n. 13, 32 n. 18, 33 n. 20, 64, 74
pathos, 21
patronage, 12, 13 n. 14
peace, 8, 11, 28, 36, 37, 84
Peirce, Charles Sanders, 16 n. 15, 89 n. 26
Perceval, 1, 24 n. 3, 58–61, 73 n. 31, 95–98, 102, 104, 106, 143–46
petitgris, 38 n. 28
Philomena (Chrétien), 102, 113–15, 118
Pickens, Rupert T., 151 n. 28
Pierre le Chantre, 25–26 n. 8
Pinasa, Delphine, 25, 31
Piponnier, Françoise, 25, 28 n. 13, 32 n. 18, 33, 43, 82, 90
Pirenne, Henri, 27 n. 12, 32

INDEX 191

Polyneices, 106, 134, 168
polyvalence, 18
Ponting, K. G., 32 n. 19
popinjay (*espapemor*), 49–50 n. 5
porpre, 46, 53–54, 58, 90, 113, 132–33, 149
Postan, M. M., 31, 33
poverty, 56–57, 59, 116–17, 156, 161
power
  acquisition of, 104, 113–15
  to change, 165
  of clothes, 128–29
  of gifts, 80, 83, 86, 89
  healing, 151, 155
  lack of, 116–17, 140
  of queen, 127
prefashion, 17
Pritchard, Frances, 33, 109
Procné, 114–15
production, 108–18. *See also* manufacture
profecy, 147–48, 154
profession. *See* occupation
prolepsis, 148, 154
prosperity. *See* wealth

quilt, 149

rarity, 20, 31, 48–49, 54, 59–60. *See also* exotic garments
recognition, 70–76, 87–88, 130, 147, 153, 161–64
reconciliation, 89–94, 105. *See also* gifts, reconciliatory
red martin, 53
religion. *See* Christianity
removal
  armor. *See* disarming
  clothing. *See* undressing
Rémy, Paul, 40 n. 30
Renart, Jean, 124 n. 4
Renaut de Bâgé, 45–47, 51–53, 99–100
rending. *See* destruction
restoration, 84, 87, 94, 157, 170. *See also* gifts, restorative
Reyerson, Kathryn L., 37
rhetoric, 12–13, 21, 45, 123 n. 2
Ribard, Jacques, 151
Rigolot, François, 147 n. 25
rings
  identifying, 70–71, 87, 162–68
  messages, 93 n. 12
  tokens, 88, 99, 129, 139
rites. *See* clothing
Roach, Mary Ellen, 20–21, 38, 43, 61 n. 73

robe, 24–27, 49, 57, 62 n. 16, 63, 72, 83, 86, 163
Roman de la rose, ou de Guillaume de Dole (Renart), 124 n. 4
Roman de Thèbes, 61, 85, 106–7, 133
Roman de Tristan. *See* Thomas of England
Roman de Tristran. *See* Béroul
romance composition, 8, 10, 11–14, 124, 166–67, 171
romance conventions, 2, 11–14, 44–45, 50, 82 n. 4
Roussel, Claude, 100 n. 17
royal power, 8 n. 3, 17 n. 18, 28
Russia, 31, 59
Ryding, William W., 124 n. 3

sable, 31, 46–47, 49–51, 59
sackcloth, 160
saddle, 67
safflower, 33
saffron, 33
samite, 27, 31, 31–32 n. 18, 35 n. 22, 45, 48, 51, 83–84, 105
sappan, 32, 33
Saussure, Ferdinand, 9, 15–16
Scandinavia, 31, 37
scarlet, 33, 33 n. 19, 36, 45, 52, 82, 84, 90
Schneider, Jane, 108
Schwartz, Ronald A., 26
seduction. *See* clothes; nudity
self-dressing. *See* dressing
sericulture, 32
sewing, 109, 111–12, 114, 116–17
sexualized image, 4, 52
shame, 25, 73, 92, 139–41, 145, 158–61, 165. *See also* nudity
shape. *See* style
shared values, 72–73
sheets. *See* bedclothes
shield, 56, 61–62, 67–68, 73 n. 31, 74–75, 112
shoes, 24, 28 n. 14, 41, 143
siege, 58–60
siglaton, 31, 31–32 n. 18, 84
signs, linguistic, 15–18
silhouette. *See* style
silk, 24, 30, 31–33, 39, 45–46, 48–50, 73, 82, 84, 86–88, 90, 109 n. 22, 116, 149, 164. *See also specific types of silk*
Simonnet, Dominique, 12 n. 13
sleeves, 24–25, 26, 88
social hierarchy, 23, 37, 39, 108
social values, 11, 37, 40, 61 n. 15

soieries, 31
Sophia, 25 n. 8
Soredamors, 88–89, 98, 126, 134
Southern, R. W., 64 n. 18
Spain, 27, 28, 30, 48, 62, 110 n. 26
spinning wheel, 28
spinning, 32 n. 18, 114–16
Spufford, Peter, 30 n. 16
Staines, David, 57 n. 9, 64 n. 19
Staniland, Kay, 33, 109
status, restoration of, 61, 86, 89, 92, 95, 115, 153–55
stockings, 24
structure, thematic, 123–25
Sturm-Maddox, Sara (Sturm, Sara), 100 n. 16, 127 n. 8, 147 n. 25
style, 17–20, 23–26, 48, 53–55, 59, 69, 73–74
sumptuary laws, 38
surplus of expression, 36
surplus of meaning, 12, 12 n. 12, 169
swaddling, 8, 156–57
symbols, linguistic, 15–18
synecdoche, 61–62, 88, 134. See also armor

tailoring, 17, 24, 59, 109 n. 23
tapestry, 3, 8, 102, 110, 114–15, 124, 171
tapestry making, 102, 113–15, 118
Tarcon, 111–12
Taulat de Rogimon, 104, 136–37
tearing. See destruction
technological advances, 27–28, 32
Tereus, 102, 113–15
textiles. See cloth
textual weaving, 1, 6, 11, 12
thematic structure, 123–25. See also clothing
Thomas of England, 70–71, 98–99
thread making. See spinning
threads, literary. See narrative threads
tisseuses, 116–18, 140, 170
topical invention, 13
topoi, 12–13, 123
tournament, 34–35, 63, 73–76, 86–87, 99–100, 103, 168
trade, 8–9, 27, 29, 37, 43, 60, 70, 121, 158
trains, 25
travel, 29, 32, 38 n. 28, 62 n. 16, 88
trim, 24 n. 3, 47, 48, 50–51, 54
Tristan, 1, 65–67, 70–71, 89, 91–94, 99, 168
tunic, 24–25
turban, 28 n. 14
Tydeus, 134

underwear, 4
undressing, 94
  narrative device, 126, 129, 130–31, 139–40, 145, 150–54
  plot device, 99, 119–20

vair, 31, 38 n. 28, 49, 82–83, 86, 90
Van Vleck, Amelia E., 71 n. 28, 113 n. 31, 130 n. 15, 133 n. 18
vassal, 34, 81
vavasor, 127
Veale, Elizabeth M., 31
veil, 67, 92, 99, 129–30, 162–64
Vinaver, Eugène, 3, 11, 123–24, 171
visual evidence, 21, 38
vows. See oaths
vulnerability. See nudity

war, 8, 11, 13, 35–37, 111–12, 134
wealth, 6, 39, 43
  acquisition of, 8, 127, 163
  distribution of, 35, 43, 80–81
  exhaustion of, 37
  foreign, 8
  lack of, 57–58, 92
  merchants', 8, 19–20
  nobles', 8, 15, 21, 25, 29, 37, 165
  sign of, 31, 38, 51–53, 55
weavers, 28, 108–10
weaving, 32, 108–10, 113 n. 31, 114, 116
wedding, 21, 34, 81–82, 99, 130–31
weft, 32 n. 18
Weiner, Annette B., 108
weld, 33
Werewolf. See *Bisclavret*
Whalen, Logan E., 87 n. 6, 123 n. 1
Williams, Harry F., 155 n. 30, 165
wimple, 51, 88
Wingate, Isabel B., 32 n. 18
woad, 33, 164
Wolf-Bonvin, Romaine, 3, 24 n. 3, 45 n. 1, 47 n. 3, 52 n. 7, 58 n. 12, 63 n. 17
women's work, 109–12
wool, 24, 27, 31–33, 62 n. 16, 66, 83, 164
work force, 27–28, 109
Wright, Monica L., 35 n. 22, 52 n. 6, 110 n. 25, 133 n. 17, 147 n. 26

Ydoine, 86, 88
Yseut, 66, 70–71, 89–94, 99, 168
Yvain (Chrétien), 1, 5, 14, 62 n. 16, 64 n. 21, 85–86, 98 n. 15, 104, 115–18, 138–40, 170

www.ingramcontent.com/pod-product-compliance
Lightning Source LLC
Chambersburg PA
CBHW031551300426
44111CB00006BA/271